# BIRD CITY

# BIRD CITY

Adventures in
New York's
Urban Wilds

RYAN GOLDBERG

ALGONQUIN BOOKS OF CHAPEL HILL
LITTLE, BROWN AND COMPANY

Copyright © 2025 by Ryan Goldberg

Hachette Book Group supports the right to free expression and the value of copyright. The purpose of copyright is to encourage writers and artists to produce the creative works that enrich our culture.

The scanning, uploading, and distribution of this book without permission is a theft of the author's intellectual property. If you would like permission to use material from the book (other than for review purposes), please contact permissions@hbgusa.com. Thank you for your support of the author's rights.

Algonquin Books of Chapel Hill / Little, Brown and Company
Hachette Book Group
1290 Avenue of the Americas, New York, NY 10104
littlebrown.com

First Edition: November 2025

Algonquin Books of Chapel Hill is an imprint of Little, Brown and Company, a division of Hachette Book Group, Inc. The Algonquin Books name and logo are trademarks of Hachette Book Group, Inc.

The publisher is not responsible for websites (or their content) that are not owned by the publisher.

The Hachette Speakers Bureau provides a wide range of authors for speaking events. To find out more, go to hachettespeakersbureau.com or email hachettespeakers@hbgusa.com.

Little, Brown and Company books may be purchased in bulk for business, educational, or promotional use. For information, please contact your local bookseller or the Hachette Book Group Special Markets Department at special.markets@hbgusa.com.

Design by Steve Godwin
Illustrations by Aimee Lusty

ISBN 978-1-64375-556-4 (HC) / 978-1-64375-558-8 (Ebook)
LCCN 2025939798

1 2025

MRQ-T
Printed in Canada

*For Angie*

## CONTENTS

**WINTER** 1
    Chapter 1: Counting   3
    Chapter 2: Belonging   22
    Chapter 3: Flaco   40

**SPRING** 61
    Chapter 4: The Moraine   63
    Chapter 5: Safe Flight   82
    Chapter 6: Morning Flight   101
    Chapter 7: Wave Day   112

**SUMMER** 127
    Chapter 8: Freshkills   129
    Chapter 9: Piping Plovers   148
    Chapter 10: The Guardian   168
    Chapter 11: The Bronx River   190

**FALL** 209
    Chapter 12: Tribute in Light   211
    Chapter 13: Hawk Watch   230
    Chapter 14: Rarities   244

    *Acknowledgments* 264
    *Author's Note on Sources* 267
    *Bibliography* 273

# BIRD CITY

# WINTER

CHAPTER 1

# Counting

On a windswept beach in New York City, Peter Dorosh and I counted ducks. But they were nothing like the ones I'd fed stale bread when I was a child. Here, there were three kinds of scoters—stocky, velvet-black sea ducks—and they plunged under waves that crashed into a long rock jetty, surfacing with mollusks in their knobby bills. The surf scoters looked especially strange. The drakes, or males, had bills that looked like squashed candy corns, and white irises that made them appear highly caffeinated. Long-tailed ducks, smaller than scoters, mixed with them in the icy chop. The males sported curved tail plumes and what looked like a white fur cap and dark earmuffs.

Peter pulled out his pocket notebook and smiled as he added the birds to his list. It was the middle of January and one of his favorite days of the year: the state ornithological association's annual waterfowl count. For over six hours, we had picked along six miles of the western Rockaway Peninsula, a narrow strip of land separating Jamaica Bay from the Atlantic Ocean, tallying roughly 1,500 ducks from 10 different species, as well as grebes, loons, and geese. Sunset was two hours away, and this was the tip of Breezy Point, our final spot.

In a city of more than eight million people, there were only four others on the wide beach: two fishermen, and, coming our way, an older couple out for a walk. Peter leaned against his scope and pulled sunglasses over his blue eyes. His face, though lined, appeared youthful, and was framed by a trim gray beard that softened its angles. A worn cap covered his bald head. Weather-deepened spiderwebs radiated from the corners of his eyes, indicating not only a life spent outdoors but a ready laugh. I had heard it earlier when we pulled our scopes out of the trunk of his Subaru in the sandy parking lot. "Do you want to bring your water?" I'd asked, pointing to a crinkled plastic bottle. Then came that laugh, a loud, free-ranging cackle. "Do you know what that is?" he'd said. "Holy water! From Pope John Paul's visit to Shea Stadium in 1979. I was there."

We waited for more sea ducks to fly toward the jetty. I was tired by that time, but Peter showed no signs of fatigue. He wore a backpack large enough for a weeklong hike on the Appalachian Trail. He had been doing this count every January for over 30 years. Sometimes he walked it all, roughly 10 or 12 miles, though today we walked and drove. Peter loved winter birding, calling it more peaceful and relaxing than at other times of the year, and he liked to end his emails with a quote about the season, along with the name of the person it's attributed to: "Andrew Wyeth: 'I prefer winter and fall, when you feel the bone structure of the landscape—the loneliness of it; the dead feeling of winter. Something waits beneath it, the whole story doesn't show.'" "Oscar Wilde: 'Wisdom comes with winters.'" "John Steinbeck: 'What good is the warmth of summer, without the cold of winter to give it sweetness.'"

But I gathered there was more to his deep feelings. Peter is deaf, and wears a hearing aid, and Breezy Point is a refuge from the city's loud noises, large crowds, and general chaos. Here, he can scan the ocean without interruption for long spells.

It was Peter's second-grade Catholic school teacher who first realized he was deaf, and when his mother took him to a Flatbush dispensary to buy hearing aids, he sprinted outside just as a fire engine raced down the street. Thinking his head was going to explode, he ran back inside and yelled, "Take one out!" Ever since, he's worn only one hearing aid.

As a child, his inability to communicate left him anxious and frustrated, but birding changed that. His mother showed him blue jays, and from their house near the Brooklyn Navy Yard, he would look for them in their sparse backyard. His window watching took on greater meaning after his father, a postal worker, died when Peter was 13. In May of the following year, 1975, he went to the window and saw on the ground a glowing red bird with ink-black wings. As with the introduction of those hearing aids, it was a combustible experience. Mesmerized, he sketched the bird, then carried his drawing to the library. The paperback third-edition Peterson Field Guide told him it was a male scarlet tanager, a songbird that each year migrated between the Andean foothills of South America and the hardwood forests of the eastern US.

In birding parlance, the scarlet tanager was Peter's "spark bird," the species whose sighting ignites a passion for birds. Coming soon after his father died, Peter thought of the scarlet tanager as divine intervention. He wondered which other birds lived beyond his backyard. His first pair of binoculars led him to nearby Prospect Park, and then the Jamaica Bay Wildlife Refuge, where he found a postcard for the Brooklyn Bird Club. The club had been around since 1909, he learned, and it organized field trips and contributed greatly to the city's scientific and civic life. In 1978, he joined his first field trip. The connection to nature gave his psyche the calm it desperately needed, and the community welcomed him.

When I met Peter days after my own spark in the spring of 2016, he had already been the club's president, newsletter editor, and trips planner. He also blogged about Brooklyn bird sightings—breaking news I couldn't believe there was an audience for. He was employed on the natural resources crew at Prospect Park, which kept him close to the action, and he lived near the park in an old brick town house, with four generations of his family.

Peter encouraged me to write to him with questions about birding—which I did, many times. I quickly realized we were living in two different cities. Peter knew New York better than anyone I had ever met—the natural side, that is. He couldn't recommend a hip place to eat or drink, the kind of details that preoccupied my mind, but he could talk endlessly about birds' migration schedules, the meteorological forces that carry them to the city, and the kinds of trees they prefer when they get here. Whenever I found an uncommon bird, Peter was the first person I told, so he could post the sighting on his blog. A year and a half into my birding days, he asked me to join him for the waterfowl count.

Though Peter had been coming to Breezy Point for almost four decades, it was still hard for me to believe I was in the same city where I had lived my entire adult life. Looking to my right, over the dunes, a jagged skyline of glass and steel began to the north, at the southern tip of Manhattan, skipped across the water, and ran through downtown Brooklyn, then over to Midtown Manhattan, all condensed onto one plane. In the foreground were the amusements of Coney Island, frozen for the season. Looking to my left, the Atlantic sparkled to the New Jersey highlands, near my childhood home. Following that ridge led to Staten Island and the Verrazzano-Narrows Bridge, which I could also distantly see from my apartment window.

Out at the horizon, we watched a river of black scoters in Ambrose Channel, the harbor's main passage for large vessels trafficking the Port of New York and New Jersey. They streamed like dark clouds hurrying across the water, rising when a container ship entered the channel. Their local numbers had grown by leaps and bounds since

Peter's first waterfowl count, thanks to a cleaner harbor and an abundance of quahogs and mussels. Some estimates put the number of black scoters at more than 50,000 during the winter, a figure that amounts to between a sixth and a quarter of their total population in the eastern US. Toward the end of winter, they and the other sea ducks here would fly north to breed in the freshwater wetlands of the boreal forest or the high Arctic tundra.

"People think the birds are out in the country," Peter said. "No, the best birding is actually in the cities." More accurately: a coastal city. Excluding escapees from zoos and the pet trade, around 430 species have been seen in New York, which represents more than a third of the species in the entire US. They're packed in just like us, shoulder to shoulder, fighting for their place here.

The couple I'd first noticed walking down the beach now approached us. Peter said hello, then turned back to his scope. Peter reads lips, and it struck me that he couldn't carry on a conversation and simultaneously look through his scope, watching birds.

"Have you seen any snowy owls?" the man asked me.

We hadn't, I said, but we also hadn't checked the dunes, which was their favored daytime roost.

"We're counting waterfowl," I explained, an answer that only got me blank looks.

Peter remained glued to his view of the ocean. Moments later, he shouted, "Eider!"

I lifted my binoculars. A hundred yards offshore was a duck larger than the scoters, patterned black and white like the classic New York deli cookie. It was a male common eider, the largest duck in the Northern Hemisphere, a species whose down keeps it warm through Hudson Bay winters. But forget the Far North. This duck looked to me like it had arrived from the *future*, a sleek, geometric black cap pulled low over its eyes.

I showed it to the couple through my scope. They grew politely interested. I grasped for words to inspire them. "It looks like Robo-Duck," I said.

"Eider!" Peter yelled again. Then louder now: "Ryan! Eider! Ryan!"

Another duck landed behind the common eider. In the second it took me to focus my binoculars, Peter screamed, "It's a kiiiiiing!"

He spun around, eyes wide, then looked startled to find me still talking to the couple. I sheepishly apologized to them as he yanked me toward my scope. Peering through, I saw a duck that resembled a melted-down Fisher-Price toy. Its strangely flattened and bulbous head was powder blue, green ombré, and bright orange. Two triangles rose like meringue peaks on its black back.

"King eider!"

It was the one duck Peter had never seen during the waterfowl count. Drake king eiders like this one rarely fly this far south in winter, leaving that to the hens and immatures.

"Follow him!" Peter cried.

As the two ducks swam toward the jetty, we tracked them down the beach, alternating between a crab-like side shuffle, scope in hands, to a hunched-in viewing position. As they turned slowly out to sea, I scrambled onto the jetty for a closer look, perhaps trying to make up for my less-than-vigilance before. Eyes on the ducks, I hardly noticed the seaweed and barnacles lacing the rocks beneath my feet.

Two steps later, my legs flew out from under me. I instinctively shielded my scope with my body, like you would for a small child. Lying on my side, I could see that its cover was cracked, but not the glass itself. I felt momentary relief, followed by a surge of pain. My right hand was cut and bleeding. My wrist throbbed.

I crawled to the nearest dry rock and slid onto the sand. Peter, who had stopped at the rocks and had his face glued to his scope, saw none of this. Tapping him on the shoulder with my good hand, I held up the bloody one. He was shocked.

At least I'd followed the king all the way, I joked half-heartedly. He said I wasn't the first birder to go down there.

Peter dug through his stuffed backpack and came out with hand sanitizer and Band-Aids. I was thankful for his preparedness. I thought my wrist might be broken, at best severely sprained.

I patched up my hand, ready now to call it a day.

"Do you wanna keep going?" Peter asked, his tone hopeful.

Really? I knew we should count more ducks on the walk back to his car; otherwise, the record would be incomplete. But couldn't we make an exception? Couldn't we place an asterisk next to it?

"Sure," I answered. "Let's keep going."

THE TRUTH IS, I should have known better. Birders love to count.

As we left the jetty, Peter posted about the king eider on Twitter, which, at the time, was where many New York birders shared sightings. Our sighting then circulated on a WhatsApp group for rare Brooklyn and Queens birds. Before long, someone asked for travel advice to the jetty, and Peter tapped out directions. Somehow, that birder reached our corner of the city just in time to see the two eiders in the gathering twilight. A drake king eider hadn't been reported in many years and was a nice addition to a life list or a state list (or both). The king was too far away for a decent photograph, the observer noted on eBird, the Cornell Lab of Ornithology's bird sightings website, since the jetty was "not climbable."

What had gotten into me? I hadn't been birding very long, but I was learning that it provokes odd behavior: intense emotional highs, meticulous list keeping, spontaneous trips where you drop everything to chase a bird. One day, I had never really looked at a bird; the next, I couldn't imagine doing much else.

I was instantly grabbed by it. On my first walk in Prospect Park with the Brooklyn Bird Club, I listened to the way people described and identified a bird, and it seemed like this required precision, accuracy, and quick thinking—skills that I, a reporter, figured I could manage. I filled a notebook that morning with the names of over 50 different birds along with short descriptions of them, none very scientific—like the "reddish chest hair" of the veery, a plump little russet bird in the thrush family. I left the park gripped by stories of arduous journeys, wild feats of migration made year after year—in the spring *and* in the fall—and the more I heard, the more I felt compelled to learn even more.

Obsession, I found, is a curious thing. My fall at Breezy Point stuck with me for more than just the shock of my stupidity. It was one of the first moments I realized there was a roving network of birders who ordered their lives around rare birds, who rushed off at the buzz of a Twitter, WhatsApp, or GroupMe message. (Now, most use Discord.) Why exactly do birders love to count? What lengths will they go to to see an unlikely bird? Why was Peter hell-bent on adding a few more ducks to our lengthy list that day? I wanted to understand, even as I started to feel the same urgency overtaking me.

In a secondhand shop in Manhattan, I came upon Roger Tory Peterson's *Birds Over America*, a captivating book about the country's bird life, published in 1948. Peterson, who published his first popular field guide in 1934, studied at the Art Students League and was a New York City birder for many years. "The lure of the list," he called it, quoting his contemporary Guy Emerson. Though ornithologists might look down on list-happy birders, Peterson rose to their defense. "The field-glass amateurs need not apologize to the professionals," he wrote. "To the beginner, advanced ornithological research seems as dull and pointless as bird listing seems to some biologists. Yet they blend, one with the other."

Compared to other animals, birds are relatively easily viewed and tallied, which makes them perfect for amateur study. Peter told me that New York state's wildlife officials used the waterfowl count to keep tabs on winter populations. Because we kept going after my fall, our records that day were complete. They were reliable. Perhaps there was something in our numbers that a scientist would eventually want to find out, I told myself. My wrist was not broken, and I got back to birding.

Or rather, I fell deeper into it. I read Peter's blog and started following citywide rare bird alerts as if they were front-page news. I birded almost every day, and quickly my life in New York—which had up until then been primarily confined to the realm of human affairs, involving deadlines, weekend plans, and scrolling at my computer—radically shifted. Wildness was all around me, and for the most part I only had to walk, bike, or get on a subway or bus to make discoveries.

When I *really* saw a bird, I didn't just see what it looked like. I saw how it behaved, where it foraged for insects, when it came and went. And in this way, I began to understand its life cycle and how it fit with the seasons. I realized I couldn't describe an organism without describing the whole environment around it. And that included me. My own spark bird—a hefty black-and-russet sparrow called an eastern towhee—was just the first of a series of spark experiences, or insights, that illuminated the world for me.

Almost a year after our waterfowl count, Peter asked me to lead a trip of my own for the Brooklyn Bird Club. Birding gave me license to explore, and in New York that exploration encompassed a surprising variety of landscapes, from the Hudson to the Atlantic, forests to grasslands, urban canyons to salt marshes. I began to see a city that was shaped by birds and by birders. But as I learned, first you had to count them.

IN 2022, ON a Sunday morning in December, I rode a nearly empty subway car uptown to Central Park. It was the 123rd annual edition of the Christmas Bird Count (CBC), and I was about to join one of its 2,625 different counts. Organized by the National Audubon Society, the CBC is one of the world's longest-running and largest volunteer wildlife censuses. Over the course of three weeks, more than 67,000 of us, across 50 states and in over 20 countries, would head into the field to count every bird we saw or heard. And I was on my way to its birthplace.

In December of 1900, Frank Chapman, then a young ornithologist at the American Museum of Natural History, looked over Central Park and proposed a bird census to replace the traditional Christmas "side hunt," a jolly competition in which two teams dashed through woods and fields looking to kill "practically everything in fur or feathers that crossed their path." Chapman's "hunt," on the other hand, asked participants to submit their sightings to *Bird-Lore*, his new magazine, along with their notes on location, time, and weather. Readers would get a snapshot of winter bird life, and Chapman's periodical would get to promote its mission of conservation.

At the time, hunting was not the only threat driving some North American birds to the brink of extinction (or over the edge, as with the passenger pigeon). The fashion industry was another. Whole colonies of terns, gulls, egrets, herons, ibises, pelicans, and spoonbills had been wiped out from Maine's rocky islands to Florida's Everglades, just so their feathers (and occasionally the whole bird) could be worn on a hat. And they all made their way to the country's fashion capital. One day before the museum hired Chapman, he parked himself with a notebook on Manhattan's 14th Street and wrote down the different birds going by on women's hats. The result was shocking: 40 different species, from warblers to woodpeckers, sparrows to shorebirds.

In the inaugural CBC year of 1900, there were 25 different

Christmas censuses across 13 states and Canada. In Central Park, an 11-year-old named Charles Rogers showed up at 10 that morning and counted a dozen herring gulls, one downy woodpecker, four European starlings, one American robin, two song sparrows, and "abundant" white-throated sparrows. (*Bird-Lore* didn't say how long he stayed or if his parents joined him.) And so the recordkeeping began, with a format that turned any citizen into a researcher and activated a distributed network of data collectors. The year was a turning point for conservation too, as the Audubon Societies seized the last few gull colonies on the Maine coast and, with armed patrols, defended them from millinery hunters.

Wanting to see where it had all started, I entered Central Park at 96th Street a little before eight to meet my team. Five tufted titmouses were foraging right on the grass. (From what I can tell, either *titmouses* or *titmice* is acceptable as the plural. The name *titmouse*, however, has nothing to do with rodents; it comes from the old English words *tit* and *mase*, meaning "small bird.") These small birds had comically oversized features, I thought, with big beady black eyes and a spiky crest. Their presence cheered me. It was a good sign, and a noteworthy one too.

Though common in suburban backyards, the titmouses' return to the city is predictably irregular, like an uncle who turns up unannounced at Thanksgiving. For weeks, they had been pouring into the city—flying over rooftops, landing on fire escapes, getting trapped in buildings—in a potentially historic "irruption," as ornithologists call such a large invasion. The tufted titmouse was once a southern bird; the first one wasn't recorded on Central Park's CBC until 1953, and the next one, not until 1957. For decades, though, as CBC records show us, they have nudged their way north, likely due to milder winters and the lure of backyard feeders. The city's first irruption occurred in 1978, which a New York City birder named Peter Post later wrote about with a detective's flair: "The first indication that something unusual was happening was an observation of a flock of Tufted Titmice moving south on October 10 at 9:45 a.m. among the trees which separate the lanes of Broadway, in mid-Manhattan."

Their scratchy calls followed me all the way to the North Meadow Recreation Center, my team's meeting point, where I joined a small group of birders in their sixties and seventies who were all friends. The glue appeared to be Junko Suzuki, a soft-spoken graphic designer with dark-gray hair who volunteered in Frank Chapman's old department at the Museum of Natural History, where she translated tiny handwritten tags on old Japanese specimens.

Our sector, one of seven in Central Park, was a rocky and mostly wooded area cut through by streams. We split into two groups. Junko volunteered to keep a written list for ours, a task nobody else seemed to want. We walked along the North Meadow ballfields and, beyond center field, saw several dozen American robins feeding noisily on the still-lingering fruit of a crab apple tree. I pointed out a dark-eyed junco, a small sparrow the color of smoke, as it flashed its white tail feathers before flying off. Once a commonplace winter visitor, it was the only one we'd see.

"Thank you for finding a junco," Junko said happily, adding it to the list. Her name, of course, has nothing to do with the bird. Pronounced *Joon-ko* (compared with *Jun-ko* for the bird), it has an abstract meaning about purity, she told me. But she didn't mind the association.

"I like that my name is easy to remember for people," she added. "I like this bird. It's simple and understated."

For New York City's various CBCs, the action is on the waterfront. Most years, forest birds are few and far between. So our group spent much of the next two hours talking rather than watching birds— except in the case of titmouses. None of us had seen anything like it.

Our sector had 79; the Ramble had 306; in total, there were 765 in Central Park. Next to the park's drive, we gathered around a scrum of them picking through leaves, and people shared firsthand reports on their diet—acorns, seeds, insects, peanuts from bird feeders, food scraps like old bread. An urban park ranger who joined us said he'd watched a titmouse pick apart a paper-wasp nest for days.

A crowd of birders in New York will inevitably draw spectators of its own. Two older women walked up to us, and one, dressed in spandex, her hair dyed neon orange, sized up the ranger's attire; he was wearing the classic dark-green uniform and khaki hat. "What are you looking for?" she asked mischievously. "Smokey the Bear?"

ACTUALLY, IT WAS a good question. What *were* we looking for? Not just birds—or at least not for the mere sake of a sighting. It was for the larger story the birds were telling us. The CBC, like a time-lapse photo, records the shifting shape of bird populations over time. Patterns emerge from the numbers, turning our anecdotal experiences into scientific stories: like the tufted titmouse, once rare, expanding its range. Now considered common, it arrives in an irregular boom-and-bust cycle.

I was building a continuous dataset of my own. I hadn't missed a Brooklyn CBC since I took up birding, and so the day before the Central Park count, I was at Green-Wood Cemetery, where I'd been asked to lead the team I'd been part of for five years.

Green-Wood opened in 1838, about 30 years before Prospect Park, and the two places, separated by a handful of blocks, form a green heart in the middle of Brooklyn. I feel loyalty to my count territory, sleepy though it is. In terms of the number of species, we always come in second to last among Brooklyn's 13 territories. We are mostly trees and meadows, and though we have four ponds, we can scarcely compete with the diversity or numbers found along the coast—in the winter, that is. During the high points of migration in the spring and the fall, when seeing close to a hundred species in one day at the cemetery is possible, there's nowhere else I would rather be.

I like that the earliest we can start is eight in the morning, when the cemetery gates open. And those gates are only a 10-minute walk from my home. But Green-Wood has its secrets too, and is typically a territory with at least one "save." Saves are species that are periodically around during the count but only in small numbers, so they're regularly missed. A save is sealed when only one team finds it.

Sometimes our save is an eastern phoebe, a small flycatcher that really shouldn't be around during winter but that pops up occasionally (and, it seems to me lately, with increasing frequency). When it does, it's easy to find, usually pumping its tail by a pond's edge. Sometimes our save is an owl. Great horned owls live in the city year-round, and each pair needs a large territory of its own, so Brooklyn holds only a few of them. We've also saved with a northern saw-whet owl, a fluffy destroyer the size of a russet potato. Northern saw-whets winter here regularly but hide so flawlessly that it takes extreme commitment to the cause to find one among the many hundreds of evergreens in which the owl might feasibly be sleeping.

Usually, the birder who gets the Brooklyn CBC's northern saw-whet save is a man known as the Owl Whisperer, out in some scrubby pines near Breezy Point. I'd heard of him for years by the time of the 2022 CBC, but I'd never met him.

Technically, Breezy Point is in Queens County, which requires a bit of explanation.

On Christmas Day 1905, a now-unidentified Brooklyn birder went to the western Rockaways in bad weather and saw a brown creeper, a couple of chickadees, and a sparrow. The next count was in 1910, but it didn't become regular until after 1937. Those early counts had long-lasting consequences, however. To standardize the census, the

National Audubon Society adopted a 15-mile radius for each count circle. In the 1950s, a border dispute between four western Long Island clubs (Brooklyn, Queens, northern Nassau County, and southern Nassau County) went all the way to Audubon's top ranks. By making a case for continuous recordkeeping, the Brooklyn Bird Club laid claim to the western Rockaway beaches, which include Breezy Point. The judgment didn't go well for Queens. Its club was forced to concede those beaches to Brooklyn (along with the west side of the Jamaica Bay refuge) plus to cede other territory to southern Nassau County. Queens birders were furious, and they apparently refused to submit their numbers to Audubon for a decade even as they kept doing their count. And so, the anomalous count territory continues by tradition.

These days, at the end of an organized count, each team reunites to compile a master list. In Brooklyn, this is best done over food and beverages. Canvassing birds works up an appetite, and not just one that is sated by pizza and beer. There's also the hunger for glory to be attended to.

WHEN I ARRIVED at Prospect Park's boathouse for the compilation that December weekend, the atmosphere buzzed, with an assortment of people as cheerfully mishmashed as the potluck dishes they brought. Much like a sports memorabilia conference, an outlier interest had brought us together, and we hovered over folding tables, in clipped conversations: "What did you see?" "What did you get?" "Remember that spotted redshank in 1992?" "How about the finch irruption in 2012?"

Because of the COVID-19 pandemic, that night was our first in-person compilation in three years. About half of the day's 130 counters turned out. The event had long since outgrown the living rooms of Brooklyn Bird Club members, relocating to this much larger—and grander—space. Though not one of the park's original structures, the boathouse was built in 1905, when Beaux-Arts gripped architects' imaginations. Its white columns, arched windows, and a row of orb lamps grace a small waterway. Blue and green Guastavino tile vaults top the interior. Prospect Park Alliance would typically rent the space for $6,000 on a Saturday night in December, but because the bird club racks up hundreds of volunteer hours to the benefit of the park, we get it free for the CBC.

I waved to Peter Dorosh. He'd been leading a Prospect Park team for well over 30 years. My first CBC, before I moved to Green-Wood, had been with him. His day had gone well, though it was without surprises. But he happily reported secondhand news: A Townsend's warbler had been seen. The Townsend's, a small yellow-and-black songbird, is a western species, but this individual had been found the previous month in Fort Greene Park, a place rarely frequented by birders in November. It should have been in Southern California or Mexico but, instead, it appeared to be surviving on sap from freshly drilled woodpecker holes.

I scanned the room for Doug Gochfeld, the original finder of the bird. In his late thirties, Doug had a messy beard and kept his long brown hair tied in a loose knot. Tonight, he wore a dark hoodie and waterproof pants. His paper plate sagged under the weight of pizza and eclectic sides. After leading a team at the Jamaica Bay Wildlife Refuge, which had started before dawn, he'd checked a large gull roost below the Brooklyn Bridge before hurrying back to the boathouse.

A professional guide who'd led birding trips around the world, Doug's record of finding rare birds in the city was legendary. The most remarkable was the gray-breasted martin he'd discovered in Prospect Park, a large swallow from Central and South America, which hadn't been spotted north of the Rio Grande since 1898. His latest Townsend's warbler was the third one he'd found in Brooklyn in two years.

A few minutes before seven, we rearranged our folding chairs around a projection screen and settled into an expectant silence. On the screen was the first slide of the night: snow goose. Starting in taxonomic order, the count compiler was going to run through every species from past counts, from common to irregular to rare, while team leaders called out their totals for each. There were 12 land-based teams and a boat team—one man who kayaked around the islands of Jamaica Bay. I kept my eye on the boat team's species count throughout the night. It always had a strong start, as water birds come at the beginning of the taxonomic order. But eventually, it would founder, and my Green-Wood team usually passed it halfway through songbirds, clawing our way out of dead last.

All of us were able to track this and other stats in real time, thanks to a unique database created decades before by a club member who worked for the Federal Reserve. It put a stamp of professionalism on Brooklyn's records and enabled immediate comparisons to past records. Each slide included historical and 10-year highs and lows, and an empty field for the new entries.

It's powerful to see your experience in a larger context, transformed into scientific analysis before your eyes. Birds are environmental indicators, and their population trends on the CBC point to ecological changes—in Brooklyn, for instance, the loss of grasslands, as told by the downward trend of eastern meadowlarks, or the closing of landfills, as seen in the plunge in gulls, or a warming climate, from the increases of historically southern species like cardinals, mockingbirds, and titmouses. The slides also show that many common species are becoming harder to find. My first compilation, back in 2017, was shocking in this regard. Watching birds like American goldfinches and dark-eyed juncos check in at multidecade lows, I was gripped by sadness for a world I had just entered. Not long after, a landmark study in *Science* revealed that one in four adult birds in North America had been lost since 1970.

At least there was a community to share the experience with. This year's CBC was as complete as it had ever been, with the most participants and territories in our history.

One by one, we went through the common birds. Some birds, though populous, were unpopular with the crowd. "This is always a fun one: rock pigeon," the emcee said to laughter. The count was over 2,000. European starlings elicited an anonymous "Ugh." There were over 2,200 of them. Then another "fun one": house sparrows. More than 800. These were some of the most familiar birds in the city, but they weren't originally from here.

Like most birders, I'd heard that starlings were introduced by someone who wanted all the birds that appear by name in Shakespeare's oeuvre to make it in the US. Regardless of the veracity of that origin story, this much is true: They made it big. Millions of starlings, for instance, now range on this continent, from the cities of northern Mexico to the forests of southern Alaska.

We took a five-minute break after the common species, then moved onto the irregular and rare birds. This was the payoff for hours spent in the field. Anyone who thought they might have a save was sitting at the edge of their seat. An eastern phoebe earned my team one, and I looked around the room for my fellow Green-Wood counters, eager to share this award with them. A dovekie spotted at Breezy Point brought a round of applause, along with 115 razorbills, football-shaped seabirds in the same family as puffins; the last dovekie had been seen in 1957. The team at Fort Tilden, next to Breezy Point, had found two northern saw-whet owls—another save courtesy of the Owl Whisperer.

Finally, when every species that had ever been seen on a Brooklyn CBC was accounted for, the compiler asked with a smile, "Are there any I haven't asked about?" Almost everyone in the room knew the answer.

"Townsend's warbler at Fort Greene Park!" someone called out. It was the first Townsend's reported in the history of the Brooklyn CBC, marking the 236th species since its inception in 1905. It made for a total of 133 species and 51,567 individual birds. Cheering and clapping engulfed the room before the crowd quickly broke up.

Leaving the boathouse, I gazed at the sky. The night was crisp and unusually clear. Mars loomed red near the ever-bright Aldebaran. I thought of the Townsend's warbler: *What a find!* But what was it doing in Fort Greene, amid the leafless trees? It doesn't belong in New York City, but everyone seemed happy about its presence.

Cheers for the Townsend's and the dovekie, but jeers for starlings and house sparrows. I understood the sentiments. In all my years of birding, I had rarely heard anyone say a nice thing about the latter. Starlings and house sparrows—toss pigeons into that category too—also don't belong here. They feed off the scraps of human civilization, and as introduced species, the Migratory Bird Treaty Act of 1918—one of the oldest wildlife protection laws—doesn't cover them. So how had they ended up here in the first place? And what made them so successful?

I began to wonder: Which birds really count?

CHAPTER 2

# Belonging

The field of invasion biology is devoted to the study of changes wrought by introduced species. Though this name was unknown to me at the time, I was familiar with some of its unsparing terminology, such as *nonnative species* or *invasive species*. I left the Christmas Bird Count with a nagging feeling. The booing at the mention of starlings, pigeons, and house sparrows had, like pinpricks blooming into bruises, grown into a misshapen and uncomfortable sensation. What made these birds so unlovable? We're the ones who brought them here in the first place.

The widespread origin story for starlings—the Shakespeare story—claims that they were introduced to North America in the late 19th century by Eugene Schieffelin, a wealthy New Yorker who wanted all the birds of Shakespeare to populate the "New World." It makes a tidy tale—one I've heard on more birding trips than I can recall. Since then, sentiments have clearly changed. Now we're dealing with an invasive species. Hoping to unravel the yarn of a maligned bird, I made the trek one January morning to the American Museum of Natural History.

There, in the back of a sterile-looking storage room, was a metal cabinet holding the preserved bodies of some of the original invaders.

Paul Sweet crouched down and pulled out a shallow tray from cabinet 59B labeled with *Sturnus vulgaris*, the scientific name for the common or European starling. Inside were three rows of faded and slumped birds, belly up. He placed the tray on a counter and began checking their tags. "We've got some old ones here," he said.

Sweet had been at Brooklyn's CBC; he led the team that included the Owl Whisperer. A native of Bristol, England, he began looking at birds when he was nine. In the back garden of his house, his parents had a "bird table," a big piece of wood on which they scattered peanuts and kitchen scraps. Sweet started collecting young—butterflies, fossils, bird eggs—and so it was fitting that he now managed a slightly larger collection of more than one million specimens from around the globe. Its scale makes it indispensable for visiting ornithologists, paleontologists, wildlife conservationists, artists, filmmakers, and lowly writers from the outer boroughs.

The first four starlings Sweet pulled out were adults, collected in Central Park by a William Dutcher on March 30, 1890. Dutcher was a founding member and early treasurer of the American Ornithological Union. Eugene Schieffelin released starlings in Central Park on March 6, 1890, according to Frank Chapman, who once curated the museum's collection, so these birds had presumably survived the weeklong steerage trip across the Atlantic from Britain, only to die about three weeks later in their new home. Though their sharp bills had already turned yellow for the breeding season, they clearly hadn't lived long enough to nest here. Two still looked slightly speckled, while the other two were spotless. Starlings molt their feathers once per year, usually beginning in the summer, and the white tips on their fresh feathers give them a speckled appearance. Eventually, the tips wear down to show feather bases that are glossy and blackish.

Sweet rummaged further. "When did you say Schieffelin's release was?"

"1890," I said.

"I don't know how this one fits in then," he said, pulling out a starling from September 23, 1889, collected in South Oyster Bay, Long Island. Up close like this, its hundreds of white feather tips were like stars filling a dark sky. A very worn tag noted that it was the 1,406th bird in the collection; from Dutcher again. But who had released this bird?

Sweet pulled out another tray, filled with starlings from faraway places. Norfolk Island, in the South Pacific, 1912; Sunday Island, now known as Raoul Island, the largest of the Kermadec Islands, north of New Zealand, 1925; Tonga, 1924 and 1925; Fiji, 1930. All former British colonies. "These birds got around," he said. Were all the introducers Shakespeare lovers or were they just partial to their homeland fauna?

I mentioned to Sweet that starlings didn't seem very popular at the Christmas count.

"Everybody in America loves to hate starlings, but they're really cool birds," he said. "In Bristol, we used to have these huge murmurations in the winter. They're beautiful, and their behavior is so interesting."

"Of course," he added, "ours is just one of dozens of species of starlings."

We were in the Sturnidae aisle, featuring a family that includes 125 species from around the world. Sweet showed me a few—the Cape starling of Africa, an acid trip of blue-green iridescence; the common myna, yellow-masked and sold as a cage bird around the world; and the Bali myna, pure white, with blue facial skin, now on the verge of extinction on its home Indonesian island. All were beautiful, and I felt time slip by as I gazed at them a century or more after they had lived. The motivations of humans seemed mysterious in that moment, the drive to collect and classify, to give shape to our lives by ordering the rest of the animal planet. Another question nagged at me: If

Eugene Schieffelin's release wasn't the first, what was the true origin story of the starlings in New York?

IN THE SECOND half of the 19th century, any manner of creature could be set free in this country. It was called the acclimatization movement. Begun in France, it spread to Britain and its respective colonies and the US. In the US, European starlings and house sparrows were the most popular choices, but Roger Tory Peterson, in *Birds Over America*, estimates that over a hundred exotic bird species were released. Acclimatization or acclimation societies mushroomed around the country, fed by a combined scientific and colonial ethos. Plants and animals were viewed like pieces in a game, to be moved around by rational masterminds to see whether they could succeed in new territories. At the time, the experiments seemed tidy and novel. As Peterson wrote: "Ecology was an unknown word then and little was understood about a bird's relation to its environment."

The center of the movement in New York was the American Acclimatization Society, of which Schieffelin was chair. Incorporated in 1871, its mission was "the introduction and acclimatization of such foreign varieties of the animal and vegetable kingdom as may be useful or interesting." But useful to whom? Farmers, perhaps. On the grasslands of England, for instance, starlings were described as "very valuable insect destroyers." If you were a fruit grower, however, they could be a "pest." In the words of one Kent farmer: "The starling is a terror, and life around here is hardly worth living, you must have a gun always in your hand, or woe betide the cherries; they come in thousands."

And interesting to whom? Schieffelin's family ran one of Manhattan's oldest pharmaceutical businesses, and his fellow members were merchants, bankers, and real estate investors, who like him joined civic clubs, supported large city charities, and spent summers in Newport,

Rhode Island. A few were early conservationists, such as Robert B. Roosevelt, the founder of the New York State Fishery Commission (and the uncle of future president Theodore Roosevelt), and William Conklin, the director of the Central Park Zoo. To them, high regard was paid to the foreign species that could adapt to a new environment.

First was the English sparrow, or house sparrow. In 1850, the story goes, the first eight pairs were sent from England to the Brooklyn Institute to curb an outbreak of inchworms on Brooklyn's linden trees. The sparrows didn't live long. The next year, though, a hundred came over. Half were released, and the other half bred in Green-Wood Cemetery. Soon enough, house sparrows became the de rigueur pest control for cities and towns throughout the country. They "multiplied amazingly," the American Acclimatization Society reported upon one Central Park release. In his 1859 poem "The Old-World Sparrow," William Cullen Bryant celebrated their arrival as a gift to farmers:

> And the army-worm and the Hessian fly,
> And the dreaded canker-worm shall die,
> And the thrip and slug and fruit-moth seek,
> In vain, to escape that busy beak,
> And fairer harvests shall crown the year,
> For the Old-World sparrow at last is here.

The house sparrow paved the way for the releases of new and increasingly exotic species. From Oregon to Massachusetts, starlings and house sparrows fluttered cheek by jowl with English pheasants, partridges, chaffinches, blackbirds, European goldfinches, bullfinches, nightingales, skylarks, Japanese finches, and Java sparrows. In July 1877, after the American Acclimatization Society released several species in Central Park, among them starlings, members predicted to *The New York Times* that they would all prosper.

Almost none did. But they continued trying. In 1890, the society released 80 starlings in Central Park, and the next year, another 40. These releases fell "under the direction of" Schieffelin, Frank Chapman wrote in 1894, but there was no reason to believe it was a solo effort. (Chapman also noted that the 1890 release included several pairs of European chaffinches.) And there was no mention of Shakespeare at all in records about Schieffelin until well after he died. While a few of those starlings ended up in that drawer at the Museum of Natural History, others finally stuck. One of their first nests was found right outside Chapman's office, on the roof of the museum. After that, they were here to stay.

FRANK CHAPMAN BELIEVED that all the starling introductions outside the city had failed, and his opinion became the conventional wisdom. But as some have suggested, couldn't other starlings have been roving the American landscape, missed by rudimentary field glasses or confused with our blackbird species, until a critical mass was reached? We'll likely never know. We tell ourselves stories, and over time, some stick. But as starlings quickly spread—at the turn of the century they had made it to New Jersey and up the Hudson—perceptions changed of these fresh city dwellers. In 1900, Congress passed the Lacey Act, which authorized the US Department of Agriculture to regulate the import of foreign mammals and birds. Starlings and house sparrows were on the unwanted list; the acclimatization free-for-all was over.

House sparrows were suddenly treated like the pests they were imported to eradicate. *Passer domesticus* became passerine non grata. That busy beak of theirs was not only partial to insects; in the era of horse-drawn carriages, house sparrows descended on half-digested oats in the street. They nested in cracks in buildings and made a racket doing so. The League of American Sportsmen declared "a war of extermination" on them, but that was a losing battle. The author of a guide to the birds of Prospect Park remarked: "There are many common names for this fellow—most of them unprintable."

There was no turning back for starlings either. By 1915, they bred from New England to Virginia; the following year, they crossed the Alleghenies. Every building, birdhouse, broken sign, or woodpecker cavity made a fine starling home. Like house sparrows, they acclimated too well. Starlings were wily. They forced swallows, bluebirds, and wrens from nest boxes, and northern flickers suffered worse. Starlings waited for those good-looking woodpeckers to excavate a tree cavity, then they seized it, repeating this trick again and again until the flickers just gave up. It was enough to inspire "a certain admiration for its superior strategy and prowess," the Massachusetts ornithologist Edward Howe Forbush wrote.

Forbush, though, believed their introduction should never have been undertaken. Many of his contemporaries shared his opinion. Ludlow Griscom, then a colleague of Chapman's, described the starling's introduction as "probably even more regrettable" than the house sparrow's. And by the 1920s, Chapman, once fond of the starling and "its long-drawn, cheery whistle," changed his own tune. His about-face matched the politics of the day. An ugly nativism had gripped the US, as immigrants from Asia and southern and eastern Europe were all but banned from entering the country. In a 1925 essay, Chapman, by then the dean of American ornithologists, wrote of introduced species: "Having with thoughtless hospitality accorded the starling, house sparrow, San José scale, gypsy moth, and other pests, including certain members of the genus *Homo*, free and unchallenged entry to our ports, we now ask (if to our sorrow, we have not already learned), 'Are they desirable?'"

The starling's song was now a "mimetic travesty," he added, their whirling flocks a "hurrying smudge" that stirred "disappointment or indifference." But the truth is, starlings were just beneficiaries of our own society's material gains. In burgeoning eastern cities, starlings roosted in breathtaking numbers in the winter on the vast ledges, windows, and doorways of so many new buildings. In Manhattan, those roosts sometimes numbered up to 200,000. The birds literally whitewashed the Metropolitan Museum of Art and the Riverside Church. They were reverse commuters. Each morning they traveled to feeding grounds beyond the city, in suburbs and farm fields, then returned home in the evening to those ledges.

Public officials objected to the mess they left behind, but what about their usefulness? Rachel Carson, taking up an argument for the starling's citizenship in 1939, noted that the USDA had studied its diet more exhaustively than any other bird's and decided that it was a highly effective insect-pest killer. Yes, the starling ate fruit, she added, but only half as much as the American robin, and nobody was calling for the robin's deportation. And yet, Carson wrote, "In spite of his remarkable success as a pioneer, the starling probably has fewer friends than almost any other creature that wears feathers."

Still, a new generation of scientists began to join her camp. Allan Cruickshank argued in his 1942 book, *Birds Around New York City*, that the starling's bad reputation was unfounded. "I lend no support," he wrote, "to the flimsy objection that the species does not belong here." Roger Tory Peterson, Cruickshank's friend, suggested a few years later that whatever damage house sparrows and starlings had done to native birds was either finished or would soon pass. And perhaps their rehabilitation would have continued were it not for the nature writer Edwin Way Teale, who asserted in 1947 that Schieffelin's desire was to introduce all the birds of Shakespeare.

Where did that come from? According to scholars who recently combed his archives, Teale merged a few different beliefs from Schieffelin's day. Over time, as other writers adorned the tale, Schieffelin became a monomaniacal eccentric, a morality play of human folly, divorced from the acclimatization movement of which he was a member. The scholars Lauren Fugate and John MacNeill Miller debunked the legend in a 2021 paper for *Environmental Humanities*. For the European starling, though, the damage was done.

THE STORIES WE tell about introduced species have consequences. Starlicide is one of those. That's the name of the pesticide DRC-1339, first registered in the US in 1967 and trademarked by the Ralston Purina company, producers of animal feed, in Missouri. (Starlings find a lot to eat at Big Ag cattle feedlots and poultry operations.) Since that time, a little-known federal government program called Bye Bye Blackbird has used Starlicide to kill starlings, taking several native blackbird species with them. In 2009, one of the few years for which the USDA has released statistics, Bye Bye Blackbird claimed a total of four million red-winged blackbirds, starlings, brown-headed cowbirds, and grackles. Outside that program, the government also allows farmers without a permit to kill birds that they claim are causing health risks or economic damage.

It's impossible to say how much of a dent this has taken out of the starling population. One recent estimate puts the current population at 85 million in North America, down from a high of 200 million. That decline can't be explained by Starlicide alone, of course, though the widespread use of chemicals, on lawns and farm fields, surely has contributed. Starlings are also seeing declines in their native Europe, and so too are house sparrows. Greater use of pesticides, changes in agriculture, and the closure of dairy farms have all been given as explanations. Starlings are now a red-listed, or regionally endangered, species in Britain—no longer the cherry-eating pests of yore.

It's hard to survey a species with such a large population, but the Christmas Bird Count makes for an excellent resource. And that shows a huge drop. For the Manhattan count I participated in, which covers the whole island and New Jersey's Meadowlands, starlings' high-water mark was 750,000 in 1978. In 2022, the year I joined, the total was 3,459. For Brooklyn, it was just over 2,200. After speaking to a few birders, I wondered if climate change has reduced starlings' need to flock to New York City in the winter, since, like robins, they now encounter little or no snow cover to prevent them from feeding on the ground. Meanwhile, the open land and farm fields of Long Island and New Jersey, which once drew starlings back and forth between their Manhattan roosts, have become suburban tract housing.

Some birders, like those grumbling during the CBC, might say good riddance. To be honest, I too had developed a habit of unseeing starlings, skipping over them like I would pigeons and house sparrows. And so as I left Paul Sweet at the Museum of Natural History that day, I decided to walk across Central Park to the Met, the starlings' old Beaux-Arts roost. The cold air would help me clear my head.

I wondered why starlings and house sparrows had flourished and not the hundred other foreign species released in this country. They'd already rooted themselves in Europe's capitals, so they were used to living among humans. But they didn't take to the US immediately; it took perseverance on our part. Was it only a matter of time and enough birds then? Was it their diet?

Both starlings and house sparrows are generalists. And they're fast breeders. Starlings will produce two broods in a season; house sparrows, more. The early ornithologist Edward Howe Forbush saw clues in their anatomy. The starling is built like a little crow, he said—hardy, muscular, and powerful. Intelligent too. But perhaps the best explanation is that juvenile starlings dispersed great distances in their first year. Even today, researchers say, young starlings continue to migrate farther than older starlings do.

As they spread westward, new populations established themselves. Wherever they ended up, they had to adapt to their new surroundings—

the dry Sonoran Desert, damp Northwest forests, the sidewalks of New York—and they did so remarkably well, on a timescale that was previously unthinkable for evolutionary change, according to recent genetic research.

Starlings and house sparrows are synanthropes—from the Greek *syn*, "with," and *anthropos*, "human," meaning species that have adapted to live around humans. Synanthropes have been described as our animal shadows, such as the pigeons that occupy every nook and cranny of the city, from playgrounds to subway stations—birds that never existed in the wild and were kicked to the curb after they were no longer useful to us. Or the brown rats and gray squirrels that ended up here, the former unintentionally and the latter brought from Europe to "beautify" our parks, one a plague and the other a pest. Or the raccoons that have always lived on this land but changed their habits to fit a new trash-rich ecology, taking their largest meals from trash cans and dumpsters.

We imagine hard edges between cities and the wild, but they're softer than they seem. Ravens are one of the world's oldest synanthropic bird species, but until about 30 years ago they were a mythical sight in New York. They now nest on warehouses, water towers, apartment buildings, the Brooklyn Bridge, and the Cathedral of Saint John the Divine, where a whitewashed statue of Saint Andrew holds their stick nest. I've watched them eat rats, bird eggs, and baby birds, not to mention pizza. I've also seen crows, their fellow corvids, poke their heads inside traffic light poles on two of the most congested avenues in New York to search for house sparrow eggs. Once these birds made the jump to living around humans, a suite of scavenging opportunities was theirs. Viral videos capture the mighty red-tailed hawk trash-can diving for rats. The American kestrel, our smallest falcon, nests inside cornices above all-night bodegas, hunting its fill of house sparrows. And the peregrine falcon, a regal symbol of wilderness, dines on a pigeon buffet from the city's tallest structures.

Once I reached the Met, about 500 pigeons lined a corner ledge at the south end of the museum, waiting for the daily bread-feeders to show up. Across the rest of the limestone exterior, nearly every flat surface was covered with an almost imperceptible fine black netting. I saw only a handful of starlings. They jockeyed for bits of french fries on the sidewalk and in the taxi-queue lane.

AROUND THIS TIME, I was lifting the blinds in my bedroom one morning when I noticed a hunched bird atop the bell tower of a nearby orange-brick church. It was a bird of prey—that was for sure. Even at a distance, its posture and its choice of perch led me to believe it was a peregrine falcon. Sure enough, squinting through my binoculars, I saw a peregrine plucking a pigeon on a metal cross. The wind carried off the pigeon's soft white feathers like so many snow flurries. It was a fresh kill. For most raptor species, the females are larger than the males, and this peregrine looked huge, so I guessed it was a female. I set up my scope for a closer look. Her dark helmet matched the gunpowder color of the cross, and she sank her yellow talons into the pigeon as she tore it apart. Twenty minutes later, all that remained of the pigeon was a skeleton, which the peregrine unceremoniously flicked off the cross. Then she faced the cold wind and kept watch over the neighborhood the rest of the day, flying away at dusk.

I would have missed this before I became a birder. I rarely scanned the sky, and when I looked around at buildings, it was for their architectural details, not their perches. The peregrine became a regular on the cross for three winters after that morning, and I tracked her many days—watching her from my apartment, while walking to and from the subway, and from the sidewalk below the church. Unlike the novelist J. A. Baker, who published *The Peregrine* in 1967, I didn't have to slog across miles of fenlands in eastern England. The peregrine didn't go far; there was no need. There were always pigeons around—on blacktop courts, lampposts, overpasses.

Peregrine time, however, moved more slowly than any schedule I was used to. It was not the breeding season, so she needed to feed only herself—which meant one pigeon, or perhaps two smaller birds, a day. For unbroken hours, she perched on the cross. I hoped she might stay and nest on a ledge of the church. This was Peter Dorosh's parish, and when I told him we might see a family of peregrines one day, he responded: "Great. We need more congregants!"

New York's peregrine population is around 25 pairs, which is thought to be the greatest concentration in the world. Introduced here in the 1980s, they've been intensely monitored ever since. Nest boxes are set up for them on skyscrapers and suspension bridges, chicks are banded, and fledglings are rescued if they fall into the harbor. One nest, at Manhattan's 55 Water Street, even has its own live camera feed. I looked to see if my neighborhood peregrine was banded, but she wasn't. Had she come from outside New York? Whatever her background, I was quite sure of two things—like those early-generation starlings, she had human fingerprints all over her, and she was well suited to city life.

I thought I knew the peregrine story—it, like the Schieffelin myth, is birding lore. In the two decades after World War II, all the peregrines east of the Mississippi, estimated at around 350 pairs, were lost to the use of pesticides like DDT. Their nests, or aeries, were usually on cliffs, like the rock walls of the Palisades on the west side of the Hudson, across from Upper Manhattan. They also fell to critically low levels in the western US and Europe. In 1962, Rachel Carson's *Silent Spring* sounded the alarm over pesticides and reported that peregrines, bald eagles, and ospreys that had ingested DDT had started laying thin-shelled eggs that cracked during incubation. A few years later, when J. A. Baker wrote *The Peregrine*, he may have thought he was watching their final days in England. In 1970, the US government listed the peregrine as endangered. Two years later, DDT was banned, and scientists and conservationists began a captive-breeding program to reintroduce peregrines to the wild.

But what I didn't realize was that before DDT, peregrines had already started making inroads into several large cities. In New York, a monumental era of bridge and skyscraper construction was capped in 1931 with the Empire State Building, then the world's tallest building. Peregrines quickly arrived on the scene of the newly towering city. In the 1940s, a pair nested on the St. Regis hotel and an abandoned building on the Upper West Side, though ASPCA agents drove them off after complaints from hotel guests and pigeon racers. In the winter, though, as many as 16 peregrines hunted from regular posts on Manhattan skyscrapers, several bridges, and a tank at a gas plant and a high school in the Bronx. Like cliffs, these elevated structures were a major appeal, but so too were the droves of starlings and pigeons that were settling nicely into the city. I shouldn't have been surprised to learn that one peregrine wintered at the Riverside Church, where it picked starlings out of the dark blizzard that swirled around it every morning and evening.

This urban adaptation became important during their reintroduction. In 1970, ornithologist Tom Cade founded the Peregrine Fund, and at his Cornell University lab he gathered a melting pot of peregrines from around the world. With only a few remaining American peregrines (*Falco peregrinus anatum*), he had to mate them with other subspecies from British Columbia, Scotland, Spain, Chile, the Arctic, and southern Australia. Beginning in 1974, their first chicks were released on cliffs and on specially built towers in coastal marshes. The young were "hacked"—kept in a custom-built enclosure and provided food through a chute until they were old enough to fly. The marsh releases proved successful, but not the releases at the ancestral aeries; without their parents around, young peregrines were picked off by the likes of great horned owls. But Cade was familiar with the history of urban peregrines, and he knew they didn't need much for an aerie—just a tray of sand and gravel on a skyscraper ledge.

In 1980, the first peregrines were released in New York on the top of the Manhattan Life Building on West 57th Street. Three years later, the first pairs moved onto the Verrazzano and Throgs Neck Bridges. Others soon occupied former winter haunts like the Riverside Church. There was no genetic memory, of course, only the fact that these superstructures suited a peregrine's instinctual need to command the landscape.

Today's resident peregrines in New York City have probably never seen a cliff in their lives. Does that make them less wild? They're certainly streetwise. In *Hawks in Flight*, the authors—Pete Dunne, David Allen Sibley, and Clay Sutton—suggest a new subspecies for North America's city peregrines: *Falco peregrinus urbanii*.

AFTER THE MANHATTAN Life release, Tom Cade met with New York City mayor Ed Koch. Koch was concerned that introduced peregrines "might become another problem like starlings," he told the ornithologist. As Cade recalled in the preface to the book *City Peregrines*, "When we told him that we would be extremely lucky to get two or three pairs established in the city, he relaxed and made a public announcement that 'these falcons are better than pigeons.'" On June 30, 1981, Koch called them "the national bird of New York City" during a ceremony at City Hall Park, where he held a peregrine in one arm and declared it Peregrine Falcon Day. Was it a coincidence, a *Times* editorial asked, that the ceremony came only two days after pigeons were key suspects in the snapping of Brooklyn Bridge cables?

There are now a lot more than two or three pairs. I took a spin up to Central Park West with Bruce Yolton, the author of a blog called *Urban Hawks,* to visit a relatively new winter post of a peregrine pair at the El Dorado apartment building. The scene was too good to pass up. For their futuristic designs, art deco buildings are a personal favorite of mine, and peregrines seem to like their geometry too. The building's two brick-clad towers rise like tiered wedding cakes, and each giant ledge acts as a cliff. Air conditioners serve a similar purpose. "I call that the picnic table," Yolton said, pointing to a unit almost 30 stories up on the north tower. "When they catch prey, they bring it there."

Yolton set up his scope just inside Central Park. After waiting a few minutes, one of the peregrines came gliding overhead toward the El Dorado. When it flapped, power rippled down its wings like the crack of a bullwhip. Yolton said it was the male. He landed on a ledge above the picnic table and announced himself with a loud, rising wail. The female soon followed. She was visibly larger than her mate, and we watched her soar above the El Dorado, a bird with absolutely nothing to fear. Yolton chuckled to himself. "It looks like so much fun," he said.

What came to mind were the ironworkers who walk high steel, graced with a view of the city we mere landlubbers can only dream about. The falcons' view across West 91st Street was like looking down a canyon to the Hudson River.

When the pair first arrived in February 2019, Yolton watched them pursue pigeons up and down Central Park West in high-speed attacks. The white on a pigeon is visible to peregrines from far away. "They're very noisy in the morning, so everybody who lives up there knows them," he said. He was invited by a resident to get a closer look.

It wasn't the first time that had happened. There was another pair of peregrines that had a nest on a nearby church, and Yolton spent many days watching them and their young. "A few of the fledglings would stay for a day or two on someone's balcony without moving, which is typical for young, scared kids," he told me. "There was a guy who lived across the street who had a terrace, and he invited me to his apartment to take some photos. And I thought, New Yorkers don't do this."

The man's daughter was in first grade, and she asked Yolton what he was going to photograph. When he told her, she said, "I know about peregrines. I'm writing a paper on them in school."

They watched them together for about 10 minutes, Yolton said, and then he told her it was Rachel Carson's birthday. "She's the reason we have peregrines again," he said.

"Yes, I know," the girl replied. "She's the person who figured out that the eggs were too thin."

Peregrines are a glowing tale of conservation success. Even kids know that. But I was trying to understand why some birds are the villains of our stories and others the heroes. Currently, starlings are unwanted and peregrines are celebrated; that was not always so. Two great releases, 90 years apart, happened in this city: Schieffelin's and Cade's. It's reductive to try to point to the murky origins of these species in our ecosystems—native versus nonnative, or said another way, introduced by humans (intentionally or not) versus not introduced by humans—since humans have been modifying or meddling with ecosystems since our first dawn. That view in itself—that we "meddle" with nature—puts us outside of it, or apart from it. Perhaps by thinking of ourselves as part of nature, we might be less inclined to judge species by how useful or interesting they are to us and take as a given the fact that their existence means there is a place for them.

Starlings and pigeons, though, are flock birds; peregrines are individualistic. The ability to track the same bird, to get to know it, helps us build emotional connections from afar. Flock birds get lost in a crowd. In that regard, raptors like peregrines and red-tailed hawks have become key characters in this city's wildlife-adaptation drama. These large, striking predators are often the first birds that New Yorkers get excited about. They make quite an impression. And they're often loyal to the same locations year after year, so it's easy to watch their behavior and understand them one by one. And if you are so inclined, you can even attach a name to them.

CHAPTER 3

# Flaco

On the first day of 2023, I went to the beach. The local chapter of the American Littoral Society, a coastal protection group, was having its annual New Year's walk at Fort Tilden, the former military base near Breezy Point. I didn't expect a large turnout, but at 11 in the morning more than 80 people had crowded around Don Riepe, the chapter's spry former director. Riepe uncorked a bottle of cheap bubbly, which sprayed into the seaside air.

"I think I hit a seagull," he said, laughing as he began pouring into Dixie cups.

We gathered beside an old wood-framed white chapel in a barren field. Beyond the field, in a patchy maritime forest, multiflora rose and bittersweet, typical invasive plants, were climbing over birches and pitch pines and bayberries, swallowing up old batteries and bunkers. Fort Tilden, like the tip of Breezy Point, is part of the National Park Service's Gateway National Recreation Area, and its rangers do little to no habitat management here. I love those pines, in part because saw-whet owls like to roost in them. On the night of the Christmas Bird Count, I had heard there were two around. The Owl Whisperer had found them in the "usual spot." Don would know where that was, but I couldn't just ask him. That wasn't done with owls.

As he opened a second bottle, I drank in the festive cheer. It felt like a reunion, and in many ways it was. Several former high school classmates, leaning on hiking poles, had been coming since the first walk in 1981. Many people had known Don, who was in his eighties, for decades. Prior to joining the Littoral Society, he'd been a ranger at Gateway for more than 25 years. (Pronounced like the word *literal*, the name comes from the Latin word for "shore" or "beach.") Though the group that day skewed older, Don had young admirers too, including an 11-year-old boy who idolized him. The boy's mother had made a chocolate cake for Don, and its icing portrayed a familiar urban scene: a peregrine sinking its yellow talons into a pigeon.

Don is robust, about five foot five, with the barrel-chested build of someone who jumps in and out of boats tying knots all day. His face, round and smiling, has a small, curved nose and sharp blue eyes that twinkle when he gets ready to tell a story. He's a joker, and I heard about one prank he had pulled on his keen-eyed regulars the previous spring. During a hike around the Jamaica Bay Wildlife Refuge, he made a show of finding three candy eggs he had secretly hidden beside the trail. "A woodcock nest!" he said, picking up the eggs. "Can we touch them?" he was asked. "One second," he said. "I wonder how they taste." He popped one in his mouth and crunched down. Cue shock and horror.

Don lives in an old cottage in Broad Channel, an island community of about 2,500 on Jamaica Bay. Its ground floor doubles as the Littoral Society's local office. As New York has become hotter and wetter, his house has grown increasingly flood-prone. A recent storm had been a doozy, so I asked him how he made out. He laughed. "You're like all the other reporters," he said, in a reedy voice shored up by an outer-borough accent. "I'm the guy people call when they wanna talk about sea level rise."

It had been touch and go. During the storm, floodwaters climbed to within six inches of his oil burner and destroyed papers and books. But he had raised his electrical outlets after Hurricane Sandy in 2012, and raised his valuables after Hurricane Ida in 2021.

It was time for a free raffle. The prizes were 10 different 8.5 × 11 photos Don had shot. Alexandra Kanonik, the director who had taken over from Don, reached into an envelope and held up a photo of a great egret standing on Don's deck.

"Edgar!" she said.

People applauded. Edgar was clearly familiar to this crowd. For a decade now, Don had been feeding the egret silversides at his house, between his springtime arrival and his autumn departure. Before Edgar, there was Egor, the first egret to beg Don for fish.

"Don't worry." Don grinned. "If you don't win this one, I'll take another and sell it to you for a thousand dollars!"

By the time the raffle ended, it was half an hour into the festivities. Don hollered, "Let's go! Double time!" and a long shapeless line snaked across the field. Once we reached the shore—the littoral zone—Kanonik handed out sparklers. The plan was to light them and hold up a large mirror to signal to the Sandy Hook chapter, eight miles across the ocean, in New Jersey. It was an idiosyncratic tradition, a message sent across a distance with little expectation of a reply; none had ever been noted. The point was getting outside on a morning when many were sleeping off hangovers, to see what lived here in the winter.

The beach was packed. Shirtless kids played soccer while others plunged in the water. It was over 50 degrees and unusually warm. Just beyond the surf, 20 buffleheads bobbed like rubber ducks as they took turns diving. The backlit silhouette of a long-tailed duck sped by in fast, twisting flight.

As Kanonik began the countdown, Don stepped over to me.

"We located a saw-whet owl," he whispered. "I'll show you afterward."

Incredible! I tried to play it cool, hide my excitement, but I couldn't help wondering what I had done to earn this privilege.

The sparklers sputtered out, unrecognized for another year. Then Don led the group back around the dunes. We filed past a hulking concrete gun battery, tufts of vegetation sprouting between the steps to its top.

Don pulled me over and pointed ahead to a sixtyish man with white hair and a white goatee who was clad in black technical gear and black sunglasses. I'd never seen a birder dressed like that. "He'll show you the owl," Don said. "He was the one who found it."

I walked up. "Are you the Owl Whisperer?" I asked.

His face broke into a smile. Indeed he was. Born in Bay Ridge, he was an IT professional who lived outside the city, in the town of Lido Beach, but he still regularly drove about an hour each way to search for owls. He was proud of his CBC record. He had at least 20 saves to his name, he told me, most of them saw-whets. He enjoyed showing them to others, especially if the saw-whet was a "life bird" or "lifer" for them, which is what birders call your first time seeing a specific species. That was the case for the boy and his mother, the one who brought the cake—they joined us.

It was easy to break off, because the group was now strung out. We followed the Owl Whisperer around the gun battery toward a grove of pitch pines. Then I heard someone ask behind me, "Where are they going?"

I turned around and saw a couple I had met earlier talking to Don. My heart sank. I had learned that they were getting into birding and that we lived in the same neighborhood. I wanted to tell them. I really did. I knew how exciting this could be for them. But there was an owl code in New York.

I was out of earshot before I heard Don's response.

YES, AN OWL code. This varies by borough. Brooklyn, my home, is the strictest. As an example, its eBird moderators (volunteers who are some of the best birders in the area) will write to people who have submitted an owl sighting and ask them to remove it. (eBird now automatically hides submissions of some highly sensitive owl species from public viewing.) We all want to see owls, but they're nocturnal, and easily disturbed during their daytime slumber. The American Birding Association's guidelines seem like common sense: Don't get too close. Don't use audio recordings. Don't publicize the location. Manhattan sits on the other end of the spectrum; Manhattan Bird Alert—a Twitter (now X) account created by a birder and retired hedge fund manager named David Barrett—will post an owl's roost down to the branch. At last check, Manhattan Bird Alert had almost 90,000 followers.

No other group of birds in New York sparks such heated emotions. Robert DeCandido, a white-haired, raspy-voiced Central Park guide better known as Birding Bob, has compared the Brooklyn Bird Club's mores to the Mafia's. "They keep things really secret," he told a reporter from *The New York Times*. The Brooklyn Bird Club's president told me about his own personal policy: He asks his friends *not* to share owl sightings with him. Consequently, he avoids some thorny questions: Who should I tell? Can they keep a secret? Who'll disown me if I don't tell them? Another friend of mine once found a great horned owl nest in Prospect Park and took me to see it. This was exciting news—there were only a few nests in the entire city. He said I could tell my wife, Angie, who's also a birder (owls aren't worth upsetting a happy home), but that was it.

If owls are the touch paper, then social media is the match. Wildlife experts suggest that an owl will be stressed by lots of attention. But for many photographers, the chance of getting a photo or a video they can share on Instagram or X—where David Barrett might retweet it—turns otherwise sane people into like-hungry fanatics. When a pair of long-eared owls recently turned up in Central Park, the New York City Department of Parks and Recreation's X account had to urge people to give them space. I have reason to think this is particular to New York. In other places, birders have shared an owl's roost with me as freely as recommending a restaurant, but they don't have to worry about hundreds of people showing up, or a birding scene as competitive as New York's. Normally, finding an owl takes time, patience, and know-how. As Bruce Yolton of *Urban Hawks* told me, "Maybe that should be the barrier to entry." But if a roost is readily publicized, none of this is required.

I can understand why passions run red-hot. Owls are incredible—mysterious, charismatic, easy to anthropomorphize, with their large forward-facing eyes and unblinking gaze. "Perhaps no other creature has been invested with such contradictory meanings across so many different cultures—as a protective spirit, a totem of erudition and an omen of death," Michiko Kakutani once wrote in the *Times*. When you see an owl, it feels like you're touching something ancient, otherworldly—the goddess Athena's companion, the Chauvet Cave in southern France—even in the middle of New York City.

I returned to Fort Tilden two weeks later with the hope of finding that saw-whet owl again. I looked in the same spot, and there it was, tucked into needles near the trunk of a short pitch pine. The small predator was visible only if you stood a few steps from the base of the tree. I marveled at how the Owl Whisperer had discovered it. The owl was asleep, but red around its bill suggested that it had eaten recently, probably some mouse leftovers from the night before. It was a blocky bird, its wide head nearly half the size of its auburn-streaked body.

Had I not known it was there, I could've detected clues from the birds that were very much alert to its presence. Two black-capped chickadees poked around the pitch pines like sentinels, and their twitchy alarm calls were answered by another curious little bird, a red-breasted nuthatch. Like the Owl Whisperer, they knew how to find a saw-whet. I left once the owl opened its yellow eyes and stared at me.

But of course, I hoped to find my own owl. So I ventured to Hunter Island, in the Bronx's Pelham Bay Park, to visit a grove of tall white pines at the rocky northern tip of the city. Pelham Bay is the city's largest park, more than three times larger than Central Park, and sits at one end of the 6 local train. The grove was a winter birding destination I'd first heard about from Peter Dorosh. Twenty years earlier, you could see four kinds of owls: barred, great horned, long-eared, and saw-whet. The trees were smaller then.

On a frigid morning, a friendly Bronx birder and I followed Long Island Sound past stands of stunted swamp white oaks on bedrock that ended up in Maine. Named for John Hunter, the man whose estate once included this parcel, the Lenape people of the area had another name for Hunter Island (which is no longer an island): Lap-Haa-Waach King, or "place of stringing beads," for the shells they gathered to make wampum. We encountered two local birders, one of whom volunteered that there was a barred owl in the pines.

"Don't advertise it, okay?" he asked kindly. His concern was for the bird's safety. "I don't put it on the alerts anymore," he said.

The barred owl wasn't difficult to find. At the grove, a pair of Queens birders pointed it out. The owl was three-quarters of the way up and conspicuous; in fact, they told us, a raven had just harassed it.

After a few hushed minutes, the bird turned its head 180 degrees to face us. Its eyes were so dark they seemed like holes, surrounded by pale, funnel-like facial disks. A striped coat framed its face like a cowl that bunched at the chest.

We sighed happily at our good fortune, and the Queens couple showed us an arrow on the path, which they had made with three sticks. The arrow pointed to the roost tree. It was meant for searching birders, but I wasn't sure I would have noticed it on my own. I could understand their motivation. When you encounter something magical, it's hard not to want to share it—to leave your own mark.

As promised, my friend and I didn't advertise it. But two days later, I saw that the man who'd shared the sighting with us had listed it on eBird. Maybe it didn't matter, I thought, because four birders from Manhattan had already done the same. That was the culture on their side of town. Perhaps they'd reasoned that the barred owl's hiding spot didn't put it in jeopardy. After all, the pine grove was hardly a secret location. But I suspect it was just a matter of friendly competition. They wanted to add one more species to their year's tally, a figure that anyone could find on eBird, and they didn't feel like waiting until the owl had left for the season.

WHEN DID THIS high-stakes struggle start? As far as I could tell, it began a few years earlier, with another owl, a female barred owl that somebody named Barry.

Barry was first spotted in Central Park on October 9, 2020, in the park's wooded north end. (I'm not too fond of naming birds, for fear of falling too heavily into anthropomorphism. For ease of storytelling, though, and sometimes for conservation value, it has its pluses, so I'll go with it.) It was the dark days of the pandemic, and there were lots of new birders for whom observing a wild owl in the heart of this great big city was a mind-splitting event. Some described their desire to see Barry as an obsession. Thanks to David Barrett's updates, she drew large crowds day and night. The gaggle itself seemed to be part of the attraction. Within a month, the *Times* had published a front-page article in its local section, headlined CENTRAL PARK'S NEW CELEBRITY BIRD SOAKS UP ATTENTION, in which reporter Lisa M.

Collins wrote with anthropomorphic glee about an owl she assumed was male: "He plucks chipmunks with his talons and devours them, seemingly unfazed by adoring fans and the paparazzi, many of whom have already made him Instagram-famous."

A *new* celebrity bird? Before Barry, that title was held by a male mandarin duck that appeared in the Pond at Central Park in 2018. He was an escaped aviary bird; local coverage branded him "the hot duck." David Barrett once tried to coax the duck into the open by tossing him pieces of a soft pretzel, and when that failed, he quacked at it.

But Barry wasn't the first owl celebrity either. In the 1940s, according to Roger Tory Peterson, a barred owl perched every day for two winters in the same tree on Fifth Avenue, and bus conductors pointed it out to their passengers. Unlike that owl, however, Barry had her every move instantly disseminated to tens of thousands of people. "This is the information age," Barrett told the *Times*. "People can report what they see."

Barry was found that 2020 night by Birding Bob. DeCandido charged 10 bucks for a nighttime owl walk, and Barry became a major selling point for him. He would blast hoots from a portable speaker to pull her into the open, then shine a flashlight on her. DeCandido later compared his tactics to fishing, saying, "I go out there with an audio lure." Back in 2008, when he charged five dollars, a *Times* reporter followed along. DeCandido's target that night was an eastern screech owl, a robin-sized cavity nester. His speaker blared the owl's whinnying call on loop, drawing out the bird at a time when it was looking for a mate. As the reporter described it: "Bird and machine called back and forth to each other, a haunting sound of longing in the darkness."

Does that sound disruptive to you? DeCandido, who holds a PhD in botany, says he's never harmed a bird, though his defense tends to be circular: "The more people see this, the more they'll like owls, and the less they'll want ice-skating rinks and things that reduce what owls need, which is woods." But he's also frank. "It's good for business," he says.

DeCandido relies on audio lures, or "playback," as birders call them, all year long. In the spring, he rolls through the Ramble with his Bluetooth speaker sounding the distress calls of songbirds. I should repeat that: distress calls. Until you've experienced it in person, it's hard to convey just how loud, obnoxious, and grating it is.

In a short *Times* documentary, DeCandido acknowledges that his behavior is antithetical to people's search for peace in nature. "To say that I'm hated, you know, that's mild." The film ends with him in the Bronx's Van Cortlandt Park at night, blasting hoots from a dance-hall speaker and shining his flashlight on a jumpy barred owl.

Using playback is against Central Park's rules. But if it sounds harmless enough, I heard a gruesome story on my visit to Hunter Island that suggests otherwise. Hoping for the perfect shot, a photographer there used playback to wake up a saw-whet owl. A barred owl in the woods responded to the recording, found the little owl, and tore it to bits in front of the photographer.

The owls that show up in New York in the winter are usually young or migrating, Bruce Yolton told me, so this may be the most difficult and stressful time in their lives—as it was with Barry. Large groups camped out beneath her roost tree during the day, and at night they tracked her as she hunted. Yolton wrote a 3,500-word blog post called "A Wild Barred Owl Is Not a Celebrity," which challenged the media coverage and profit-making focused on Barry and her "'Beatlemania' type fan base." Yolton was a vocal critic of DeCandido and Barrett, but he was a lonely voice in the wilderness.

Unusually, Barry didn't leave the park to seek a mate, and she stayed through the summer of 2021. She became atypically active during the day, another sign that perhaps something was not right. Early one day in August, around 2:30 a.m., she died after colliding with a maintenance vehicle on the park's drive. #RIPBarry trended on Twitter. Public records reporting by *The City* showed that the owl had high levels of rat poison in her bloodstream, leaving her at risk for a fatal collision. "There's a lot of us who are devastated today," a photographer told the *Times*. "We always knew she might fly away and start a family, but none of us were prepared for this."

I was slightly turned off by the crowds following her, so I never went to see Barry. I felt for those who grieved her, though, even if it was an outcome that was not all that surprising. City rats make for easy, available prey, and many urban raptors, from owls to red-tailed hawks, fall victim to poisoning each year. But I couldn't help but wonder what influence Barry's paparazzi may have had on her ability to hunt more freely and with less interference.

A MONTH AFTER my New Year's Day walk at Fort Tilden, there was a break-in at the Central Park Zoo. On February 2, 2023, someone scaled the waist-high fence of the Temperate Territory section, walked past snow leopards, snow monkeys, and red pandas, and cut open the steel-mesh enclosure of a Eurasian eagle-owl named Flaco. At 8:30 p.m., a zoo employee reported the vandalism to police. By then, Flaco was gone.

But he didn't travel far. He was spotted about six blocks away on the sidewalk of Bergdorf Goodman, where he drew a crowd. A photo posted on Twitter showed Flaco surrounded by yellow crime-scene tape and flashing red lights. Officers from the New York Police Department's 19th Precinct stood next to a small pet carrier. "Apparently in case he wanted to surrender," ABC News later reported. Flaco looked terrified; his head, with its big orange eyes, was literally spinning. Before zoo staff could arrive, he flew into the fountain outside the Plaza Hotel. He spent the freezing night in a tree on 59th Street.

*Flaco* is Spanish for "skinny," which seemed an odd name for a bird of his kind. The Eurasian eagle-owl is among the world's largest owls, a more imposing cousin of the great horned owl, with wingspans that can exceed six feet. Flaco, however, had not been able to flex his wings much. He hatched at a bird park in North Carolina on March 15, 2010, the seventh of 20 owlets hatched by captive parents over a nine-year period. Flaco's siblings ended up in zoos around the country, including the Bronx Zoo. Sent to the Central Park Zoo, his first pen was outdoors, but he was then moved inside to one with a painted mountain vista, some tree branches, and fake rocks. It was barely twice the width of his spread wings. Birds like this are window dressing for zoos, one ornithologist told me, the kind you can order on the internet. Flaco lived on a diet of dead mice. One visitor described him as "grumpy" and "slightly pudgy." In the wild, Eurasian eagle-owls live in the woods, farmlands, and mountains of Europe and Asia, often in areas with rocky outcrops and cliffs. Some live in cities too. One pair, for instance, raised three chicks on a windowsill planter in the Belgian city of Geel. But they do not live free in US cities.

Flaco flew into Central Park the morning after his escape. I say "flew," but he crashed into branches while making short flights from one tree to the next, tiring himself out. He was terrible at hiding, a necessary skill for any owl on the outside. Owls roost in conifers during the winter, but he perched more than 60 feet off the ground in a bare deciduous tree. He was lashed by the wind and spooked by a squirrel.

I followed this news at home, but I didn't feel a great urge to see Flaco in real life. His every move was covered by Manhattan Bird Alert. Here was another celebrity bird. It was a Manhattan thing, a curiosity, an oddity, a fluke. Some birders even tried to list him on eBird, but those entries didn't constitute scientific data—captive escapees don't "count." Flaco had no experience in the wild. It was only a matter of time until zoo employees recaptured him. Or worse.

Flaco wasn't eating, because he didn't know how to hunt. But he made himself difficult to catch by staying off the ground. So on his sixth day outside captivity, I finally decided to go see him with Bruce Yolton. Yolton had been watching him every day until around midnight. Though he acknowledged the strange circumstances, Yolton was enjoying observing Flaco's adaptation. Flaco had begun choosing more concealed roosts. He had hopped around in a tree. He was growing stronger. He was learning by trial and error. And he seemed to be tapping into some repressed instincts. Two nights before, Yolton had heard him hoot 20 times in 10 minutes. Zoo employees had told Yolton they'd only ever heard him hoot around once a year.

As Yolton and I walked up, Flaco was roosting in an ivy-covered tree right outside the zoo. "He's getting good at hiding," Yolton said. There were about 25 people watching him, a mix of curious passersby and birders. Five photographers, one of whom was dressed in head-to-toe camouflage, had set up giant telephoto lenses on tripods. Yolton shared notes on Flaco's progress with a few others. "This is the one owl we can share the location of!" he said, to laughter.

Yolton set up his scope and shared close views of Flaco with anyone who wanted to see him. He was beautiful—you could search for meaning in those orange eyes—but of course I had no way of knowing what all this was like for him. He did look more settled than on his first night outside the zoo. This was one of the busiest entrances to the park, and over the next hour, I counted a dozen different languages spoken from the tourists who stopped to look. The group swelled, spilling into the center of the road. As a young French couple peered through Yolton's scope, a horse-drawn carriage burst past and nearly ran them over. The driver hollered, "I know the owl is there, but you have to get out of the way!"

Standing apart from the fray were zoo employees carrying walkie-talkies and binoculars. They looked solemn. They were under instructions to not speak to the press, so I didn't try talking to them. For years, they had cared for this animal, but the situation was spiraling out of their control. I told Flaco's story to three women from Poland and said the zoo was waiting to bring him back.

"I hope not," one of them said. Walking away, she cried, "Freedom!"

I left at dusk, feeling a sense of unease. Nobody knew what was going to happen next, and that seemed to be part of the appeal. Few people wanted to see Flaco confined again, but he wasn't a cuddly pet; in the wild, eagle-owls are apex predators.

Flaco wasn't wild, but he was big news now—international news. The hashtag #FreeFlaco began trending on Twitter. Several friends who had never expressed the slightest interest in birds peppered me with questions. I shared my ambivalence, noting that a free Eurasian eagle-owl could attack the native birds like red-tailed hawks or peregrine falcons that nested in or around Central Park, driving them or their young away to claim the territory for himself. One friend accused me of xenophobia and called me a MAGA birder. Why did it matter that Flaco was not native if he was able to survive on his own? he asked. Did I want him tossed back into his cage?

No, I replied. But I really didn't know the right answer.

THE NEXT NIGHT, Flaco tried to hunt. He parked himself by some exposed Manhattan schist and waited awhile for a brown rat to run over it. There was a neat echo to the fact that wild Eurasian eagle-owls are drawn to rocky outcrops.

Zoo staffers also made their move. While playing audio recordings of female Eurasian eagle-owls, they tried to capture Flaco with traps baited with a lab rat. Flaco pursued the bait and briefly got tangled in the netting, but he flew off as staffers rushed forward. And they were far from the only humans on the scene. David Barrett was using the #FreeFlaco hashtag on Manhattan Bird Alert as he live-tweeted about the recovery efforts. Yolton told me that 30 people he had never seen birding in the park before arrived during Barrett's play-by-play, and they milled around the traps like bodyguards. Jim Breheny, the director of the Bronx Zoo, castigated Barrett on Twitter: "Whatever your intent, your need to seem relevant or involved in this effort is not at all helpful." But Barrett, it appeared, didn't want to help.

The next day, a wildlife photographer named David Lei posted a photo on Twitter that he had taken of Flaco holding a rat in his beak. He had finally caught one the previous night. For the next two days, the zoo still tried to lure Flaco to traps, but he ignored them and continued hunting. The zoo decided to call off its capture attempts, sending out a statement that read, in part: "Several days ago, we observed him successfully hunting, catching and consuming prey. We have seen a rapid improvement in his flight skills and ability to confidently maneuver around the park. A major concern for everyone at the beginning was whether Flaco would be able to hunt and eat; that is no longer a concern."

Ten days after his escape, Flaco was free.

I KNEW VERY few birders who traveled to Central Park to see Flaco. Was it because they couldn't list it? Or because of all the media attention? Did they share the unease I felt? One friend told me his feelings about Flaco changed after Flaco started hunting; suddenly, this was a real bird doing bird things, not a helpless zoo animal. Around that time, the mayor's office was looking to hire a well-salaried "rat czar," whose job would be to reduce rat numbers. People joked that Flaco was the perfect candidate.

Like a diet made up of brown rats, adaptation isn't always pretty—but consider all those synanthropic species carving out an existence in New York City's liminal spaces. It was to their advantage. As Flaco settled into Central Park, all the birders I knew were instead eager to see a native bird—a Swainson's hawk—that had ended up at a recycling plant on Brooklyn's industrial waterfront. I saw parallels between the two birds' odysseys.

The Swainson's hawk was a juvenile, and it was extremely lost. It should have been in South America, feeding on grasshoppers in the Pampas of Argentina. Swainson's hawks migrate between the Northern and Southern Hemispheres, with round trips that can exceed 12,000 miles—the second-longest among raptors, surpassed only by Arctic-breeding peregrine falcons. As they leave their breeding grounds in western North America in the fall, hundreds of thousands of them routinely pass through bottleneck land passages in Veracruz, Mexico, and Panama City. The occasional stray ends up on the East Coast, and a few have been observed in New York. But until 2023, never during winter.

When I went to see the hawk on a cold March morning, I hopscotched across rutted streets and pressed my face against a chain-link fence outside the Sims recycling plant, a multiwarehouse campus that collected most of the city's curbside recyclables. It was not on any New York City birding map, but the place was teeming with birds. Gulls and crows swirled overhead, and from that ruckus I heard a raven's croak. A red-tailed hawk, perched on a lamppost, looked over hills of rubble and rebar, and its relaxed posture suggested that it knew its way around. Hundreds of starlings, fish crows, and pigeons picked from a small mountain of plastic. A giant green claw reached into a dockside barge and dropped on it a fresh snowpack of single-use. Out in the harbor was the Statue of Liberty. *The United States of Trash*, I thought.

Another birder rushed up. "Are you on it?" she asked.

I said I wasn't.

"This is my third time here," she explained.

I turned around and watched two birders on bikes swerve around big rigs pulling in and out of the facility. Despite our good nature, Sims had denied birders access to the plant. So we waited outside the fence with our scopes and ran through the hawk's strange trip. It had been found two months earlier on the Staten Island waterfront, where it ate rats on the shore. It left after two days, but then, like a phantom, reappeared some weeks later at Green-Wood Cemetery. One clever birder thought it might be getting by on the easy meals down here, just half a mile from the cemetery, so he staked out the facility and caught it flying in.

An hour passed, and then someone in the group picked out the hawk hunched down on a light fixture in the eaves of the receiving warehouse. It had probably been there all along, eyeing rats in the new stuff. Its appearance was fearsome: stout and neckless, its bib and streaks were the color of milk chocolate. It flexed its right wing—like a scimitar, one person said—which almost reached its tail, then hopped onto that mountain with the other city birds.

I'd seen enough. This really wasn't my kind of birding. But that *was* my stuff in there.

AFTER THE CENTRAL Park Zoo's statement, Flaco relocated to the Loch, the quiet woods that Barry the barred owl had roamed. The Loch was conveniently located across from a construction site at the Harlem Meer, where Flaco was photographed from a distance eating rats on top of a yellow excavator. Seeing that, I couldn't help but smile.

I decided to visit him again on the first afternoon of spring. I entered the park at 103rd Street, and a tufted titmouse whistled, cheery-sounding, from a leggy oak in the sunshine. I assumed the tree had supplied it with acorns during the winter months. For all I knew, I had counted this same bird on the Christmas Bird Count. But its departure was coming; spring was everywhere. In truth, it had been kicking around for a while. Daffodils popped in large patches. Buds of red maples poked out, the color of Matisse's Venetian red. Benches were full of people.

I walked down a series of rock steps and under a stone bridge, following a stream into the Loch. Frederick Law Olmsted and Calvert Vaux, Central Park's designers, had created the Loch, but the stream itself, once called Montayne's Rivulet, was ancient; sections of it still flowed along its old bed until it drained into the underground Harlem Creek.

Several hundred yards into the woods, I saw around 20 people spread out on either side of the creek. Flaco, his head tucked in, rested in the crook of a tall red oak that bent over a gentle waterfall. The dark streaks on his back matched the oak's runners, lending some camouflage. It was around four, and over the next three hours he'd have a steady watching party. Hundreds of people paused briefly to look up at him—dog walkers, joggers, groups of schoolchildren. They all knew his story.

Soon, Flaco woke up and began hooting. He put his entire body into each hoot, one every 15 to 45 seconds, raising his tail and leaning forward in a slo-mo Hungry Hungry Hippos move. The combination of the dark feathers at the bottom of his face and his fluffy white throat feathers brought to mind the Cheshire Cat. Flaco's hoots echoed through the Loch. Then he walked across the branch to warm his tawny body in shoots of sunlight; he puffed out his feathers and preened, cleaning his wings and talons.

I sat on a wooden fence and heard conversations in English, Hebrew, Spanish, and Mandarin. A familiar refrain was, "Are you going to stay for the flyout?" The *flyout* is the sweet spot for respectful owl viewing, the twilight moment when these nocturnal predators rouse from their daytime slumber and venture into the night.

I eavesdropped on a conversation among five older women that told me a lot about Flaco's fandom. To them, the boundaries between wild and captive were loose. They shared stories about a great horned owl in Central Park named Geraldine, and about Gus, the Central Park Zoo's late polar bear who swam laps in his pool for up to 12 hours a day. They chatted about Flaco the way people of an earlier generation must have talked about the first moon landing. Where were you when you heard... he was at the playground? In the evergreen? Outside the zoo? Uptown? One of the women had a camera; none had binoculars. They were animal lovers. "He's used to us," one said of Flaco. "He's adapted. He likes people." They grieved Barry. "She gave people an excuse to come to the park during COVID," said another.

Looking around, I realized that the people waiting for Flaco to fly out were as diverse as the city itself. This was a social gathering, an owl-watching commons. There aren't many spaces left to meet in New York that don't require you to spend money, I thought. A park is one, and this might explain the growing popularity of urban birding. But one bird had brought this crowd together.

About 40 minutes from sunset, Flaco turned to face the construction site and resumed hooting. His hoots sounded louder now, or maybe the park was just quieter. Only the die-hards remained, including a small band of photographers on Huddlestone Arch, who were hoping for a head-on shot as Flaco flew to the Harlem Meer. I noticed Bruce Yolton on his own, off to the side of the creek, and I walked over to say hello. He had just returned from two weeks in southern Africa, but he was quickly back on the Flaco beat. Yesterday,

Flaco had nibbled on a rat he'd saved from the previous day, Yolton told me; the owl used to wolf them down whole but now was stashing for the future. Yolton—and countless other observers—would be there along the way. Almost a year later, he was still blogging about Flaco.

Who would have imagined the months ahead? The jokes on late-night TV, the murals of Flaco around the city, the worldwide media coverage, his weeklong trip downtown, and then his return to the fire escapes, windowsills, and air conditioners of the Upper West Side, like so many rock ledges. His one-year anniversary on the loose won him stories in the *Times*, *Gothamist*, ABC News, the Associated Press, and many, many more news outlets. He was world famous. Yolton also thought Flaco was confused. He would hoot for hours at night on a water tower or some other promontory, and, of course, no mate would ever answer. "No wild Eurasian eagle-owl hoots that much," Yolton told me. And though Flaco didn't lose his appetite for rats, he was also seen eating pigeons. The zoo's employees continued to monitor him. Manhattan Bird Alert made sure people kept watching.

I didn't know it then, but this was the last time I'd see Flaco. Three weeks after his one-year anniversary, he was found facedown in a courtyard on West 89th Street. A necropsy showed acute body trauma. Either he had collided with a building or with the ground on impact. As with Barry, the manner of his death suggested a weakened state. Front-page obituaries mourned him for the celebrity he was. It was later confirmed that he was indeed a very sick owl. The flip side to his life of freedom was the rat poison he had ingested and the pigeon herpesvirus he had contracted. Were it not for the traumatic injury, he would have died soon enough from severe tissue damage and inflamed organs.

Right around sunset that first night of spring the year before, a warm breeze blew through the Loch and ruffled Flaco's back feathers. He raised himself and his tufts, then bobbed his head side to side, up and down. He flexed his wings and took off, circling around to a branch close to Huddlestone Arch. In flight he was massive, his wings rounded and broad. He resumed hooting, then flew over my head toward the Meer.

As I turned to leave, a scruffy guy in his twenties walked up to me.

"What kind of owl is that?" he asked.

I thought everyone who had stuck around already knew Flaco's story. "Eurasian eagle-owl," I said, unsure how much to explain. "He's not a native owl. He came from the zoo. His enclosure was vandalized and he escaped."

He was intrigued. "Activists?"

"I think so."

"Was it you?"

I laughed. "No, it wasn't me."

He looked unconvinced, and his long stare unnerved me.

"Okay," he said, walking off. Then he stopped, turned around, and whispered, "Keep fighting the good fight."

# SPRING

CHAPTER 4

# The Moraine

For me, spring hasn't started until I've seen a pine warbler. "Have you seen a pine yet?" is a familiar question among birders in March and early April. Though not the earliest spring migrant—common grackles and red-winged blackbirds land in early February—the pine is the first of the warblers, a popular family of small, colorful songbirds whose members, by and large, migrate between the tropics and the temperate zone of North America. Most pine warblers, however, winter in the southern US, where they eat seeds beside sparrows on subdivision lawns.

As relatively new birders in 2017, my wife, Angie, and I found that spring's first pine warbler in Prospect Park, foraging in—yes—a pine sapling. The date was March 9. I alerted Peter Dorosh, and soon we heard the chugging of his work-issued Toro cart as he rushed over. The earliest record of a pine warbler in the park was 20 days later, he told us when he arrived, a mark set in 1968. He wondered if we'd mistaken it for another yellow bird, like maybe a goldfinch. Then the pine warbler flitted to another branch. "Son of a gun," Peter exclaimed, looking into his binoculars.

In New York, as in all cities, birds can end up anywhere during migration—a Virginia rail on the roof of a car, an ovenbird on an uptown subway platform, a Kentucky warbler in a community garden—but knowing their habitat choices allows you a better chance of finding them. For the pine warbler, I knew some places to look.

On a warm March morning in 2023, I left my apartment and walked less than a mile to Ocean Hill, inside Green-Wood Cemetery. Roughly 200 feet above sea level, the hill is one of the highest points in Brooklyn. A string of tall pines, which I can see from home, marks its wide crest like a row of ship masts. As I walked up its steep southern slope, I heard some sharp notes coming from an eastern white pine. Looking up, a male pine warbler, bright as a lemon, hopped along a sunlit upper branch. His yellow spectacles stood out against the olive of his head and back. He probed for caterpillars. Soft, easy to digest, and full of protein, they were the perfect food for recovering his energy.

Some pine warblers never leave the Southeast, where they nest high in the pine plantations that replaced the old growth, but this one would have ridden warm winds up the coast. His migration wasn't over, though. He would be gone in a matter of days, perhaps flying east to Long Island's pine barrens or tracing the coast up to New England, at which point he would stake a territory and woo the next-to-arrive females. There was hardly any time to spare. After swallowing a bug, he lifted his tiny head and let out a liquid trill that shook his entire body. Spring had arrived.

More than 650 species of birds breed north of the Mexico border, and like this pine warbler, around three-quarters of them are migratory. Of those, 80 percent migrate at night, guided by a suite of celestial clues, as well as more mysterious ones like low-frequency sound waves, polarized light, and the earth's electromagnetic field. Well over 200 species will pass Green-Wood's hills before June, a good deal of them coming from the tropics, spurred north by instinct to breed in North America's insect-rich forests and wetlands. Their goal is simple: to perpetuate their species. By some accounts, 270 species are regular migrants to New York City. Southwest winds deliver the best spring days, funneling birds from the Appalachians toward the natural and unnatural barriers of this water-bound city.

Migration follows a rather predictable schedule, which is why I expected to find a pine warbler. Songbirds, or passerines, come in waves, prompted by changes in daylight and allied with environmental and ecological factors like the greening of vegetation across the continent. In each wave, the birds share certain traits, like their choice of wintering grounds or diet. Short-distance migrants like the pine warbler usually arrive first. The pace quickens in May. Long-distance migrants follow, and they make up the largest and most colorful waves. The leaves are out, and the birds most skilled at catching flying bugs roll through.

We know what migration looks and feels like in New York thanks to a few centuries of stories, recordkeeping, and field guides, but we now know the size of it and can visualize it on a continental scale thanks to BirdCast. A big-data project created by the Cornell Lab of Ornithology, BirdCast pulls from weather radar the number and flight direction of birds in the air at any given time. In the spring, somewhere around five million birds cross New York. That alone doesn't make it a large hotspot; in the spring, for instance, Chicago sees around 50 million birds, as they take advantage of the jet stream that flows up the center of the country. But in New York, the paucity of green space concentrates them in places like Green-Wood. For birders, that makes for spectacular viewing.

Most species don't complete their entire migration in one flight. A few shorebirds do, like the bar-tailed godwit, which sometimes leaps off the North Slope of Alaska and flies across the Pacific to New Zealand, an open-water trip of more than a week. Shorebirds (and waterfowl) tend to congregate at familiar sites during their long-haul migrations, timing their stops to known food sources, like horseshoe crabs laying their eggs on the Atlantic coast. (As an aside, some birds like ducks and geese migrate not only by instinct but by learned experience.) Songbirds migrate across a broad front, however, and make localized decisions on where to stop—more off the cuff while on the wing. They touch down more frequently, often in unfamiliar or less-than-perfect habitats, island-hopping across the continent.

Green-Wood's a "stopover" site; ornithologist David Mehlman likens its kind to a convenience store for migratory birds—a spot to restock on immediate essentials. A migrating bird is a well-calibrated athlete, balancing enough fat but not too much to weigh it down on its flight. In stays lasting from a day up to more than a week, they must eat enough, rest, and avoid being picked off by predators before speeding off to their breeding grounds. Finding the right stopovers is crucial to their overall success—studies show that the birds that return earliest in the spring end up laying more eggs and raising more young.

Songbirds cross all landscapes, tracking so-called leading lines such as rivers and mountains to their desired places. Though the stopovers they make aren't predictable, most hold a high fidelity to their breeding location, returning to the same one year after year. Migrating is perhaps the most dangerous feature of their lives, and some birds spend up to a third of each year doing it. But in the long history of migration research, scientists have primarily focused on birds' breeding or wintering grounds—the ends of their remarkable journeys rather than the waypoints. Only in the last 30 years, with great advances in the use of weather radar data, has the study of stopovers developed more fully. For instance, migration ecologist Freda Guo, along with several colleagues, recently mapped stopover hotspots across the eastern US and found that landbirds concentrate in deciduous forest fragments in otherwise heavily deforested regions. In other words: the parks and cemeteries of New York. One reason for this concentration, a subject I'll return to later, is the pull of artificial light on migrating birds.

As the eastern sun unveils the concrete city to northbound nocturnal migrants in the spring, whether they're crossing the Narrows between Staten Island and Brooklyn or coming over the ocean from Sandy Hook, Ocean Hill is likely the first wooded high point they see. Many of them spend most of their lives in forests or jungles; they need trees for insects and for shelter. Standing on the hill, I can see the cemetery's utility. Outside the gates, crowded neighborhoods stretch for six miles to the Atlantic. Their street trees, backyards, and pocket parks offer only a lifeline. Mehlman, the ornithologist, calls those "fire escapes," his lowest stopover category. According to lore, Green-Wood's founder, the wealthy Brooklynite Henry Evelyn Pierrepont, believed the cemetery to be sufficiently far enough from Manhattan that the area around it would never be developed. Almost two centuries later, it's hemmed in by an electrical substation, a bus depot, a train yard, warehouses, fast-food joints, car washes, schools, a church, and apartment buildings. The millions of birds that come up the Atlantic coast in the spring, then return this way in autumn, are forced into the few places we've left for them.

In fact, the story of Ocean Hill helps explain why this place became a cemetery. Green-Wood sits on a terminal moraine, a ridge of rocks and earth laid down by the farthest advance of a two-mile-high ice sheet that once blanketed most of Canada and the northern United States. When the ice began its retreat some 18,000 years ago, meltwaters carried sand and sediment south to form a broad outwash plain leading to Jamaica Bay. Looking at a map of New York, you can discern the moraine's path by the ribbon of parks, golf courses, and cemeteries strung across Queens, Brooklyn, and Staten Island. Here, the sandy glacial soil is easy to dig up for graves, and it's well drained.

Southwest of Green-Wood, the moraine bends toward Staten

Island. Some 13,000 years ago, titanic floodwaters surged down the ice-age Hudson and punched a gap through it between Brooklyn and Staten Island—the Narrows. On Staten Island, the moraine climbs another 200 feet to Todt Hill, the highest point on the Atlantic coastal plain from Florida to Cape Cod. The names of neighborhoods around the moraine underscore this glacial history: Jamaica Hills, Cypress Hills, Crown Heights, Park Slope, Bay Ridge, Lighthouse Hill, Arden Heights, and so forth.

Green-Wood, after Dutch settlers forced out Lenape inhabitants, was farmed—but never very well. It was too rocky, sandy, and steep. But those same features made the moraine resistant to development. A "considerable portion" of the cemetery's first 178 acres, purchased in 1838, was then an impenetrable old forest, "left to grow wilderness-like," according to early reports. The soil, for the most part, "had been exhausted by bad farming and by neglect." David Bates Douglass, the civil engineer who designed the cemetery, emphasized its existing topography. Carriage roads led through pond-filled valleys and climbed wooded hills to ocean and harbor views. For humans, Green-Wood became a place to hold and honor the dead; a place for contemplation and culture; a retreat from the hue and cry of city life. For birds, it's now much more: a refuge necessary for survival.

On this March day, cemetery life was stirring all around me. I took stock of the birds that might have spent the winter here. Birds like dark-eyed juncos and white-throated sparrows had migrated this way in the fall, spent the next months together in seed-searching flocks, and were now about to return north to raise their young, from the forests of the Adirondacks to the edge of the Labrador Sea. From headstones, eastern phoebes sallied out to catch bugs. The phoebe my team found on last year's Christmas Bird Count survived the winter here on leftover berries and insects. The rest had flown up from the southern states. And out toward the edges of a pine, hanging upside down like circus performers, were three golden-crowned kinglets.

Each weighing only as much as two pennies, they're one of the smallest birds to make it through northern winters, feeding on overwintering insects and their eggs. As darkness falls, the kinglets sometimes will huddle together for warmth inside tree cavities. Many perish in subzero temperatures, but their high breeding rates—they lay lots of eggs and oftentimes two broods a year—compensate for their short lives. I find them in pairs and trios in early spring—an extension, I'd like to believe, of those winter survival skills, but more realistically the fact that there are just so many, upward of 30 or 40 on the best days.

Watching them poke around pine needles for spider eggs, I got a flash of the orange feathers that crown their striped heads, the feature that inspired their genus name, *Regulus*, meaning "little king."

To the birds' liking as well as mine, the cemetery's horticulturists have allowed the woodlot on Ocean Hill to grow more naturally. Sweetgum and black cherry saplings sprout from a rich seed bank into a leaf-covered understory. Poking around that litter were common grackles and red-winged blackbirds, making a racket of whistles and squeaks. Five or six decades ago, local records had these birds reliably arriving by February 15. With increasingly mild winters, though, they've forged ahead by several weeks, and small groups of them never seem to leave. Both are in the blackbird family, a name that belies their rich colors, from the male red-wing's ruby-and-gold epaulets to the grackle's midnight iridescence.

As I walked closer to get a better look, an American woodcock flew out of the leaves in front of my path, wings whistling. Woodcocks go by many nicknames—bogsucker, timberdoodle, night partridge—all of which speak to their eccentricity. Big-eyed, oblong, and long-billed, they breed in marshes and wooded edges, where at dusk and dawn the males attract a mate through elaborate aerial displays and nasal *Peent!* calls. Though you won't see their sky dance at Green-Wood, the cemetery remains one of the best places to see them during migration. Their cryptic patterning makes them all but invisible in a bed of leaves, where they probe for earthworms and occasionally do a bizarre, gyrating strut, which some ornithologists think helps them digest.

I reminded myself that spring migration was only just beginning. I began to daydream about the waves of May that crest with the "neotropical" migrants: eastern kingbirds from the western Amazon River basin, cerulean warblers from Andean mountainsides in Peru, scarlet tanagers from the Bolivian rainforest, bobolinks from the Pampas of Argentina, Baltimore orioles from shade-grown coffee farms in Nicaragua, and so on. As I watched the kinglets, phoebes, and blackbirds, those other birds probably hadn't left their winter homes yet, still gorging themselves on insects ahead of a much longer trip. Most would cross the Gulf of Mexico, a nonstop flight of over 600 miles that would take from 12 to 18 hours and cost them a third of their body weight.

Instinct drives these migrants to traverse continents, and they only touch down a short while in the city. Over the years, I had learned why they came, but I wanted to know more about how they got around New York, the dangers they faced, and where they ended up. For answers, I turned to Doug Gochfeld.

I MET DOUG at a mostly empty Brooklyn diner one afternoon. As you may recall, Doug was a star of the Christmas Bird Count, indeed the whole Brooklyn birding universe. I knew I wouldn't get many chances to tap his brain on migration. He's a busy guy. When he's not in New York, for up to half the year he's guiding birders through the world's richest avian environments. Recent or regular tours of his include the Pribilof Islands, Borneo, Papua New Guinea, Sichuan Province, Veracruz, and southern Argentina. Locally, he goes birding with at most a few other crack birders. We had rarely crossed paths in my years of birding; to a novice, his reputation was intimidating. As he sipped hot chocolate and spoke between messy bites of a Reuben, I drank coffee and listened.

"Migration is the most dynamic time of the year, and it's the most dynamic part of most birds' lives," he said. "No two days are the same. Birds are so sensitive to the environment and the time of year that they're making decisions based on more inputs than we know. It's an interesting time to be out. And as a birder, you want to maximize what you're going to see."

We were two blocks from Prospect Park, which is where Doug began birding at age six with his father, a retired city planner and lawyer and a former editor of the Brooklyn Bird Club's newsletter. His uncle is an ornithologist and seabird expert. The conditions were right for him; like a child learns a language, birding came naturally. In his field guide, which he'd memorized, he would draw the birds he saw, eventually illustrating whole scenes of them, like marshscapes. But Little League baseball knocked birding to the sidelines, and for years, he kept the old obsession to himself.

He picked it back up when his father gave him a pair of binoculars for his 18th birthday. He was a beginner twice, he said, but the past knowledge lay just below the surface, and he quickly became one of the city's best birders. At 23, he was hired as a fall migration counter in Cape May, New Jersey. This was like grad school for migration—one of the premier places to learn its dynamics. He rotated between three famous counts: the hawk watch, the sea watch, and the songbird flight. "In Cape May, you only look at birds in flight," he said. He learned to identify them by repetition—looking, listening, standing next to experts who had watched the sky for decades. He observed how birds moved around the landscape. This was active migration—for the birds and the counters. He did that for several seasons, then returned to master New York's migration dynamics.

As Doug explained, New York's geography makes it a unique corner of the country for people and for birds. Because of its location on the eastern shore of North America, European people created a center of commerce here. For bird migration, the coast also serves an important purpose. Birds come to a crossway in Brooklyn and Queens at the western end of Long Island, with east-west routes along the Atlantic or north-south routes up the harbor or down to New Jersey. Coasts tend to concentrate migrants that don't want to get blown offshore, he said. And the city consists of 520 miles of coastline, which are leading lines, like the terminal moraine—visual markers that birds follow during daylight hours. Only the Bronx technically sits on the North American continent; the rest of the city is an archipelago that lies within several estuaries, a rich ecosystem where fresh water and salt water meet.

But where the broad front of nocturnal migration meets the concrete city, there's not much leeway. Today, approximately 12 percent of the city's area is considered "natural"—10,500 acres of forests, 5,700 acres of grasslands, and 4,800 acres of wetlands. Another 29 percent is "landscaped," a category that includes athletic fields, lawns, and grassy medians, while the remaining 59 percent is "built environment," meaning all the buildings and transportation infrastructure humans have created. Twelve percent doesn't seem like a lot—and it isn't. What's more, the NYC Parks Department, the agency tasked with managing much of that acreage, is funded at one-half of 1 percent of the city's budget, an expenditure less than the NYPD's *overtime* expense. (In the 1970s, during a legendary fiscal crisis, the agency was still allotted 1.2 percent of the city's budget, and it employed 12,000 workers, or 4,000 more than in 2024.) For migrating birds, the airspace narrows like a funnel to these green spaces. Given their rather limited choices, they flock to the largest parks with the most tree cover, like desert wanderers to an oasis. The outcome is an extreme concentration of birds, the so-called Central Park effect. Roger Tory Peterson called Central Park, which makes up 6 percent of Manhattan's land area, the "most famous bird trap of all."

But dig deeper, Doug said. New York City is about 300 square miles of land (304, to be exact; another 165 is water). Take a 40-mile-wide front of birds. "How much of that is suitable habitat for a bird to be in?" he said. Then he paused.

Was that question for me? I assumed it was the 12 percent of remaining natural area. "Around thirty-five square miles of land?" I stammered.

"Depends on what bird you are," he said.

"Of course," I said. I nodded.

"If you're a saltmarsh sparrow, very finite," he said. "If you're a clapper rail, very finite." These are marsh birds, and there's only about 15 percent of their habitat left, dating to European arrival. "If you're a house wren," Doug said, "you can probably spend the day anywhere—well, not anywhere, but still, you have more options. If you're a ground-dwelling bird, you need one of the big green areas. You can have a cerulean warbler singing in front of your house in Park Slope in May, but you're not gonna have a Bicknell's thrush hopping around on the concrete. You've got forty miles' worth of birds condensed into much smaller areas. To compound that, you're right on the ocean. So any birds that are offshore and coming to shore, they're hitting the city first."

I'd never thought about it that fine-grained. I recalled David Mehlman writing about stopovers in the ornithology journal *The Auk*: "A given convenience store may better serve the needs of some species than of others." A cerulean warbler, a near-endangered long-distance migrant, depends on mature forests on its wintering and breeding grounds. But a fire-escape option—a sidewalk oak—can do in a pinch. A Bicknell's thrush, meanwhile, an endangered bird the color of brown leaves, needs an understory for food as much as it does for cover. This is how birds read the landscape.

"Want some Reuben?" Doug offered me his half-eaten sandwich.

"I'm good," I said. I wasn't in a pinch, not yet.

"From a bird's perspective," he continued, "New York City is very important during migration."

Taken together, the 12 percent of natural area is made up of a mosaic of habitats, though they're mostly fragments. So how effective are they for migrants? Are the birds finding what they need? Radar ornithology shows you the big picture, but not exactly the local scene. One of the few studies about New York was done over 15 years ago by a New York–born ornithologist named Chad Seewagen. He wanted to know if birds crammed into small spaces, fighting for food, were able to adequately refuel in the city. Was it an oasis, or really a mirage? Seewagen set up banding stations in Bronx Park, Prospect Park, and Manhattan's Inwood Hill Park, and after several seasons he learned that the warblers and thrushes he'd netted *were* finding enough food on their stopover. They seemed to fatten up just as well as the birds he'd banded, for comparison, in much larger suburban parks. In short: The city was an oasis.

More recent studies have confirmed this. One study led by ecologist Frank La Sorte found that a 50 percent increase in the tree canopy of New York City green spaces led to a 23 percent increase in the nocturnal songbird migrants in them. Put simply: More trees equal more birds.

"Any bit of green space you have in New York City is gonna provide an outsized impact on a bird population, because you're getting double or triple or quadruple your money for the land area," Doug said.

He tapped his mug with his spoon.

He was right. Several parks smaller than a hundred acres—

Brooklyn Bridge Park, the Battery, Ridgewood Reservoir—claim records of around 200 species. Even green roofs have proved to be adequate stopover habitats. Most birders favor the large parks with the most trees. Doug, however, likes birding the seldom-visited and undersurveyed marginal ones—those fire escapes again. And not only because he might find something unusual. Fire escapes plug important gaps in the stopover network, researchers say, but they're rarely protected and thus most in need of conservation. Across the world, the last pristine forests are disappearing; they left New York four centuries ago.

"Marginal habitat is the future," Doug said. "Yes, we still have tracts of land elsewhere, but we're traveling in one direction: urbanization. We're in the Anthropocene. We have to allow animals to thrive in cities as best as possible."

His favorite places in New York, he said, are the pinch points of land and water, what I'd call "the ultimate fire escapes." Nocturnal migrants often land in these places in the early hours of the morning after finding themselves over water near sunrise. But if the habitat can't offer them much, they quickly take off again in search of a more suitable stopover. These are the places to see migration in action; to see birds as they negotiate land, water, and wind; to see the most and greatest diversity of them at once. "The result can be spectacular," Doug said. And you can witness it all over the city: from points on the Hudson River, Long Island Sound, Jamaica Bay, and the Atlantic, in Central and Prospect Park, even from the Empire State Building.

"It's called morning flight," he said.

"When is it best?" I asked.

Fall migration is the best time, he said, but there are chances to see it in spring. It depends on a whole host of factors, like wind, cloud cover, temperature, precipitation, and time of year. "It's endlessly interesting," Doug added.

Artful, mysterious—morning flight! I was ready to jump out of my seat to go find it. Doug said I could join him in May.

LEAVING OCEAN HILL that March morning, I walked down to the southern flats of the cemetery that lay outside its original boundary. Unlike the hill's rewilding slopes, the trees were spaced out as you would expect to find in a modern cemetery. Straight rows of headstones lined putting-green lawns, a shift in cemetery design that followed the rise of gas-powered mowing equipment. The manicured spaces didn't help most migrating songbirds, but they weren't empty. This was the land of mockingbirds.

Each headstone was a possible stage for these mimics, and they sang for hours. I listened to one impersonate the clucks of a robin, the rattle of a belted kingfisher, and, most surprisingly, the springy *Chick-burr* of a scarlet tanager. That was obviously from last year's soundtrack; tanagers wouldn't land here for at least another month. Mockingbirds' mimicry travels easily in the cemetery, and its small shrubs and berry bushes offer food and homes for their tight stick nests.

Northern mockingbirds were once a more southern species, until they began pressing north around the middle of the 20th century. Early New York City bird-finding guides, like Ludlow Griscom's, included sporadic reports from the late 19th century, but it was generally thought that those were escaped cage birds. Griscom was suspicious of that logic, since he'd found records after the pet trade for mockingbirds had closed. Where the mockingbirds were coming from, though, was a "mystery which still awaits solution," he wrote.

The answer was range expansion. Those first-generation mockingbirds weren't really migrating; they were dispersing, as it's known, seeking new places to breed in the great green patchwork of urban and suburban lawns. The Brooklyn Bird Club's *Birds of Prospect Park*, published in 1951, included only one record of an overwintering mockingbird in the winter of 1945–46. "There is no way to predict this bird's occurrence in the Park," the entry said. "If it's there, be thankful!" It has long since become a permanent resident.

Northern cardinals followed a similar trend. I began hearing one sing from my apartment at the end of January—yes, January—to get a jump on his neighborhood rivals. It was a rapid-fire wake-up call I hadn't asked for, and which by May would sound as early as four thirty. Weaving between graves, I counted cardinals on two hands. Through the end of the 19th century, New York had been their northern limit, according to Griscom, but the clearing of woods and thickets destroyed their haunts—the same leveling that opened pathways for mockingbirds. By 1920, cardinals were all but gone from the whole state. But two decades later, they began their return, adapting to this new landscape and a changing climate.

Older birders tell younger ones these stories all the time, about the once rare but now common species. Mockingbirds, cardinals, tufted titmouses, Carolina wrens, red-bellied woodpeckers—birds we think of as backyard birds—have all rapidly extended their ranges, partly in response to warmer temperatures. Looking back toward the ridge, I heard the familiar call of a red-bellied: great barks of laughter. I found it flying between a series of tree cavities, presumably searching for a place to nest. It was a male—the whole of his head was Day-Glo pink. Had I counted him on my Christmas Bird Count? Our territory had 22 that day, far more than any other woodpecker. Red-bellied woodpeckers are residents, and they usually don't migrate. But they had to get here somehow. Their Latin name, *Melanerpes carolinus*, speaks to their traditional home, and in the South, they love cypress swamps. In the first half of the 20th century, they appeared in New York City only as vagrants, or chance visitors. But their "colonization," a word ornithologists use for establishing more permanent populations in new territories, began with six different sightings in May of 1961; the next spring, their spread grew to more than 30 sightings. They began breeding throughout the city in the 1980s. One explanation for their success is their talent for keeping starlings out of their nest cavities.

In these expansions, I see parallels in the forces that shaped this land. After glacial retreat, plants shifted north to a bare but fertile territory: First, it became tundra, then a conifer forest, and then, as the climate stabilized about 4,000 years ago, a deciduous forest dominated by oaks, hickories, and American chestnuts. The moraine is a reminder that New York exists "at a crossroads," writes ecologist Eric Sanderson in the fantastic book *Mannahatta*, "between the northern flora of boreal Canada and the southern flora of Virginia and the Carolinas. It's as if New York's plant life draws from those two great traditions—the South's and the North's—and as a result, there are many more plants here than there are in many cities of similar latitude and position; both peat moss and magnolias once marked time in New York City."

But those were slow changes. All around us now they're coming fast. Gulf of Mexico temperatures continue to break records. The Atlantic Ocean's circulation stands at its weakest point in more than a thousand years. Spring is coming sooner, with plants budding before many birds' arrival. The links between trees, their insects, and the birds that feed on them look ready to snap. Birds' geographic ranges aren't permanent; field-guide maps only capture them at a particular moment in time. They evolve, sometimes quickly, sometimes slowly, often in response to environmental changes—ice ages, for instance, or anthropogenic global warming. The short-distance migrants on Ocean Hill, like the flats' cardinals, mockingbirds, and red-bellied woodpeckers, are thought to be more capable of shifting their ranges to adapt to rapid disruptions in weather and food supplies. As for long-distance migrants, which I'd see in May, scientists say their departures appear largely hardwired. With longer to travel—and travel time itself varying with local weather conditions—chances are that their timing will fall worryingly out of step.

BATTLE HILL, AT the northern extreme of the cemetery, is the highest natural point in Brooklyn, around 220 feet. It may not seem like a great height, but this is a coastal plain, so every foot counts. During the Battle of Brooklyn (also known as the Battle of Long Island), George Washington's Continental Army and the British both knew the importance of holding the moraine; Washington chose to defend New York from this hilltop, then called Gowanus Heights. His men were overrun by the British on August 27, 1776, but the battered troops escaped across the East River to fight another day.

The summit is now a hawk-watching spot for Brooklyn birders. Its panoramic views are spectacular. On clear days, you can see the Watchung Mountains in New Jersey. The mountains are another leading line, same as the waterways that feed the harbor; together, Allan Cruickshank once wrote, they are "marked highways of migration upon which thousands upon thousands of transients pass each spring and fall." I'm fond of the view. In the harbor, the Statue of Liberty lies in the center of a constant coming and going of container vessels, cruise ships, barges, tugboats, sailboats, and ferries. Carried by steamships into this port city, millions of immigrants once looked upon Lady Liberty's copper promise. In recent years, tens of thousands have arrived in New York on buses or planes, seeking refuge from the climate disasters laying waste to their homelands in Central and South America. The birds I couldn't wait to see in May were about to leave from some of those same places. And those same disasters—drought, deforestation, despoliation—are challenging them to adapt more quickly than they've ever been forced to in their evolutionary histories.

In the grass around Battle Hill were more early birds—northern flickers, eastern phoebes, dark-eyed juncos—and they looked crisp, wearing their best dress. Behind me, they could rest and feed in meadows, trees, and ponds. Imperfect though it may be, Green-Wood was one of the few places they could land safely between here and the Watchung Mountains. But land they must. To the north, skyscrapers rose like one great unbroken Jenga. One World Trade Center loomed tallest. Were they going to cross the harbor toward that steel-and-glass barrier? I knew the perils of that. I had seen it myself a few weeks earlier.

That evening, I went to a concert at Federal Hall in Lower Manhattan. Walking on Pine Street, our group was stopped cold in our tracks by a plump oval-shaped bird lying dead in the middle of the sidewalk outside a Duane Reade pharmacy. It was an American woodcock. The bird might have passed through the cemetery, I considered, but what had killed it was apparent: Duane Reade's two-story glass storefront. After a brief silence, I photographed the victim of the fatal collision. We didn't want to leave the bird there, but we hesitated—how to pick it up? Angie closed one hand around its body, and with the other lifted its head by the tip of its long bill. It was so light and so soft, she said. And still warm. We looked around for a tree, for a decent burial in some soil, but we didn't see one. On this block of Pine Street, there were no trees. Angie moved the bird to the edge of the sidewalk, in the shelter of a parking meter.

Inside Federal Hall, I tried to push the incident aside. The concert was made up of six scores written by composers who'd participated in a backcountry trip to the Alaskan wilderness. As the music bounced off the vaulted ceiling, I imagined the atmosphere of the boreal forest, the breeding grounds of so many migrating birds. Once in that wilderness, they have everything they need to raise their young (for now, at least). But to reach it, they must cross vast distances. Glass is what killed that American woodcock, and it is ubiquitous across the US landscape.

When we got home, Angie and I uploaded the photo I took to dBird, for "dead bird," an online database where people can submit reports of collisions in New York, or anywhere else in the country. That woodcock was one of the city's early victims that season, and it wouldn't be the last. NYC Bird Alliance estimates that upward of 230,000 birds are killed each year by the city's glass windows, most of them during migration. Nationally, the annual toll is thought to be up to one billion, making it second only to feral and free-roaming cats as the leading human-caused hazard for birds. But these problems have solutions; unlike the climate crisis, they could be addressed now for immediate results.

*One billion birds a year.* In the days ahead, I couldn't stop thinking about that one.

CHAPTER 5

# Safe Flight

On a cool May morning, the last thing this magnolia warbler saw was the reflection of trees and sky in the glass of One World Trade Center. Melissa Breyer crouched down and picked up the dead songbird. "Still warm," she said. It was a male—bright yellow with a gray cap and a neat jet-black mask and necklace. Melissa shook her head. "Can you believe how beautiful this bird is?" Seeing it lying in her hand like that, I couldn't.

More than 30,000 birds had flown through Manhattan overnight, and though it wasn't a large number for the spring—a few nights that season would see over half a million—this wave of neotropical migrants was crashing headlong into the city's glass facades. Melissa hadn't slept much. She'd woken up every two hours to check Bird-Cast, the Cornell Lab of Ornithology project that provides real-time updates on nocturnal bird migration. After midnight, birds flew at an average elevation of 800 feet, more than halfway up One WTC if you don't count the spire (its overall height is 1,776 feet). She looked over her shoulder. "Every time I walk down that first expanse of sidewalk, I'm braced to see birds everywhere," she said.

Then, like a forensic investigator bagging evidence, she took a photo of the magnolia warbler and slid the bird into a Ziploc bag. On it, she wrote the time and location: *6:15, Building 16, Facade C*. But there was no mystery at this crime scene. We knew who the killer was.

These details are necessary for Project Safe Flight, NYC Bird Alliance's collision-monitoring program for which Melissa, a writer, photographer, and the editorial director of the Martha Stewart website, is one of its longest-serving volunteers. (NYC Audubon changed its name to NYC Bird Alliance in 2024; to minimize confusion, I'll use its new name even while writing about its pre-name-change activities.) There were about 30 volunteers in Project Safe Flight when Melissa joined in the fall of 2020. Now she's one of more than 200. "It's very popular with the newbies," Melissa said. They walk 15 routes in all five boroughs, checking approximately 80 buildings during five months of spring and fall migration. Her route, which includes four World Trade Center skyscrapers within a three-by-five-block radius, sees the most collisions.

Dark-haired and tall, Melissa wore a gray wool cap and cardigan. In her backpack were brown paper bags for the injured. She would bring them uptown to the Wild Bird Fund, the city's only wildlife rehab center and a key Project Safe Flight partner. The others end up in Ziploc bags. Each year, the Wild Bird Fund averages about 1,200 window-strike intakes. Most of them are migrating songbirds. Melissa drops off well over a hundred each year.

After finding the dead woodcock on Pine Street, I wanted to learn more about the problem in New York. What better way than to join the people who find them, I thought. Project Safe Flight is different from dBird, the database where I had submitted my report. The latter, which NYC Bird Alliance launched in 2014, was designed for incidental observations. Project Safe Flight, on the other hand, which a corporate communications officer named Rebekah Creshkoff started in 1997, depends on standardized data collection. Volunteers are asked to do one circuit of their buildings and record what they find. But once Melissa finishes her circuit, she usually circles again and again, sometimes walking up to 12 miles so she can rescue any survivors. She tries to stay until birds stop hitting the glass.

Most mornings, she's locked in a race with the maintenance staff of these buildings, especially from One WTC, to get the incriminating evidence before they sweep it into trash cans. A spokesperson for One WTC has said its lower floors are bird-friendly, since they're encased in nonreflective glass fins. But when I looked up to the spot the magnolia warbler struck, I could see a reflection of trees and sky.

Today, there are many products to make glass bird-safe, such as tight patterns of dots and lines, or UV coating. Birds can see those. But they don't perceive clear or reflective glass as a solid surface, just as we humans don't until we're taught at a young age. What birds see are the illusions of trees or sky—a place to feed, a place to fly through—and not an obstacle they're about to crash into. In 2020, New York City enacted legislation that mandated bird-safe materials for all new buildings. It was a tremendous victory, but for one million existing structures—the city's estimate of its building stock—the law applies only when they undergo major alterations.

As we embarked on her route, Melissa walked quickly. The early-morning streets were quiet enough to hear the thin calls of warblers still flying up in the clouds. Most collisions, she explained, occur after daybreak and with the lower floors of buildings. While migrating birds zip through the urban landscape looking for places to rest and feed, they end up trapped in a maze of mirrors. Skyscrapers themselves aren't the problem; studies show that across the country collisions happen for the most part at houses and low-rise buildings, but the density of glass and artificial light within the narrow canyons of Lower Manhattan intensifies the danger.

Still, the walkability of cities makes possible a program like Project Safe Flight, and Melissa's priority is getting injured birds off the sidewalk. They're easily stepped on by people or eaten by gulls, cats, squirrels, and rats. About 70 percent of the birds she finds are already dead, she told me. By recording them on Project Safe Flight, dBird, or iNaturalist, a website where she posts photos of the victims, she believes their deaths did not happen in vain. To her, the data point is their obituary. She documents all the collisions she finds on a Google spreadsheet. That magnolia warbler was number 1,840.

Since most are songbirds, they're small enough to fit in her hand and easily missed in the immense gray hardscape. Melissa checks for them in streets, bike lanes, and gutters, on sidewalks, ramps, and tunnels, and in planters. What I thought was a bird often turned out to be a leaf, a fast-food wrapper, or a plastic tumbleweed.

After finding the magnolia, Melissa climbed onto a nearby planter and walked around its ledge to look down on the flowers inside, something a happy-go-lucky kid would do. She paid close attention to windows that reflected greenery and to the glass corners of buildings, an intersection where a bird would believe it was crossing into the clear. Melissa pointed out a cantilevered awning on the south side of One WTC. Warblers land there when they strike the windows above it, she said, and gulls stalk the ledge for an easy meal—dead or alive. I shuddered, remembering a herring gull, all pale gray and white, I had earlier watched fly across Broadway. "It's like a nature show down here," she said.

But what kind of nature? I wondered. The landscape was intensely artificial. Until 400 years ago, as the birds' genes surely told them, this part of Manhattan was a primeval forest. Their ancestors traveled this way, and so they did too.

Fresh out of Mexico's Yucatán Peninsula or the West Indies, the magnolia warbler Melissa found had likely been bound for a northern stand of spruce or hemlock, where he would have sought a mate to pass on his genes. (Alexander Wilson, the early Scottish American ornithologist, gave the bird the Latin species name *magnolia* after the tree he collected one from in Mississippi in 1810, but the English name he gave it was far more accurate: black-and-yellow warbler.)

By the main entrance to One WTC, Melissa said hello to a security guard, a bubbly older Caribbean woman. "Did you find any birds?" she asked Melissa.

"I found a few today," Melissa said.

"Really, where did you find them?"

"We found one right around the corner," Melissa said, pulling out the bag with the magnolia warbler.

"Dead be gorgeous," she blurted out. It was as stunning to her as it was to us.

The guard was one of Melissa's few allies at One WTC. She told Melissa that if she found any dead birds of her own she would hide them in a nearby concrete planter next to a NO SMOKING sign.

"You're the best," Melissa said.

We pushed on to the other buildings on Melissa's route. I noted some of their tenants—McKinsey, Uber, Spotify, Chase, Moody's, Bank of New York Mellon—and the LEED-certified green symbols at their entrances. "They're greenly killing all the wild birds around them," Melissa said bitterly. As we turned the corner to the north side of 240 Greenwich Street, also known as 101 Barclay Street, she spotted a small gray shape on the sidewalk. "I think that's an injured bird," she said.

We were about 50 feet away. The bird, facing the building, was a male common yellowthroat, a tiny round warbler with a black Zorro mask. He was clearly very stunned. Then we noticed a young woman dressed in business attire walking toward him, looking straight ahead. "Oh no," Melissa gasped.

A second passed, then two. I started to panic. Should I run up? Would Melissa? But if we did, the bird might rush into the glass. In that moment, there was just one bird on Earth, and it was that common yellowthroat. Another second passed, the woman closed in, and the bird didn't move. He was that dazed. I felt my body stiffen. She missed him by only a foot.

Another office worker followed, but Melissa now dashed forward, waving her arms to get his attention. She pointed at the bird, but the middle-aged man didn't break his stride. He skirted the common yellowthroat while showing no emotion. I guess he was dazed too. Melissa scooped up the bird from behind—he offered no resistance—and placed him in a brown bag and clipped the top. *Building 14, Facade A*, she typed on her phone.

Finding a dead bird had been awful, but this felt even sadder to me. Melissa was mortified. "Did you see how close those people came?" she said.

"Well," she added, "it looks like I'm going to the Wild Bird Fund today."

It was now close to seven. Honking on Church Street made the idyll of our day's start about an hour earlier feel like a lifetime ago. Melissa's Project Safe Flight round was finished, but she wasn't. She wanted to check a death trap across West Street, the glassy complex of Brookfield Place.

Around the back of one building, the facade looked harmless enough, compared to the waistcoats of plate glass worn by the World Trade Center towers or Brookfield Place's Winter Garden glass atrium. But, sure enough, we found a black-and-white warbler on its side beneath some narrow windows. It was a female, and still warm. "I knew we'd find one over here," Melissa said. As she took a photo, her face broke into a look of great sadness. In her four years as a monitor, she had picked up more black-and-white warblers than any other species. I noticed her phone's photo album was an endless roll of dead birds on pavement, like a memorial to devastating design choices.

Melissa wanted to do another loop, since birds were clearly still coming through. But she had to get home soon. At the front of Brookfield, a female black-throated blue warbler was slumped in a corner, facing out. "The front approach is impossible unless they're really conked out," Melissa said, crouching toward it. As she slowly lowered her hand, the small bird flew weakly up into an ornamental tree above a sidewalk café. Then we cut back to One WTC. As we neared the facade that killed the magnolia warbler, Melissa abruptly stopped talking.

I followed her gaze to a dead ovenbird at the edge of the sidewalk. Two guards were talking in front of it, oblivious to the little warbler right by their feet. When alive, it struts like a chicken across the understory. I had heard one sing earlier, from the 9/11 memorial grove; its loud, rising *Teacher... Teacher... Teacher!* rang around the concrete plaza. I'd been worried then, and my fear was justified. Melissa leaned down, silently picked it up, and dropped it into a Ziploc bag.

Outside the subway station, we took stock. All things considered, it wasn't too bad, she said. During fall migration, when birds are more numerous because of all the juveniles, she finds seven times more collisions than in the spring. She had six warblers in her backpack and one warbler, the common yellowthroat, that was alive.

Or was it? Given the shape it was in earlier, Melissa wasn't optimistic it had survived the last hour. She mulled it over. She didn't want to walk into the Wild Bird Fund with a DOA. It was seven thirty, and she had to get home by nine. It was a 90-minute trip to the clinic and then to Brooklyn. Reluctantly, she pulled out the paper bag. It was risky; if alert, the bird could fly through any crack of daylight. As she gently pulled up the clip and got ready to peek inside, the tiny bird flitted around.

He was downright jumpy by the time Melissa reached the Wild Bird Fund, she told me later. "Hopefully a good sign," she said.

I IMAGINE IT was harrowing being the first. But as Rebekah Creshkoff told me, she possessed the conviction of a "lone lunatic" on her "peculiar quest." In April 1997, Creshkoff began checking some of these same buildings in the first organized attempt to monitor collisions in New York. The name Project Safe Flight came a couple years later. As Melissa put it: "Rebekah was the person to wonder what the hell was going on and why."

Creshkoff was a writer on Wall Street. A graduate of liberal arts universities, she stumbled into the corporate world in the early 1980s and stuck around because, as she liked to say, the money men couldn't write. Always a nature lover, she began birding in Central Park in 1991. Soon after, she learned about Fatal Light Awareness Program, or FLAP, a Toronto-based nonprofit that monitors collisions. FLAP's findings, devastating as they were, motivated her to action. She wanted to call building managers in Lower Manhattan and ask them to turn off their overnight lights during migration—light being the lure that confuses and traps birds before they crash into glass surfaces. But Michael Mesure, FLAP's executive director, advised against that. Before they'll change anything, he told her, you need to show them data. You need to find dead bodies.

In 1997, she went out every morning in April and May and from September through November. She would generally leave her Upper West Side apartment at a quarter to six and bike downtown on quiet avenues. It was an eight-mile, 45-minute trip. Having raised the handlebars of her Specialized, she rode as straight-backed as the Wicked Witch of the West. Arriving downtown, she would check five buildings of the World Financial Center—today's Brookfield Place—and five of the six World Trade Center towers. The courtyard-like design of the latter penned birds into a gigantic glass-walled box. Creshkoff noted on hand-drawn maps what she found and where, along with the weather and moon phase. On her worst day, she found 65 birds, all dead.

The primary victims haven't changed. White-throated sparrows slumped in dark corners. Black-and-white warblers flat out on the pavement. Common yellowthroats trying to escape the deadly maze. Ovenbirds flying out of bushes to a cruel fate. Their injuries were grisly: broken necks, legs, and wings, busted eyes and beaks, concussions, internal bleeding. Creshkoff would often lie in bed at night thinking of their awful ends.

That year, she found 413 dead or injured birds, representing 58 species. About 70 percent were dead on the spot. Close to 95 percent were songbirds—warblers and sparrows mostly. But she knew she wasn't finding everything. She didn't always outpace the sweepers, and on the days she had time to make a second or third round, she usually found more bodies. Under the Migratory Bird Treaty Act, she couldn't pick up the dead ones. She took the severely injured to an at-home rehabber and released the "merely" stunned by the trees of the nearby Battery. Years later, she met the park's gardener, who told Creshkoff she'd found lots of carcasses.

There was at least one bird Creshkoff went to great lengths to see survive that first spring. Against a revolving glass doorway at the World Financial Center, she ran into a crowd of people standing around a male scarlet tanager. "I'll handle this," she announced. She tucked the injured bird inside a pocket of the vest she was wearing, then called her boss to say she had an emergency dental appointment. She rode the subway to Central Park and released the tanager in the Loch, far from Manhattan's skyscrapers and closer to its ultimate destination.

"It was difficult to see it only as a data-driven effort," Creshkoff told me when I called her at her Catskills home. She left New York City in July 2013, one day after she accepted an early retirement from JPMorgan Chase. As she spoke, I heard in the background the faint chirping of tree swallows competing for nest boxes in her yard. "Oh my goodness," she said breathily. "I'm watching tree swallow sex right now."

After her first year, Creshkoff wrote about the few highs and many lows of her experiences. "Fellow birders ask, 'Isn't it *depressing*, finding so many dead birds?' Of course it is," she explained in NYC Bird Alliance's newsletter. "But the sense of mission—of gathering data that may eventually help resolve this problem—is a strong motivation to keep on going. Even more powerful is the incomparable joy of releasing an injured bird and giving it a second chance." She asked for help, but, she realized, loving nature doesn't automatically translate to working to protect it. Only a couple of other birders offered to join her.

One was Kellie Quiñones, a member of NYC Bird Alliance who worked as an administrative assistant for Merrill Lynch at the World Financial Center. She had found dead birds on the sidewalk outside her office and had wondered if they were falling out of the sky. Creshkoff's project was the kind of hands-on conservation work she had dreamed of doing. Quiñones grew up in Brooklyn's Bed-Stuy neighborhood, the oldest of three raised by a single mother who came from Puerto Rico in her youth. She'd loved watching nature shows as a kid, but since they were hosted by old white men, she never thought they applied to her life. "I thought nature was a white thing," Quiñones, who identifies as Afro-Boricua, told me. On her rounds, she would tear up when she thought of the birds' arduous journeys.

Another volunteer nicknamed their group the Dawn Patrol. In 2000, when NYC Bird Alliance took on management of the effort, Creshkoff suggested the name Project Safe Flight. Another monitor, Patrick Harty, an IT specialist who worked in the World Trade Center's south tower, built a web program, which Creshkoff called Bird Bash, where they could enter their records. Harty had joined Project Safe Flight after meeting coordinator Allison Sloan on a day when warblers crowded into the London plane trees outside the Twin Towers. Harty thought that was great; Sloan, who lugged two shopping bags that Harty didn't know were packed with injured birds, felt differently. A hulking Bronx native with the accent to prove it, Harty coded Bird Bash on his laptop during his commute to Grand Central Station.

By the spring of 2001, they had earned a few small victories. Harty watched a nightly webcam of the World Trade Center to figure out which tenants kept on their lights, and the group convinced the insurance company Marsh & McLennan to turn theirs off across six upper floors of the north tower. Creshkoff also persuaded the Port Authority of New York and New Jersey, the buildings' owner, to install fine-mesh garden netting over the ground-floor windows on four sides of the Twin Towers. She watched with joy as birds bounced off them like a trampoline, and hoped to see the treatment extended to additional floors.

Ahead of the fall season, there was a guarded sense of optimism. Two weeks into it, on a clear September morning, Creshkoff was in a meeting a couple blocks away when a colleague barged in and shouted that a plane had flown into the north tower. Simultaneously, Harty was sitting at his desk on the 67th floor of the south tower when he heard a terrifying explosion and looked across to see the north tower's upper floors in flames. He took off down a stairwell and reached the 50th floor, but he and a few colleagues returned to their desks upon hearing instructions over an intercom to stay in place. Harty watched several people jump out of the north tower. He quickly typed an email to Creshkoff and Sloan: *In case you didn't hear, a plane hit tower one, I'm safe in tower two.* As he hit SEND, an explosion sent him rolling across the floor.

Having sprinted outside, Creshkoff watched the second plane strike the south tower. As a teenager growing up in Montclair, New Jersey, she had watched the Twin Towers rise across the river. Now, she watched them fall.

Meanwhile, Harty ran to the elevators, but they had caved in like a collapsed mine. He thought of his wife—they had been married only nine months—and the family he'd pictured having together. He was in his late thirties. "I'm going to die *now*?" he said to himself. "I was a reckless bachelor for so long. I'm sober, I'm married, and *now* I'm going to die?"

Smoke filled the floor. Harty and others forced their way around rubble into the only open stairwell. In the south tower, the few people who had survived from above the 81st floor, the floor where the second plane hit, came through there. Inside the stairwell, an elderly woman blocked the way. Her eyes closed, she gripped both handrails. "I'm afraid," she cried. "I'm not going." Harty, a six-foot-four ex-bouncer, broke her hold and carried her down seven flights, then handed her to another person who offered aid. Firefighters climbed up the stairwell. Only then did Harty hear that a second plane had struck their tower. *What are the odds?* he thought.

As they escaped the lobby, bodies fell from the sky around them; they literally followed a path of blood into the sunlight. Harty would never forget the faces of a young female police officer who led them out and a male firefighter who desperately struggled to pry open an elevator door. Harty walked a mile to a pay phone and called his in-laws.

A week later, he found Creshkoff in the phone book—all of his contacts had been on his work computer—and he called her to say he was still alive.

THE DAWN PATROL was too shaken up to patrol much the rest of that fall. Among the thousands killed was the Port Authority manager who'd overseen the installation of the bird-protective netting and several security guards the volunteers had come to know well. Marsh & McLennan, the insurance company that adopted the lights-out program, had lost 295 employees.

Rebekah Creshkoff's office moved uptown. She pulled back from Project Safe Flight, but she knew it was in good hands. Patrick Harty's office moved to the West Side, and he purchased a fold-up bike to ride to it from Grand Central. He wanted the exercise, but, most of all, he wanted to find new buildings to monitor. He crisscrossed the streets around Bryant Park, finding several candidates, and then, reaching the Hudson, he came upon a shiny glass box covering five city blocks—the Jacob K. Javits Convention Center. No need to look any further, he thought.

Named after a US senator, the Javits Center, designed by James Ingo Freed of the award-winning firm I. M. Pei & Partners, opened in 1986. The megastructure echoed the design and principles of what was arguably the first truly modern building: the Crystal Palace exhibition hall in London, designed by gardener Joseph Paxton for a world's fair known as the Great Exhibition of 1851. And like that supersized greenhouse, the Javits Center embodied the idea of progress, of a limitless industrial future—reflected not only in its endlessly extendable space-frame structure encased in glass, but its official business as a showplace displaying the latest inventions and technologies. Sited beside the Hudson rail yards in a desolate part of town, New York state saw the Javits Center as the anchor for a West Side revitalization, targeting the big bucks of the highly competitive trade show industry. It was like a monument to glass; even the utility areas, loading docks, and storage rooms had walls made of it. Aglow at night, the glass appeared transparent, but during the day it was opaque, a dark mask that earned it the nickname Darth Vader.

For many, the glass box was—and still is—the architectural ideal. You only need to look across the island of Manhattan to Park Avenue. In 1952, the glass curtain walls of Lever House marked the dawn of the glass-and-steel age, followed that same year by the United Nations Secretariat Building. In 1958, the bronze-glass Seagram Building went up across from Lever House. These structures were symbols of a modern era, inspiring a radical change in the use of glass around the world, in large part due to cheap oil and advances in heating and cooling. Freed, the Javits designer, had briefly worked for Ludwig Mies van der Rohe, the visionary behind the Seagram Building, who argued that glass fused nature, humans, and structures in a "higher unity." But glass was killing nature. Or at least its birds, some of its most visible representatives in New York City.

Of course, none of this was on Harty's mind that first morning on the West Side. Instead, it was reaching the white-throated sparrows he found collapsed on the sidewalk below the Javits Center's tree-lined south side. The janitors he encountered wanted to know what the hell he was doing. Why was *he* picking them up? It was their job.

Harty defused the situation. He could talk to anyone. The third of seven children, his parents were Irish Catholic immigrants, and the family lived in what Harty called the Bronx's "apartment building jungle" on Fordham Road. But in that jungle, he'd discovered blue jays and cardinals, and then, his spark bird, an elegant-looking mourning dove traveling within a pack of pigeons.

Harty won over the janitors with his commitment to showing up every weekday morning. More than half his Bird Bash entries, in fact, were of birds they'd found and set aside for him. When they asked him why he was doing this work, he said, "It's not like I run into orphans every day on my way to the office." But he did see dying birds, so he decided to do something about it.

The Javits Center turned out to be the decade's worst Project Safe Flight building. Its location on the Hudson, a migration corridor, made it supremely deadly. The Javits was 15 stories at its absolute height, but most of the sprawling structure was much shorter; its reflective surfaces were the cause, not its height. Harty checked the Javits Center for four or five years, a monitoring career that stretched longer than that of most volunteers.

"It was not a happy project," Susan Elbin, an ornithologist and NYC Bird Alliance's head of conservation and science between 2007 and 2019, told me. As the organization's dataset grew, however, she and her staff were able to use it to take targeted action. And the Javits Center presented the first major opportunity.

In 2009, the state decided to pay for an environmental retrofit at a cost of half a billion dollars. Bruce Fowle, a noted architect of skyscrapers, was hired to design it. Inside NYC Bird Alliance's Manhattan office, you could hear the cheers. A proponent of sustainable design, Fowle was well aware of the Javits's dire situation, since his wife, Marcia Fowle, was on NYC Bird Alliance's board and had served as its executive director. His firm, FXFowle, had used bird-safe glass for the first time in a recent design of the Wildlife Conservation Society's Bronx Zoo headquarters, a project that brought together several experts in the field and was a laboratory for different technical solutions. The science behind bird-safe building design was still embryonic. "We didn't know much in those days," Elbin said. Without a market for bird-safe glass, manufacturers chose not to invest in R&D. But slowly, this began to change, especially after San Francisco, in 2011, became the first US city to enact bird-friendly building standards.

Because of Harty's efforts, NYC Bird Alliance could access years of detailed records about collisions at the Javits Center. FXFowle's architects wanted them all. But Fowle couldn't sell the state on bird-friendly design as his primary objective—his marching orders were for energy efficiency. Still, the two overlapped. They decided to remove a third of the glass and replace it with stainless steel panels, and for the rest they installed less-reflective glass treated with a coating of tiny ceramic black dots known as frit. Though almost imperceptible to human eyes, birds perceive it as a solid barrier. With less reflective glass and less glass overall, the building became easier to heat and cool, lowering annual energy costs by about a quarter in the first five years. The extreme makeover didn't stop there. A green roof, then a greenhouse and fruit orchard, were added.

The Javits went from being a sink to a source, from killing many thousands of birds to providing habitat for them. In the spring of 2013, monitors found only two collisions there, and NYC Bird Alliance removed it from Project Safe Flight.

Its staff deserved a victory lap, but, as Elbin told me, they also knew they needed a legislative answer, like San Francisco's standards. A year later, One WTC opened with far more glass than the Twin Towers it was replacing, making it the tallest building in the US and a symbol of a Manhattan being remade "as a giant bird killer," as the landscape architect Kate Orff described it. There is a lot you could say about how the city finally changed the building code, enacting a law I mentioned earlier, but I'll summarize it like this: In 2019, the very people who in some cases had been working toward this goal for 15 years—scientists, lawyers, architects, and advocates—united and got in the ear of the right people on the New York City Council, and showed off tremendous public support, and didn't stop until they won.

I wasn't optimistic a bill would pass. I didn't think the real estate industry would accept a mandate that added costs, however marginally. FXFowle's Dan Piselli, in testimony before a City Council hearing in September 2019, noted that measures like frit add only a fraction of a percent to construction costs, but that building owners "will not do this on their own, and that's why legislation is necessary." Piselli was one of 40 people who testified, all but one in support.

The most powerful testimony came from three young Project Safe Flight volunteers. One of them, Elias Markee-Ratner, a fourth grader, said: "Many kids my age have never held a bird, live or dead. I've been lucky enough to hold many live birds. But I've held even more dead ones, and every time it makes me sad." He added: "Before I started volunteering, I thought the idea of these beautiful birds hitting windows and dying was terrible. But actually witnessing it is ten times worse."

The bill passed 43–3 and entered New York City's building code as Local Law 15. Every kind of structure was included: skyscrapers, single-family homes, residential apartment buildings, bus stations, municipal buildings, and commercial storefronts. Bird-friendly materials had to be installed on 90 percent of facades up to 75 feet, and up to 12 feet above green roofs. Major conservation groups called it the most comprehensive bird-friendly building legislation in the nation.

Buoyed by the success, Project Safe Flight volunteers expected to take to the streets the following season, but when COVID forced the city into lockdown in March of 2020, the program went on hiatus for the first time since 1997. Of course, some volunteers still kept tabs on their buildings, since the new ordinance wouldn't be going into effect until the following January and it didn't initially apply to existing structures.

Melissa Breyer was glued to Twitter, and she happened upon a photo of 26 dead birds—warblers, thrushes, and a scarlet tanager—lying on the pavement outside Circa, an 11-story curved-glass apartment building on the north side of Central Park.

Circa was an FXFowle building. But despite hiring the firm that had done a lot for the cause, the developer chose not to make it bird-friendly—same as every other New York City apartment building up to that point, which further supported the need for the recently passed law. The photo shocked Melissa. With so much death around at the time, it seemed even more senseless.

Having grown up in California, she loved the outdoors and considered herself a "passive" birder, who enjoyed the feeder birds that hung around her backyard. By joining Project Safe Flight, she thought she was going to rescue lots of birds. "When I got ready for my first season, I had my little net, I had my little warbler guide, I had my little binoculars. I was like Girl Scout Melissa," she told me.

But one morning, after a quiet month on a Financial District route different than her current one, she found 12 dead songbirds. She sobbed as she dropped off the only survivor, a black-and-white warbler, at the Wild Bird Fund. It dawned on her that rescuing birds was not the main feature of this endeavor. Most of the birds she's found—82 species in all—have been lifers for her. Dead lifers. "I'll never get used to that concept," she said sadly.

For a while, she channeled her anger into posting heartbreaking photos of dead birds on social media and shaming the culprits. And sometimes it worked. Once, she and another monitor, Calista McRae, found a line of dead sparrows and warblers beneath a glass railing in a small park near the World Trade Center. They exposed it on Twitter, and the park's owner, the Port Authority of New York and New Jersey, responded by treating the glass with bird-friendly dots. Another Port Authority building, a glass ferry terminal behind Brookfield Place, where Melissa discovered gangplanks covered with dead warblers, was also a success story. Her office was conveniently located inside Brookfield Place, so on the days she wasn't assigned to her shift she still looked for collisions. And when she was home in Brooklyn, she checked her neighborhood's luxury condo buildings.

Most New Yorkers I speak to have no idea the city exacts such a heavy toll on migratory birds. Many birders do, of course, but like Rebekah Creshkoff, I don't know that many birders who've committed to Project Safe Flight. I asked Melissa if she considered herself a birder. "I'm not a real birder," she said. "I'm a dead birder." Collision monitors are often forced to make a trade-off, since the worst mornings on our sidewalks are usually the best ones in the parks.

I joined Melissa several times in the spring of 2023, and I dreaded each outing. I left feeling angry and hopeless. Memories of radiant little broken bodies very often slipped into my waking thoughts. And I didn't see the worst days. Once, when I had the chance to join Melissa after a big night of migration, I chose instead to go birding at Green-Wood. Yes, there was reporting I could do there, color I could capture, but I wanted to be surrounded by the living. Most birders feel reassured that somebody else—somebody like Melissa—is keeping tabs on the problem. I felt selfish.

I told her I'd see her again in September. But before then, I had to ask: Was it easier or harder for her since she began this work?

Normally sure-footed, she struggled to answer. Her voice turned sad. "I have to wonder what this does to one's psyche," she said. But then she put on a brave face. "I'm a Capricorn, though. I can put up a few walls and be fine."

CHAPTER 6

# Morning Flight

At five in the morning, I waited for Doug Gochfeld on a dark rain-slicked sidewalk in downtown Brooklyn. Private garbage trucks that looked more like armored tanks raced down Atlantic Avenue at breakneck speeds. Rats slipped through sidewalk mounds of trash—this is how the city still manages its waste, as if we're stuck in the 19th century. It was a Monday in early May, right within the sweet spot of spring migration. Doug had told me to meet him here. I wasn't sure where we were going, but I knew it was to see morning flight.

Our conversation in the diner had left me excited. Morning flight offered the thrill of seeing migration in action. And there was a mystery to it I wanted to understand. Take the fact that the morning flights of some birds aren't a simple extension of their previous night's migration; birds will often fly *into* the wind, back the way they came, as if retracing a few of their steps. It seems counterintuitive. So to prepare for the event, I sought out Andrew Farnsworth of the Cornell Lab of Ornithology, an expert on migration and the director of BirdCast. Farnsworth, who grew up in the New York suburbs and as a teenager went birding in Central Park, lives in Manhattan and watches morning flight from the terrace of his East 52nd Street apartment. "It's a widespread thing," he said. "If you look up."

Though it happens inland too, morning flight occurs on a much larger scale at the coast, Farnsworth said. He groups it into two broad categories. The first deals with course correction. Imagine nocturnal migrants—warblers, orioles, tanagers—drifting overnight on a strong wind that forces them toward the coast or over a large body of water. After landing, daybreak shows them to be in a place that doesn't have enough resources to support them for long—a poor choice of stopover. So they pick up again. The second category of morning flight is more optional. This covers birds that migrate during the day, like hawks, eagles, geese, finches, blackbirds, robins, and blue jays. They aren't correcting for wind drift, but just following the land toward their migration objective. For birders, the best times and places are where the two categories overlap: warblers beside blackbirds, tanagers next to goldfinches.

But what's driving the course-correction type of morning flight is still unclear, Farnsworth said. While finding more suitable stopovers is a major feature, it's clearly not the only one. "If it were, then the birds would presumably stop when they found habitat, but that's not the case," Farnsworth explained. "They often continue, and you can see morning flight happening for several hours. But we don't know how far they go or where they eventually land."

To Farnsworth, this suggests the birds are relying on some combination of magnetic, visual, and experiential factors. Unraveling those mysteries poses implications for conservation. If we know where nocturnal migrants concentrate for morning flight, then we can protect those places. And if we know the paths they take around the city, then we can mitigate the risks of buildings and glass they're inevitably going to encounter. Until now, scientific studies of morning flight have relied on stationary counts, the kind of on-the-ground observations

I was about to embark on with Doug. But soon, Farnsworth thinks, advances in tracking devices on individual birds will allow us to eventually connect the dots better than any count.

In the meantime, Doug pulled to the curb in a blue Subaru, and I got in. "We're going to Breezy Point," he said. As we turned onto the Brooklyn-Queens Expressway, he explained why. After he woke up, he checked the cloud cover, the wind at surface level and at 2,000 feet, and the weather radar. Overnight, the wind flowed up from the southwest, he said, carrying birds our way, and the westerly component was pushing some over the ocean. Breezy Point was bound to be the first landing strip they saw at the break of day. Still, the wind had flipped to the north a few hours earlier, a shift Doug had hoped would occur later, only after we reached the beach. That would encourage the birds to continue their migration, since a headwind gives them more control while taking off. "I haven't done this exact thing before in spring, but I've done it in fall," he hedged. "Still, it's always interesting out at Breezy. Whatever happens, we'll have a data point. It's going to be exciting. We might see zero birds."

As you can tell, Doug doesn't go birding like you and I do. He's like a storm chaser, and, yes, when storms crash into New York, he's out there looking for seabirds that get hurled toward shore. During Hurricane Sandy, he opted for Philadelphia over Brooklyn, a decision still tinged with mild regret, though both were "amazing," he said. He's not very interested in watching birds in a tree, which until I met him was usually how I watched them (and how and where I think almost all other birders watch them). He wants to see them in active migration. To collect that data in the field amounts to split-second identifications by sight or sound of small bodies in fast overhead flight. Besides excellent optics, it takes supreme ability, forged from experience. Few birders in the country—and I mean *very* few—possess it.

After graduating from college with a degree in economics, Doug figured he'd end up working a desk job for 20 or 30 years, but it was the Great Recession of 2008 and he became a working birder instead. In Alaska, he chased Hudsonian godwits around the bogs of St. Paul Island. On the flats of Suriname and Brazil, he studied semipalmated sandpipers. And in Israel, he led migration counts. Then he began guiding. His dad still encouraged him to look for a "real job," but after some time he realized that he'd become, well, a birding guide.

"It's still a weird thing," he said, turning onto Flatbush Avenue. "That's not my character, though it is what I do."

The night sky began to lighten as we crossed the Marine Parkway Bridge over Rockaway Inlet. It was around five thirty and close to sunrise. I gazed down the peninsula and saw among the bungalow communities only a few places for migrating birds to put down. To my left was Jamaica Bay, and off to my right was the ocean. Each year, I thought, birds are getting funneled into a smaller patchwork of stopovers in an increasingly inhospitable landscape. And this season was slow so far. After an early April heat wave, trees practically leafed out overnight, at least a week sooner than was considered normal. Birders fretted, asking each other: Will songbirds bypass us and head straight to their breeding grounds? Will they have enough to eat? Climate instability weighed on everyone and everything.

And yet today, I felt anything was possible. Doug agreed. "The reason I like morning flight so much is because it has the highest likelihood of surprise," he said.

Ten minutes later, we pulled into the lot at the tip of Breezy Point where Peter Dorosh and I had parked for the winter waterfowl count. A slick of clouds hung low over Brooklyn and Manhattan. A few thousand birds were still flying 700 feet above us in the dim sky, coming lower, getting ready to land somewhere in the city. I tensed with anticipation. Opening the passenger-side door was like entering a high-fidelity studio filled with bird songs. Familiar mnemonics blitzed me: *Sweet, sweet, you are so sweet* (yellow warblers), *Wichita, Wichita, Wichita* (common yellowthroats), *Drink your teeeeaaaa* (eastern towhees). But these birds weren't newcomers. They'd claimed these precious dunes for breeding territories days or even weeks ago. So had the mockingbirds that shamed the ones I'd listened to at Green-Wood. "The mockingbirds here are the most skilled around," Doug said. "One year, I heard one mimic twenty-four different species in four or five minutes."

Doug pulled on a trucker hat, aviator sunglasses, and knee-high muck boots, and we trundled into the wet dunes on a northwest tilt, careful to avoid sensitive vegetation like bayberry, beach plum, and a tiny lichen with green stalks and bright-red caps called British soldier lichen. The dunes are federal land and off-limits, but Doug had a permit from the National Park Service to enter them. I tried to keep pace, but I couldn't help but look behind me every few moments to watch the sun rise over the Marine Parkway Bridge.

In the rolling dunes, light and shadow jogged alongside us. The violet-pink sky was so clear across Rockaway Inlet that I could parse the Manhattan skyline from One WTC to the matchstick towers of Billionaire's Row. I was conscious of the fact that some of the birds we saw today might not survive that gauntlet.

A black-and-white warbler darted out of the dune grass in front of us, followed by an ovenbird. They must have just come off the ocean. Two small groups of solitary sandpipers—slim shorebirds with big white eye-rings—flew over our heads. "A little solitary movement happening," Doug remarked. In the boreal forest, where they were headed, the females would lay their eggs in the old nests of songbirds—a shorebird in the treetops.

Doug stopped after a few minutes at a knoll where a green plastic chair slumped on its side. We stood on the last line of dunes that face the inlet and, beyond it, Manhattan Beach and Coney Island. I felt a surge of anticipation. We had to be ready for any of at least a hundred different species. For Doug, a bird's flight style, size, shape, and behavior would crystallize into a snap identification. In a way, it was like watching a friend walk toward you from down the street—you can tell who they are by how they carry themselves. But listening was as important as watching. From a rainwater puddle, a northern waterthrush sang on a loop. The electric zip of an indigo bunting marked its passage out of sight. And a Baltimore oriole sang its sweet liquid song from a bare cottonwood. I assumed they had also just landed.

The air was calm. The north wind Doug had hoped for had not yet materialized. Still, warblers began to pop out of the dunes. A blast of yellow was a prairie warbler; it pumped its tail and hugged the vegetation before the dunes fell away. Then a small flock flew into a thin bayberry five feet from us. I held my breath. There were yellow-rumped warblers, another boreal-bound bird, but also a northern parula—a peppy sky-blue warbler, which is small even for its Lilliputian family. He clung to an outer branch, and his yellow chest glowed in the fresh sunlight.

"Let's see what they do next," Doug whispered. "They just made it, and they're moving north through the dunes. They clearly want to be moving in that direction, but they don't want to cross all that water."

I'd seen hundreds of parulas before, but for that individual I felt an affection I still struggle to unpack. Where I'd seen them in city parks, they were usually singing and feeding. Here, I watched this adult male forced to make a vital decision on where to go next and whether to go alone or stay with the pack. How he made that call, of course, I'll never know. He and the rest of his flock stayed in the bayberry for 15 seconds, then flew east to another bush, sticking for now to the safety of the dunes.

"I think if there was wind, they'd utilize it and jump off," Doug said. "There was supposed to be a north wind! Another thing: Forecasts are not always what they say they are."

"What makes them cross?" I asked.

"I don't know. You'll have to ask them," Doug said, seemingly annoyed by my simplistic question.

After a moment, though, he offered an explanation. "The big problem with a water crossing this size is that they're very vulnerable. There are peregrines. There are gulls. They'll probably wait until tonight. Typically, there's an urge-versus-fear balance, and I guess when it gets to a certain point where urge strongly overtakes fear, they go."

As we waited, a red-bellied woodpecker flew past us, then another, and they called to each other as if they were in on their own little joke. A third answered from the center of the dunes. This took me by surprise, since red-bellied woodpeckers aren't truly migratory—though I knew they have greatly expanded their northern range. Some birds are known to wander south in the winter to avoid cold weather, but I wanted to think these birds were pioneers embarking toward new frontiers. The trio flew all around the dunes as if they were lost. "This is what birds that don't like crossing water do when they get out here," Doug said.

But we'd found something of a runway. Three red-breasted nuthatches now grouped around us. Though they looked like toy birds, small with striped heads, they showed no fear. One honked its nasally call, then took off, followed by the other two. Interestingly, they pointed south, over the ocean. I was confused. Shouldn't they be going north to the conifer forests where they breed? They spiraled upward like tiny pill-shaped rockets.

"They're up there trying to figure it out," Doug observed. "They're three hundred feet up, so the wind is going to be stronger." He urged me to keep watching through my binoculars. "A lot of people would stop looking once they go south... and wouldn't know that they *just* turned north, toward Coney Island."

We followed the first nuthatch until it became a speck. Then we noticed five warblers in the same patch of sky, well beyond our range for identification. Scanning across, we found more specks. I wondered why that was. Shouldn't they be lower? "When it's calm, as it is now, warblers move a lot higher," Doug explained. "On a windy day, that wind is down here. You see, when birds migrate at night, they depend on a strong tailwind to cover a lot of ground. But in daytime, birds tend to fly *into* the wind, because that gives them more control—just like airplanes."

We moved around now, tracking the crest of the dunes in search of other runways. Toward the last rise, we spotted a birder we both knew, a gentlemanly Brit named Tom Preston. As we walked toward him, one of the first red-bellied woodpeckers jetted out in front of us. An hour had passed, and it had finally decided to take off. This whole time, the trio had been gathering information on the wind, figuring out the most aerodynamic path, based on the flights of the smaller birds. It jumped off heading south—like those red-breasted nuthatches.

"Is that red-bellied going? What do you think—is it gonna go?" Doug asked.

He wanted my answer on the record. I said I thought they were serious this time.

"Second one following. Watch 'em, watch 'em. See what happens." A third one sprang out of a small cottonwood and set off in pursuit. Another two we didn't realize were in the dunes appeared and joined the flight. "Five went out. Let's see. They're gaining altitude offshore."

I watched one—alone in my view of the sky—pump its wings. Quickly, the bird became a shrinking figure, leaving only the flapping and none of its finer points. The leap of faith, if you could call it that, was stirring. Following Doug's instruction, I stayed glued to that woodpecker. The group banked right, turned north over the inlet, and within a few minutes passed over Coney Island's towering Parachute Jump, the famous old amusement park ride, on the far shore.

When we reached Tom Preston, he was wearing a floppy wide-brimmed hat and baggy khakis, looking out over the Breezy Point jetty—yes, the same one I'd slipped on that day with Peter on the waterfowl count.

"Morning!" Tom said cheerily.

"Red-bellied-palooza, huh?" Doug said by way of hello.

"Yeah!" Tom said. "At first, there were only a couple around, but now there's loads of them."

"Three went, then two went, and now one is calling," Doug said.

"How's it going, Tom?" I asked.

"Good, I think." He was sweating. "It's a real schlep up here."

"Eh," Doug grunted, like it wasn't really.

"If you're old, it's a schlep," Tom clarified. "I figured you might be here, Doug, but not you, Ryan," he added.

I told him I had joined Doug to write about morning flight.

"Quasi-morning flight," Doug interjected.

Though it fell short of the epic morning flights of autumn, which entail much larger numbers than the spring, I still found it interesting. Morning flight at Breezy Point included both categories Andrew Farnsworth described for me: corrective flight and diurnal migration. And the latter was beginning to pick up, with blue jays, eastern kingbirds, several kinds of swallows, and those red-bellied woodpeckers. Common terns, their white coats gleaming, had just returned for the breeding season from Brazil or Argentina, and they plunge-dived for small fish off the jetty. Doug and Tom picked out 60 black scoters flying into the inlet, where they joined a raft of 135 surf scoters near a low-tide sandbar. Two common eiders, a drake and a hen, dozed on the lee side of the jetty. But it was getting late for them; it was time for my weird-duck winter companions to get back to the Far North.

Since it was only quasi-morning flight, Doug left us, to check some ponds in the dunes. For the next few minutes, it grew quiet. Tom and I chatted about recent sightings until we realized that we hadn't seen a new bird in a while.

Tom shook his head. "It's amazing," he said. "The birds show up when Doug's here, and when he leaves, suddenly there's no birds. I know *I* can find birds. Sometimes."

Doug returned, and so did the birds, bouncing through the dunes. A wood thrush called *Pit-pit* from a grove of aspens, while another red-bellied woodpecker shot out of the dunes. "Hummingbird!" shouted Doug. Looking up, we saw a ruby-throated hummingbird, weighing but a tenth of an ounce, chasing after a yellow-rumped warbler. "Hummingbirds are such assholes," Doug said.

The wind was finally beginning to pick up out of the north, so we looped back toward the parking lot, to a berm where we could face that direction, assuming birds would fly into it. Sure enough, we ran into a flock of woodland birds reading the situation together: six Baltimore orioles, a few rose-breasted grosbeaks, and three scarlet tanagers. A young grosbeak perched on a sapling and sang a few quizzical notes of its wobbly song. Then a female scarlet tanager, all yellow and green with blackish wings, landed in a tiny sumac before the dunes sloped down to the shore. It wasn't quite the westernmost shrub on all of Long Island, but it was pretty close. The tanager hesitated there.

Because the thin Rockaway Peninsula rounds off almost 120 miles of coastline, from Montauk to Breezy Point, birds of all kinds—and from all kinds of places—can be expected to show up here, allowing us to witness their navigational choices. "They have to make a decision, or at least a decision visible to us," Doug said.

As for the tanager, I stared across the inlet, thinking that there were no woods until Prospect Park, six miles away. Grosbeaks, orioles, tanagers, warblers—these are forest birds, but often they have no choice but to pass through urban way stations now and again.

"Imagine if this was all condos out here," Doug said. "These birds would be arriving and landing in, what, a couple of London plane trees? Terrible."

It was a little after eight now, and we'd been in the dunes for two and a half hours. Four more red-bellied woodpeckers flew past us, and it was only from our spot inside the dunes, I realized, rather than from the shore, that you could appreciate the full scope of their morning flight. As we walked on, more pairs winged their way out. Doug checked his red-bellied tally: 21 in all, a new high for the location. "New York is the new Carolinas," he said.

With the car in sight and the warm sun on our backs, we couldn't pull ourselves away, hard as we tried. Birds are always on the move in May, and there's always something new to see. We watched swallows arc up the harbor, glossy ibises float by on a light breeze, and eastern kingbirds flap low over our heads, the contrast between their dark backs and white bellies like the light and shadow that rippled around the dunes earlier. I wasn't ready to cross the water to Brooklyn, back to ordinary life.

Out here, an endless series of captivating little dramas was playing out, and though I couldn't grasp the purpose or meaning of every act, I could let myself simply be astonished by them. We stayed there for another hour, watching groups of blue jays—from several up to almost 40—flow like an outgoing tide to the east, hugging this narrow strip of sand that was invaluable to them and all these birds, whatever their destination. Seems they weren't ready to cross either.

CHAPTER 7

# Wave Day

Some birders I know take vacations during the second week of May and yet never step foot outside New York City. The thing they're hoping for—we're all hoping for—is a wave day.

"A wave is generally due to unfavorable weather damming up the birds moving northward for several days," Allan Cruickshank wrote back in 1942. "If such a spell is followed by a rise in temperature and a light southerly wind, the delayed birds rush forward *en masse*."

In 2016, I experienced my first wave at the end of my first week of birding. That was the day I met Peter Dorosh. The week had been cold and soggy, but that hadn't stopped me from birding. Having been told that spring migration—which I knew absolutely nothing about days earlier—was reaching its intoxicating finale, the thought of it ending felt apocalyptic.

I was possessed by a manic energy to make up for this time that I'd had no idea I'd lost until that moment. I'd gone on three Brooklyn Bird Club walks and was becoming familiar with some of the regulars. One encouraged me to go on Peter's Mother's Day trip to Green-Wood Cemetery. Another commented, upon running into me again several hours later, "During migration, everything stops." (She meant for us, not the birds.)

The conditions before Peter's walk were perfect for a wave, though I didn't realize it at the time. Overnight, the winds had shifted to the south. Then, shortly after sunrise, it began to rain—the kind of downpour, Peter explained, that would ground any flyovers. Seven of us waited at the cemetery's entrance, huddled inside a dim stone gatehouse on Prospect Park West. If only the weather would break, Peter said, we would find lots of birds out there.

An opening arrived after 20 minutes, and Peter led us into the misty cemetery. Just past the security booth, we found a flock of warblers and followed them a short distance down a valley, toward Ocean Hill, catching up to them at a red oak hosting a frantic convention of small birds. Exhausted and hungry after their night flights, they hurriedly gleaned caterpillars from the oak's catkins, the tiny pollen-filled flower clusters that hung like miniature drapes. The rain had forced them all down. Peter called it a fallout.

The other birders matched the birds' feverishness, and I struggled to keep up. "Blue-winged!" "Black-throated green!" "Worm-eating!" "Chestnut-sided!" "Blackburnian!" I fumbled with my new binoculars. I didn't want them to get wet. They fogged up anyway. I tried to wipe them. I couldn't get a clear sight. For the first time, I felt that distinct birder's panic—the desperate scramble to focus your binoculars on a bird before it vanishes, like trying to pluck confetti from the air. I was overwhelmed. The birds moved quickly, and I could pick up only flashes of color.

Meanwhile, Peter's ability to quickly identify them rapid-fire in the dense leaves seemed preternatural. Because he couldn't hear their vocalizations, he had long ago trained his eyes to notice the slightest movements. He also had a feel for the behavior of each species—how it moved up or down branches, how it fed, which part of the tree it favored. Peter greeted them all like old friends, and for him they were, back in town for a short visit.

It struck me that this kind of information wasn't in my field guide. I decided then that I wanted to learn these birds as Peter had.

"If you wanna see warblers, look for the oaks," Peter told me. No other family of trees offered as many insects, especially caterpillars, he said.

I hardly knew the birds. "I should know the trees too?" I asked.

Well, he said, warblers make birders do obsessive things. "I have a name for it, OCWA: obsessive-compulsive warbler affliction."

I didn't realize that OCWA is the banding code, or shorthand, that birders and ornithologists use for the orange-crowned warbler, one of Peter's favorite warblers. "In my early days, I often wondered about the time I spent out during warbler migrations," he went on. "If I were married, I'm sure my spouse would resort to an all-points bulletin to find me!"

Peter pulled up his rain jacket to show me a faded T-shirt from the Biggest Week in American Birding, a 10-day festival at Ohio's Magee Marsh, a premier warbler-sighting destination. He'd visited years ago, and the shirt featured the breeding males of all 37 eastern species (the yellow-breasted chat has since been assigned to its own group), in their yellows, blues, blacks, oranges, and greens.

Their main appeal wasn't actually in their songs. What I was hearing in Green-Wood was dry, buzzy, and insect-like, with hardly any warble at all. That was a bit of a misnomer; early ornithologists from England found these small birds to resemble their native country's warblers, even though biologically they aren't closely related. And while Old World warblers are renowned for their voices, here, ours are known for the beauty of their plumage.

On a day like this, Peter said, you could find more than 20 warblers in New York's large green spaces; we'd nearly seen that many in this one tree. But in a couple weeks, they'd all be gone, up to their breeding territories, he said. Like the birds themselves, brilliant but short-lived, their migrations through the city shine brightly but quickly flame out.

Later, I visited Peter's blog to read his summary of the day. The reports he gathered between Green-Wood and Prospect Park accounted for 28 warbler species, most of his T-shirt lineup. "Mother Nature appropriately incited some fallout conditions on Mother's Day," he wrote. "You can tell it was a BIG day," he added, "at least in the sense of how long we impatient birders have been waiting for the blast out to happen."

I've been chasing waves ever since.

ON A WARM May morning in 2023, thrushes sang in music-box voices as I climbed the stairs of Prospect Park's Lookout Hill. It was six o'clock, and the air smelled of black cherry flowers. Once I reached the Butterfly Meadow, I found four other birders milling around in the pale light, saying little. We'd all checked BirdCast and knew that more than half a million birds had flown through Brooklyn overnight. More were coming, and their altitude was low. The birds we'd waited all year to see were looking for a place to land.

Lookout Hill is the most important place in Brooklyn for migratory birds, according to Peter; it sits on the moraine, and its wooded slopes are a strong visual cue for birds in flight. And the Butterfly Meadow, all of three acres just below the hill's summit, can be a place of concentrated magic. I chose my waiting spot at the southwest corner of the meadow at a juncture of paths that Peter—and only Peter—calls the Golden Triangle.

Looking at it from above, it's not really a triangle but a Y shape, with the arms defined by one line of elms and one of pin oaks. The meadow, ringed by more oaks, fills their V, overflowing it like a giant bubble in a martini glass. What makes the whole thing "golden," for migrating songbirds and thus birders, is in the cornucopia dished up by those elms and oaks.

A pin oak on the south side of the meadow was the first to catch the sun's slanting rays. Warmed up, the tree's glossy leaves lit up with bugs like a marquee sign flickering to life. A tugboat horn sounded off to the west, probably from the Red Hook docks. Then birdsong rose around me like fizz rushing to the surface of a shaken soda, voiced overwhelmingly by four different kinds of warblers: northern parula, black-throated blue, black-and-white, and magnolia. Their songs were buzzy and bright, slow and clear, squeaky like a rusty bicycle chain, clipped and whistled. I had eagerly memorized them in the years since my first wave day. Quick darting movements peppered the tree. A warbler sprang out of the foliage onto a bare branch to snatch a flying meal.

Our sunrise crew paused in the auditory storm to zero in on a male Blackburnian warbler foraging in the treetop. This flame-orange little bird may have been in Peru or Bolivia only a few weeks ago. "The sun just hit its throat," someone said. "I can see it sing," said another. The last note was ear-splittingly high, and I was glad the city's soundscape hadn't dulled my ability to hear it.

Like Peter that day at Green-Wood, I expected to find different warblers in each strata of the tree. At the top were Blackburnian, Tennessee, Nashville, and Cape May warblers; what those names don't tell you is where they're going, which on the whole are breeding grounds in Canada's boreal forest. Blackpolls, another treetop lover, were more aptly named, for the black cap they wore in the spring and summer. Below them were mid-canopy specialists: magnolias, parulas, American redstarts, and a bay-breasted warbler, a bird that brought a subtle beauty to the scene's bright palette.

Each had a biological niche, which encompassed not only their preferred habitat but also their behavior. Parulas, between singing their rising trills, gleaned bugs from the edges of leaves, while redstarts sallied like flycatchers, and black-and-white warblers crept along the branches like nuthatches. Still, there's flexibility—birds go where the food is—and I was delighted to see the caramel head of a worm-eating warbler near the pin oak's crown. These birds are normally found around the forest's floor, picking through dead leaves for arthropods, not worms, but this one hung upside down and pecked at some leftover catkins.

Watching them, I suddenly felt the weight of an ancient, unbroken cycle. Back and forth across the hemisphere, these warblers returned every spring and autumn with the regularity of day turning into night. I basked in this day's abundance, but knew how contingent the experience was. A complex choreography was at play, and I wondered about my role—or the role of my species—in the web of relationships.

My frustration of that first wave day at Green-Wood was long gone, but I still felt overwhelmed. I was learning of the dangers these birds face, and I knew days like this were becoming rarer. Over the next couple hours, birders would find 27 warbler species in Prospect Park alone, almost an entire season's worth compressed into a morning. One birder called it an "extreme birdpalooza."

A friend at Central Park's Summit Rock told me the wave of migrants had rolled through there for three hours. "We only have a few truly amazing days like that in a season," she said.

But how much longer, I wondered, would we have birds in these numbers? I was at a loss. The best thing, I decided, was to just enjoy the moment.

THAT DAY, IT was May 11. My first wave day experience at Green-Wood occurred on May 8. A Linnaean Society newsletter from 1952 pegs the famous "warbler wave" as May 10. According to BirdCast, spring migration in New York City peaks between May 7 and May 22.

Migration is influenced by local conditions like weather, but the overall schedule has remained relatively consistent. Historically, the springtime arrivals of migrating passerines or songbirds closely follow the budding of leaves in the continent's "green-up" or "green wave." Vast numbers of caterpillars, waking from their winter slumber, begin chewing the new foliage. And in turn, birds follow the trend northward, feasting on those insects during their stopovers and depending on them to feed their chicks. As I looked around Lookout Hill, though, I sensed that the relationship was falling out of sync. It had been lush and green since the last week of April. Catkins blanketed the ground like a yellow carpet. Peter, who knows Lookout better than anyone, thinks its trees leaf out at least a week earlier than two decades ago, though without long-term data it's impossible to say for sure.

Scientists tell us that spring's coming sooner, a shift that's accelerating. How are migrating birds adjusting to this rapid climatic change? A study by researchers from Oklahoma State and several other universities recently attempted to answer that question. The headline doesn't sound scary—DECOUPLING OF BIRD MIGRATION FROM THE CHANGING PHENOLOGY OF SPRING GREEN-UP—but its conclusions are terrifying. Comparing almost 20 years of eBird records against phenological trends—patterns in the timing of seasonal events like plant budding—the researchers concluded that the migration schedules of most species of birds may not be keeping pace with the green wave. The fear is that as this synchronicity continues to fall out of alignment, more and more birds won't be able to find the food they need to feed their young.

Like those red-bellied woodpeckers at Breezy Point, we often see firsthand birds changing their geographic range. Some birds—perhaps if they're more flexible about their diet or breeding habitat—are better able to adapt than others. Migratory patterns—some combination of instinct and learned behavior—are flexible. And evolution doesn't stand still. Scientists point out that bird migration on this continent has already evolved, largely as a response to a changing climate, the last two-million-plus years of glacial advance and retreat.

But can birds evolve again in what is, geologically speaking, the blink of an eye? Some species, like the Eurasian blackcap and the house finch, have changed their migratory patterns within a few generations. A warmer planet may benefit some. In the last 30 years, for instance, black vultures have followed their turkey vulture cousins north during spring migration. A resident pair in Queens now warms itself in the winter on the chimney of a Catholic school. A study of black-throated blue warblers in New Hampshire found that they were sometimes hatching two clutches instead of the usual one because they arrived ahead of schedule. So far, though, they seem to be the exception.

Birders who've been around long enough will tell you that wave days are fewer. And there have been reports confirming this as far back as the late 1980s, when the ornithologist Sidney A. Gauthreaux Jr., using over three decades of archived radar images, was able to show that the frequency of springtime migrant waves across the Gulf of Mexico had decreased by almost 50 percent. But has the *timing* of wave days changed today? Not really. Hundreds of different species are crossing the Gulf around the same date as they always have, according to radar studies led by Colorado State University's Kyle Horton. However, they *are* speeding up their migrations after they make landfall, presumably by cutting back on stopovers to try to catch the green wave now way out in front of them.

"The first several days of May and the last days of April now have a lot more birds than they did twenty or thirty years ago," Roger Pasquier, an author and Central Park birder who keeps records going back nearly 70 years, told me. "The first arrivals of many species are now at least a few days earlier, even if the bulk of birds may still peak around the tenth of May."

In late April, I'd seen singles of Cape May, blackpoll, and bay-breasted warblers, some of the northernmost boreal breeders. Though not entirely unexpected, I was still taken aback. John Bull's *Birds of New York State*, published in 1974, is a classic among an older generation of birders partly because of his well-researched arrival dates. Bull's "extreme arrival," meaning an unusually early arrival date, for bay-breasted warblers was April 30, the same date I'd seen one. For blackpolls, the last common migrant to arrive in large numbers, it was April 28. "Rare before mid-May," Bull wrote.

Long-term banding studies provide the clearest picture. In southwestern Pennsylvania, for instance, researchers found that several species, including wood thrushes, are returning only about five days sooner than they did in the 1960s, according to a 2022 *Audubon* essay by Scott Weidensaul, whose book *Living on the Wind* is a classic on migration. They're breeding more than three weeks earlier, though. The wood thrushes, writes Weidensaul, "have managed to compress what should take weeks into mere days, perhaps by abandoning a period of rest and recovery after they arrive and before they mate."

Birds that migrate thousands of miles each year need plenty of things to go right for them. And until very recently, many things had been going right, as their evolutionary history suggests. Ornithologist Benjamin Winger theorizes that long-distance migration is in fact a survival strategy. One reason, Winger believes, is seasonal: It is more economical to fly between food-rich tropical forests and food-rich northern forests than to eke out hard and unpredictable winters in the latter. Doing so gives a Blackburnian warbler, for instance, a better chance of living longer than the golden-crowned kinglets I'd seen at Green-Wood. And indeed, Winger's research has found that long-distance migrants enjoy higher survival rates than their short-distance counterparts.

But there's a trade-off. Kinglets may not live as long, but being closer to their breeding grounds means they'll produce more offspring. Long-distance migrants, by spending less time on their breeding grounds, produce fewer young. That squares with what biologists call the "slow-fast continuum" of life history, Winger points out. Elephants live slowly but produce few young; mice live fast but produce many. (It follows that those species that live faster evolve more quickly than slow-lived species, since producing more generations in the same amount of time contributes to more genetic variance.) A long-distance neotropical migrant may be more like an elephant than a mouse, says Winger. But this fine balance depends on the Blackburnian, for instance, leaving its winter home in the Andes and making it back to Canada alive. It doesn't have the luxury of just being able to produce more offspring each year.

Glass windows, predators, shrinking habitat: These are extreme threats that keep all these migrants from coming back alive year after year, raising doubts over how many more waves of birds I'll see. So, short of immediate decarbonization, what do they need? As Scott Weidensaul writes, they need enough to eat and they need room to adapt to a warmer planet, which means better-managed forests and native trees—like the oaks Peter went on about the day I met him—and protected areas or corridors to allow for a shift north.

Whether that happens or not depends entirely on us.

PETER PULLED UP to the Golden Triangle in his Toro a little after seven. His workday had just begun, and this was his territory. Each member of Prospect Park's natural resources crew was assigned a zone in the park, and Peter, several years earlier, had asked for Lookout Hill, the place he calls his "sacred birding shrine."

But the shrine had a few cracked steps. Peter walked over with a slight limp, looking a little worse for wear. All week he'd been hacking away at Norway maple saplings, and he complained of plantar fasciitis. "Lookout is the toughest terrain in the whole park," he said, with some pride. "In some parts you're working at almost forty-five-degree angles." In almost 25 years on the job, he'd pulled out something like 30,000 Norway maples. And that was just one of his many invasive archenemies, which include mugwort, Japanese knotweed, garlic mustard, porcelain berry, multiflora rose, and paper mulberry. Working the moraine's steep, slippery, and eroded slopes was taxing, and Peter was no spring chicken. "I look forward to retirement someday," he said. But somehow, I couldn't imagine that day coming.

Peter had his weekly volunteer crew scheduled to tackle the mugwort in the Butterfly Meadow, so he took a moment to look around. He fetched a pair of old binoculars from the passenger seat of his cart. He'd seen the alerts from the still-young morning. "My phone wouldn't stop vibrating. Blue grosbeak, Kentucky warbler, cerulean warbler. It sounds like a wave day. What have you seen?"

Where to begin? I named a few, like the Blackburnian, and told him it had been the best morning of the spring. At last check, I said, there were 12 warbler species in that nearest pin oak.

"It's a twister," he said. "That's where you see many warbler species together in the same tree."

I visualized a storm of birds whipping through one tree, then quickly moving on. I noticed that more birders had arrived, and they hurried back and forth between the oaks, as if caught in the middle of a twister themselves.

That had once been Peter—"in my youthful days," he said—but he was no longer a warbler chaser. His goal for the season was 25 species. "I used to see thirty-two or thirty-five every spring, but those days are gone."

A lot had changed in the years since our Mother's Day wave—even since our waterfowl count. Since then, Peter had begun to suffer from glaucoma, and he was no longer able to rely on his once-impeccable vision. His eyes had become extremely sensitive to light and cold, and could no longer fix on small, fast-moving birds; they ended up looking like a blur. He leaned now on a combination of patience and luck, and sometimes the help of others, preferring to wait for warblers at their tried-and-true spots. To do that, you had to know the trees, of course. "Boiding the easy way," he called it. "As one gets older, finding birds by sight alone can be hard."

I knew it would be impossible for him to locate upper-story birds like the Blackburnian, so I mentioned a few that were in the lower strata.

"Have you seen a chestnut-sided?" he asked.

The chestnut-sided warbler was one of my favorites too. Unlike some in its family, it's named well; it has chestnut-colored feathers along its flanks. It also has a golden cap. And its song is cheerful, often written out as *Pleased, pleased, pleased to meetcha!* I'd seen several, I said, but not within the last few minutes. So I left Peter and edged my way around the meadow, hoping to hear one for him.

It struck me that in part we had Peter to thank for this terrific experience. He was doing the backbreaking work of stripping Lookout Hill and planting oaks to create better woodlands for migrants. How many birders here realized that? Peter had known the area was in bad shape when he'd asked to be assigned to it. There were still great old trees, but several slopes had been entirely choked out by deep-rooted invasive plants. Given his seniority, I assume he could've asked for a less difficult post. But Peter knew Lookout as well as anyone, both as a birder and a landscaper, and he had ideas on how birds moved across it on their way through the park. His best birding days had been here.

When Peter lived nearby and worked at Republic National Bank, a job he got through the Center for Hearing and Communication, Lookout Hill was his first stop on his way to the office. Wearing a sport jacket and tie, he would give himself two hours to walk from there to Flatbush Avenue, birding the whole way. A good migration day was 15 warbler species before he had to move on. On weekends, though, he would go all out. One day in May 1993, he and his friend Glen Davis, a phenomenal ear-birder who was only a sophomore in high school, spent 14 hours in Prospect Park, returning often to Lookout on their all-day warbler quest. Minutes before sunset, they stared into the fading light and found in a white oak near the hill's northwest corner their 25th species—a golden-winged warbler, the day's rarest. Next to it was a Lawrence's warbler, a hybrid offspring of a golden-winged and a blue-winged warbler. Exhausted, they lay down on some stairs and looked straight up with their binoculars.

In his bank job of 16 years, Peter investigated errors in the check-processing unit, and it bored him. Then he found the natural resources crew. His office, he liked saying, grew from five feet to 500 acres. He'd thought working at the park would give him more time to see birds, but it turned out to be the opposite. The rest of us got the enjoyment; he had to keep his head down. Still, he felt like he was creating something for birds and their future.

Peter's work on Lookout marked the start of years of restoration. Despite the aches and tiredness, he felt happy with what he was doing. "We should at least give birds a chance, give them food and shelter, so they have enough nutrition to make the next leg in their journey," he told me. This season, he had gone with a new quote in his email signature, attributed to Bengali writer Rabindranath Tagore: "The one who plants trees knowing that he or she will never sit in their shade, has at least started to understand the meaning of life."

Now at the other end of the meadow, I heard the song *Pleased, pleased, pleased to meetcha!* I sent a text to Peter, and he came running over. The chestnut-sided was on a low branch, but like all hungry warblers, it was not about to stay in place. I pointed, I turned Peter's shoulders to face the bird, I gave directions, but I couldn't get him to spot the bird. After it flew off, I broke the news that the chestnut-sided had left. By then, Peter wore a pained expression. Disappointed, he walked back to his cart.

His eyesight had been a superpower, and I wondered if he had made peace with its disappearance. Sometimes I heard him grumble about those who could go birding every day while he labored. That was a privilege some had—I included myself in that—because of flexible jobs or wealth or retirement savings. But he told me his motto was to be happy with whatever popped up in front of him.

As I began to think about leaving Lookout, the chestnut-sided flew back into the same tree. I wavered about whether to text Peter again. I was certain he would find one this season, eventually, in his own time. But I did, and he rushed back. For a split second, the bird paused in a gap between the thin leaves.

"Niiiiiiiiiiice," Peter said. He pulled down his binoculars, and I could see a sparkle in his blue eyes. He grinned and fist-bumped me, then got to work pulling mugwort.

# SUMMER

CHAPTER 8

# Freshkills

Aldo Leopold once wondered "what a thousand acres of Silphiums looked like when they tickled the bellies of the buffalo." Little remains of the tallgrass prairie, where the yellow silphium flowers grew on stalks as tall as your head: less than 4 percent of 170 million acres. But I didn't have to search for the remnants of the prairie in places like the Flint Hills of Kansas. I only had to borrow a car and drive to the west shore of Staten Island.

The prairie at Freshkills Park was knee-high when I met ecologists Shannon Curley and José Ramírez-Garofalo there on a broiling July morning. We stood in a gently swaying sea of switchgrass, Indian grass, and big bluestem, and listened for furtive grassland birds rarely found elsewhere in the city. The Manhattan skyline was visible to the north but only as a dim outline. Wildfire smoke from Canada had drifted down and, at times, created a scary orange haze over the city. On several headline-making days that summer of 2023, New York's air quality was the world's worst.

Out here, though, it was blue sky and green grass, as thick as a shag rug. Tidal creeks that looked wide enough to be called rivers snaked between four large earthwork mounds. We were at the north end of the East Mound, 120 feet tall. Below us, great egrets and snowy egrets stalked the shallows of an emerald-green marsh. Off to our right, upland woods stretched across a ridge of ancient serpentinite, and behind us, the prairie reached clear to the horizon. By August, its grasses would climb almost six feet, tall enough to obscure any hint that you hadn't ended up in Leopold's dream—without the buffalo, that is.

"I won't walk into them," said Curley, who was about a foot shorter than that peak. "I make José do it. Otherwise, I'll get lost forever."

Curley, in her late thirties, tied her long auburn hair in a knot to keep it off her neck on the sweltering day. Red-faced, she began to sneeze. "I'm the worst grassland biologist," she joked. "I'm allergic to grasses."

Ramírez-Garofalo, the park's head of science and research development and a doctoral candidate at Rutgers University, wore a serious demeanor behind aviator sunglasses. A decade younger than Curley, he was writing his dissertation on the geographic responses of species to climate change, namely through a phenomenon called vagrancy. In those tall grasses, he had found a Gulf Coast tick, a scary little arachnid that had journeyed up to the Northeast from the South. That was an example of vagrancy: a species found well outside its normal range.

Curley, who lives on Long Island, was a postdoctoral researcher at the Cornell Lab of Ornithology, where she was studying offshore migration using the same tools as her BirdCast colleagues. Cutting-edge radar ornithology also provided significant allergic relief.

Curley and Ramírez-Garofalo have studied the park's birds for almost a decade, along with its other animals, insects, and plants. But their schedules had kept them away from Freshkills for much of that spring and summer. I couldn't have entered without them. Nearly all of the park was closed to the public, though it's projected to open in phases through 2036. The first 21 acres, or less than 1 percent of its 2,200 acres, opened in the fall of 2023, but this segment is accessible only by car, and its entrance is tucked behind an abandoned shopping center, a self-storage facility, and a Fairfield Inn.

When the park is fully open, though, it will be one of the largest parks in New York, with grasslands making up over a thousand acres. Such an extraordinary amount of undeveloped space was only made possible by the mounds of capped trash we were standing on—yes, 150 million tons of it. This was once Fresh Kills, for a time the world's largest dump.

Few areas in New York City are large enough to meet the breeding needs of most migratory birds, so summer is typically quieter for birders. Freshkills, Jamaica Bay, Rockaway beaches like Breezy Point, and a few large parks like Pelham Bay are exceptions. Staten Island's marshes and its wooded spine—the Greenbelt, which I could see clearly from the East Mound—also offer valuable breeding habitat, hosting thrushes, scarlet tanagers, various warblers, and even pileated woodpeckers. Although Staten Island, the city's least populous borough, suburbanized rapidly after the Verrazzano Bridge connected it to Brooklyn in 1964, its tree canopy cover remains around 31 percent. By contrast, Brooklyn, the most populous borough, has under 18 percent cover.

You won't find many urban grasslands outside of Freshkills. And in the Northeast, several generations of abandoned farms and grasslands became woods and forests through ecological succession. Eastern tallgrass prairies, like the Hempstead Plains, which once stretched more than 50 square miles across Long Island, are all but extinct. Indeed, since they're easy to build on or plow under, 90 percent of the world's grasslands have been grazed, cleared, or otherwise corroded. It's no secret what that's done to the specialized birds that nest in them. Since 1970, grassland birds in North America have declined by 53 percent. No other group has decreased so precipitously.

But not in New York City; at Freshkills, they're having a renaissance.

From within the prairie, a song that sounded like a dial-up modem—high, thin, a fast trill when you connect—came at us from all sides. It was Savannah sparrows. Some birders refer to certain drab sparrows as "LBJs," or little brown jobs, but to me the Savannahs have an understated appeal: a yellow tint to the face, a neat head pattern, fine streaking. Over 600 pairs breed across the park's four mounds, the most of any bird. They aren't choosy. "Savannah sparrows will nest in a plant pot," Ramírez-Garofalo told me. "If it's flat and grassy, they'll nest there." Having arrived in late winter or early spring, the males were singing for their second clutch of the season.

I hadn't come to see Savannah sparrows, though. We picked through their dial-up chorus to listen for the insect-like buzz of the aptly named grasshopper sparrow. Unlike Savannahs, grasshopper sparrows *are* picky, which partly explains why they've disappeared from many parts of North America. Instead of something as simple as a plant pot, they need large, unfragmented native grasslands. Grasshopper sparrows began breeding at Freshkills in 2015, and their colony had grown to over 120 pairs, one of the largest in the region and possibly the densest anywhere in the country. Though they made themselves hard to spot, we soon heard one. The tiny singer was some 50 yards away on a dark-green clump of bayberry. Potbellied, flat-headed, and rather plain, the bird recalled a caricatured old French chef.

"Chonky," Curley said.

"They're the crown jewel of the park," Ramírez-Garofalo added.

*Crown jewel?* The bird flew weakly into a thick patch, where its nest might have been.

Grasshopper sparrows may look bland, but their scarcity has attracted our attention and concern. At Freshkills, Curley and Ramírez-Garofalo have intensely monitored them in the form of surveying, banding, and radio-tagging. Picky though they are, the birds obviously like it here.

Once clued in to their soft buzz, I heard several more, then watched one hop onto a blade of Indian grass. Golden seed heads brought out the sparrow's subtle tan hues. Bird and grass swayed together. I found myself coming around to the crown-jewel description. After all, these birds are a big reason why these extensive grasslands will feature prominently in the city's largest park in over a century.

BEFORE FRESHKILLS WAS a tallgrass prairie and before it was a trash dump, it was one of the largest and richest tidal marshes in the Hudson River estuary. The Lenape people, who left great piles of oyster and mussel shells on the island, called it Aquehonga Manacknong, or "place of the bad woods." The Dutch named it Staaten Eylandt, and its waterways "kills," from the Middle Dutch word *kille*, meaning "riverbed" or "water channel." The Fresh Kill flowed from the Arthur Kill, the tidal strait that twists up Raritan Bay and divides Staten Island and New Jersey. Its marshes drained half the island, and they were bountiful. In colonial years, disputes arose between English governors on either side of the Arthur Kill over who held the right to harvest its salt-meadow grass. In 1695, a surveyor reported that his compass was stolen after he set it down "on a certain parcel of meadow (the grass whereof being cut downe)."

Mentions of Fresh Kills followed in the chronicles of other visitors. In 1748, the Swedish naturalist Pehr (or Peter) Kalm described coming upon its swampy meadows in "a wretched half-rotten ferry." By then, all the island's woods—bad or otherwise—had been replaced by wheat and rye fields, apple orchards, and cherry trees. Nearly every farmhouse, Kalm wrote, boasted a cider press. A young Henry David Thoreau later rambled along the island's South Shore, picking through the shell middens at Fresh Kills. He wrote home in 1843: "The whole Island is like a garden, and affords very fine scenery."

The borough held its natural beauty longer than the rest of New York. In 1892's *Days Afield on Staten Island*, the naturalist William T. Davis wrote that he could ramble for miles on summer days without seeing anyone. While almost 1.2 million people lived across the harbor in Manhattan, the island's population of 39,000 was spread mostly among farming and shorefront communities; beyond a few hotels on the beach, he said, "much of the old time quietness still remains." Its glacial hills, wooded again, "give you the impression of life, as if somehow the ridge that you saw in the distance was the dorsal crest of some monstrous beast," Davis wrote.

But by then, the city's policy toward wetlands was already becoming clear: They were considered wasted land. Using fill was a way to grow New York. "By the nineteenth century," notes historian Martin V. Melosi in his tome *Fresh Kills*, "water lots and marsh filling added 137 acres of land to Lower Manhattan." By the middle of the 20th century, all but 15 percent of the city's 30,000 acres of tidal wetlands were filled or dredged. City officials were hungry for development opportunities for parks, real estate, industry, and garbage disposal. Robert Moses, New York City's famous urban planner, was a singular proponent. What good was a marsh anyhow? In his writings, Davis had waxed lyrical about the marsh wrens and pied-billed grebes that "alone claimed absolute ownership" of Fresh Kills. But he was proved wrong; they didn't hold the deed.

Jamaica Bay's salt marshes were some of the first to go. They bore the brunt of two airports, Floyd Bennett Field and Idlewild (later renamed John F. Kennedy), and a string of parks once Moses built the Belt Parkway. Queens's Flushing Meadows Corona Park, home to the 1939 and 1964 World's Fairs, had once been a thousand acres of marshland. And Great Kills salt meadows on Staten Island became a trash dump, before it was capped and opened as a park in 1949. A similar fate awaited Fresh Kills. Before the dump opened in 1948, Moses promised that three years of marsh-fill would remove "an unsanitary mosquito breeding swamp" and give the west shore of Staten Island a base for industry, housing, roads, and parks. He won over the Staten Island borough president by promising him funds for the construction of a highway, the West Shore Expressway, which would eventually run the length of the island.

Fresh Kills was an attractive location for a landfill—easy to reach via the Arthur Kill for barges from the other boroughs and still relatively far enough from most Staten Island residents. Melosi makes clear that it was meant to be a stopgap until incineration became the city's primary method of waste disposal. But those plans were undone by environmental concerns, making Fresh Kills permanent. In less than a decade, it became the world's largest landfill; its trash-print grew large enough to cover Manhattan from the Battery to 25th Street. Where Thoreau once celebrated its landscape, Staten Island now became associated with garbage.

Despite their grim nature, landfills—like the recycling plant I visited to see the overwintering Swainson's hawk—appeal to some birds and birders. "It is a standing jest among bird watchers along the coast that there is no place like a good garbage dump for birds," Roger Tory Peterson wrote. One of Peterson's favorites was Hunts Point, in the Bronx, where he'd found four snowy owls one winter and, in another, 12 short-eared owls in an adjacent marsh. But gulls ruled. "On the big city dumps," Peterson wrote, "they swarm by thousands; brown gulls, gray gulls, white gulls, young ones, middle-aged and old ones, rising in windrows at our approach and dropping to the rear among the grapefruit rinds, chicken legs and coffee grounds." At its mid-1980s peak, when Fresh Kills received up to 29,000 tons of trash per day, over 100,000 gulls congregated there, a concentration that could rival any in the country.

For many birders, the chance to see that many gulls on a windless winter day was worth braving the smell. In 1996, Richard "Dick" Veit, a no-nonsense seabird researcher recently hired by the College of Staten Island, went to Fresh Kills for the first time, with Lars Jonsson, a famed Swedish artist and ornithologist who was visiting and wanted to study North American gulls. Veit had gone birding at other city landfills, but to him Fresh Kills was the Yankee Stadium of dumps—the best and biggest. Veit remembered an old New York City birding book that gave directions to Fresh Kills by bus or car. Easy enough, he figured—he and Jonsson would drive in. But security had grown tighter, and they were turned away. So they snuck in through a hole in a fence.

They almost got flattened by one of the many dump trucks that barreled past them. "It was objectively dangerous," Veit told me. The trashscape spread over four square miles. On the West Mound, bulldozers, cranes, and trucks moved garbage around an earthwork the size of Prospect Park. Veit and Jonsson watched thousands of herring gulls and great black-backed gulls trail the machines in screaming pursuit. Plastic bags flew into the men as they scrambled for a closer view. They were happy.

On the other hand, Staten Island residents had had enough. Between 1950 and 1990, the population had doubled—new housing went up so quickly after the Verrazzano Bridge was finished in 1964 that entire South Shore neighborhoods lacked sewage systems—and this growing electorate helped deliver victories to Republicans from Albany to city hall. Their reward in return was a state law passed in 1996 that required the closure of the landfill by December 31, 2001. Over the next two years, the North Mound and the South Mound were closed and capped with an impermeable plastic liner and layered with industrial soil.

Veit, on official business now, made several trips each year, including for the Christmas Bird Count. After tallying the gull hordes, he and others would scope the place. Through ecological succession, it was transforming into a strange kind of grasslands. Mugwort and goldenrod grew on the closed mounds. It was the making of a whole new landscape.

On March 22, 2001, a blue barge full of trash left Queens bearing red, white, and blue banners that read LAST BARGE and LAST GARBAGE BARGE TO FRESH KILLS. The landfill site's future looked brighter. On September 5, 2001, the city announced the start of an international design competition to solicit ideas for a transformative park. But one week later, the West Mound reopened to accept the wreckage from the Twin Towers. About 1.4 million tons of material—blasted steel, concrete, and glass—was brought to the landfill, and for 10 months thousands of forensic investigators and recovery workers screened and sifted through it for the traces of missing people. Over 20,000 human remains were found and brought to the medical examiner's office. The leftover material was covered with clean soil on a 48-acre plot.

The winner of the competition was eventually chosen in June 2003: Field Operations, a landscape architecture firm that would also soon design Manhattan's High Line. After public feedback, the firm's team drafted a master plan in 2006, which was like a road map for the park, now called Freshkills. The team dreamed big, calling for ecological restoration—40 miles of trails and paths and hundreds of acres of marsh and creeks that could be paddled—and all kinds of recreation and development opportunities: a major sports venue, an equestrian center, a golf course, wind turbines, a solar farm, fields for archery, skeet shooting, Frisbee, and more. An east-to-west road that cut across the East Mound figured prominently. But for any of this to happen, the landscape would have to be highly engineered to make it safe for visitors: A complex underground system of soil and plastics would keep the trash sealed in, while wells and pipes would capture offshoots like methane, which could then be sold to heat local homes.

In 2011, it was the East Mound's turn to be capped, but unlike the first two, it was seeded with warm-season native grasses, like a prairie. And on a sunny May morning in 2015, Dick Veit brought his ecology class to "the dump," as he still called it, and heard an insect-like song. Then another. Veit was surprised. He remembered finding grasshopper sparrows in the past at a short-grass prairie of bluestem and bayberry on Nantucket that had once been fire-managed by Indigenous people. He thought the birds were picky about their habitat. In other words, he didn't think a former landfill would satisfy them. He laughed about it later, telling me, "They seemed to think it was a pretty good place."

IN THE EARLY 1800s, Alexander Wilson traveled through Staten Island while researching what would become his illustrated nine-volume classic, *American Ornithology*. The bird he named the yellow-winged sparrow was "very numerous," he wrote, and the male's song was "a short, weak, interrupted chirrup." A female he found was sitting on five grayish eggs in a nest of dry grass lined with hair and fibrous plant roots. The sparrow was new to Wilson, a species never described in Western scientific literature, so he didn't know the extent of its range, but he rightly guessed that it migrated to the southern states. Though numerous on Staten Island, he called it "the scarcest of all our summer Sparrows."

Even after a name change, the grasshopper sparrow didn't exactly attract a fan club. In 1929, Edward Howe Forbush, the same Massachusetts ornithologist who'd written about the starling's introduction, described it as "a queer, somber-colored, big-headed, short-tailed, unobtrusive little bird [that] did not come by its name because of its fondness for grasshoppers, though it is never averse to making a meal of them, but because of its grasshopper-like attempt at song—if song it can be called." Grasshopper sparrows were still numerous in

New York City and Long Island meadows, especially the Hempstead Plains, which, according to John Bull, "held over *100* pairs" in the 1920s. The italics were his; that was a lot. But like marshes, meadows are another easy place to pave over. The last few Bronx breeders were seen in the early 1970s at Ferry Point Park on the East River, an area that was once a landfill. Decades later, it was capped and leased to Donald Trump to build a public golf course. Prior to Veit's discovery at Freshkills, the last pair of grasshopper sparrows known to nest on Staten Island did so in the early 1980s on a scrap of coastal meadow near the Verrazzano Bridge.

Grasshopper sparrows aren't endangered in New York state, but they are classified as a species of "special concern," and according to breeding-bird surveys their population declined by almost 10 percent annually from 1966 to 2005. But in the summer of 2015, 30 pairs nested on the East Mound. "Then everything changed," said Cait Field, an ethologist and sailing captain who had been hired by the NYC Parks Department to create a research program at Freshkills.

Also in 2015, Shannon Curley began co-teaching Dick Veit's ecology course. Studying grassland birds wasn't on her mind. Her interest was in the responses of North American birds—especially waterbirds—to climate change. But the first place she visited within the park was the North Mound, which overlooks the city skyline, and she was blown away. "In New York, it's hard to see that much nature in front of you," she told me. Born in Brooklyn but raised in the Long Island suburbs, Curley had loved animals from a young age. Her family spent Thanksgivings at the Bronx Zoo, where today her uncle is the director and her aunt is the curator of animal encounters. While attending community college, Curley worked part-time at a pet store that specialized in selling exotic birds, and her interest in birds advanced from there to academic research.

José Ramírez-Garofalo knew Dick Veit from Staten Island's small birding community. He had started birding at a young age, often with his mother. Both of his parents worked as rangers for Gateway National Recreation Area, the park that stretches along the coast of New York City to Sandy Hook in New Jersey. Ramírez-Garofalo was five when Fresh Kills received its last barge, so his memories of the landfill were few. But when he ran into Veit after the first grasshopper sparrows showed up, Veit asked him, "Are you interested in birding at the dump?"

Veit, Field, and others recognized the importance of documenting the wildlife changes at Freshkills. For grassland birds especially, capped landfills in the US could be a lifeline. In 2016, they began regularly surveying the grasshopper sparrow colony, and in 2019 they set up a banding station on the East Mound. In 2020, Field secured grant money to hire Curley and Ramírez-Garofalo to continue the research. But in the summer of 2022, a drought cleared out the birds. Out of 120 pairs, only about 5 percent had any breeding success in the straw-yellow prairie, Curley told me. Most just left, practically overnight. For the researchers, the rest of the summer felt like a vigil. "I was so nervous they wouldn't come back," Curley said.

On my visit, however, we confirmed that they had. Curley and Ramírez-Garofalo suspected their numbers had even shot up. Driving along dirt trails in Ramírez-Garofalo's jeep, we found small groups of singing males on the East Mound whenever we pulled over. And the colony, having evidently reached a saturation point on the East Mound, was now expanding to the West Mound, the last to be capped, in 2021. It, too, was seeded with the "right stuff," Ramírez-Garofalo said.

As we rumbled on, he slammed on the brakes. "Bobolink! Bobolink!" he shouted. We jumped out of the car. Two buffy females zipped through the tall grass, followed by a male, still in its reverse-tuxedoed look of the breeding season. Bobolinks typically come to Freshkills in July from other grasslands in New Jersey or upstate New York and gather in large, roving flocks, then molt their feathers before embarking for the vast plains of South America, the return leg of an incredible 12,500-mile round-trip migration. Bobolinks had bred at Freshkills in previous years, but not lately. "They're absolutely beautiful," Ramírez-Garofalo said.

We drove onward to the South Mound on a winding, bumpy road tucked into zippered trash hills. Unlike the East Mound, trees had popped up here and there, and the grass was low and yellow. Capped years before the master plan, this landscape was shaped by natural dispersal. Consequently, the birds were different. Five species of swallows flew past our car and roosted in a bare tree, their mud nests somewhere nearby, inside pipes or underneath bridges. I was reminded of Roger Tory Peterson's commentary on their opportunistic family, the Hirundinidae: "They will never allow civilization to displace them." Indigo buntings and American goldfinches sang from roadside shrubs. A blue grosbeak, a darker shade of indigo, flashed past the car, and we stopped to hear it sing. The bird's husky warble had a muffled quality, like a distant memory.

A few pairs of blue grosbeaks started breeding at Freshkills the same year as grasshopper sparrows. They are one of several southern species for which Staten Island sits at the northern limit of their range. Not surprisingly, given its geography and open space, the borough is often the first one to welcome birds dispersing north due to a warmer climate. In fact, weeks before my visit, birders had found an American white pelican, an anhinga, and a neotropic cormorant—all three species familiar with the Gulf Coast. The anhinga and the neotropic cormorant were firsts for Staten Island. (An anhinga that drew many observers in Prospect Park may have been the same individual.) And just days before, about 15 brown pelicans had pitched up on breakwaters off the island's south shore; adults were seen carrying sticks toward existing rookeries in the harbor.

Since Curley and Ramírez-Garofalo also study waterbirds, I asked them about it.

A smiling Curley started to answer, then stopped. "I was going to make a joke," she said.

"I know you were," Ramírez-Garofalo said. "So say it."

He parked the car. "We're not leaving until you tell your joke."

Curley refused. "You know more about pelicans than I do, so you answer."

"Fine," he said.

"There are two things happening," he explained. "One, waterbirds are really good dispersers. And two, with climate change happening at a faster and faster rate, southern species are moving north across the board to track their climatic optimal. It's called tropicalization. It's the only way they can survive climate change. Since waterbirds are visible to a lot of people, we're able to see that they're dispersing. They're becoming vagrants, and then they're looking for places to breed. And after a couple years, they're settling in those locations."

Brown pelicans hadn't bred north of coastal Maryland, Ramírez-Garofalo said, though they had tried and failed in New Jersey in 1984 and 2002. "I think what we're seeing is that they want to nest on top of those breakwaters," he said.

Curley waited a beat. "But right now," she said, "they pelican't."

When the master plan for Freshkills was drawn up, there were no grasshopper sparrows. There were also no sedge wrens.

Around 11 in the morning on August 6, 2020, Shannon Curley, José Ramírez-Garofalo, and Cait Field started rolling up their banding-station mist nets on the East Mound when a staccato rattle stopped them in their tracks. It was unusual for them to hear a song they didn't immediately recognize. Just as Ramírez-Garofalo walked into the tall grasses, hoping to find the bird, a streaky little thing with peachy flanks flew right up to their net. They yelped. It was a sedge wren.

Sedge wrens are also very picky grassland birds, and they like wet meadows. Largely found in the Midwest, they nest up through the prairie potholes into southern Canada. But it was one day after Hurricane Isaias had rolled through New York, and standing puddles studded the East Mound. Curley and Ramírez-Garofalo assumed the bird was migrating and drawn in by the storm, but they knew they couldn't rule out an unlikelier scenario. Sedge wrens are itinerant breeders, an exceptionally rare group of birds that breed (or attempt to breed) in multiple different areas in the same season. They first nest at higher latitudes across the Upper Midwest and Canada, but if they can find another suitable place during their return migration to the Gulf Coast, they'll nest again in the late summer at a lower latitude, such as on Staten Island.

After an hour, two more sedge wrens began singing, and later a fourth. For small birds, they were loud. It was 100 degrees in the sun, but the three scientists stayed and listened happily the rest of the afternoon.

Sedge wrens hadn't bred in New York City since 1960, but Freshkills seemed like a perfect match. Three males decided to stick around and pair off with females, building their nests in some sedge about 250 feet apart, and Curley and Ramírez-Garofalo later observed at least three fledglings. Their observations were important. Sedge wrens are among the rarest breeders in the state, and their threatened status comes with legal protections; with them around, the NYC Department of Sanitation was forced to delay mowing the East Mound by two months. Eight showed up the following year, but while a storm had lured them to Freshkills before, another now scattered them. Not long after their 2021 arrival, Hurricane Ida clobbered the city, and the birds haven't been seen at Freshkills again.

On my visit, we listened for sedge wrens at both ends of the East Mound. With rain overnight, I was full of hope. "We'll hear them if they're around," Ramírez-Garofalo said. "They don't shut up." He and Curley discussed how little recent research had been done on sedge wrens. A paper they wrote in 2021 about the birds of Freshkills was one of the few publications. It was all part of Dick Veit's original vision to create a body of research on the management of a reclaimed landfill.

"Does anybody really study these birds?" Curley asked.

"Nobody wants to," Ramírez-Garofalo said.

"I want to," Curley said.

"Me too. But we're different."

Things are changing constantly at Freshkills. For example, opportunistic predators, like red foxes and deer, now prowl the mounds for bird nests, and as a result, a few regular species have all but vanished during the breeding season. The mounds themselves are changing too, deflating ever so slowly as the trash settles. Less methane is now being off-gassed, the sale of which, to the National Grid utility company, has funded some of the park's operating budget. And there are certainly more avian surprises ahead. Several rare visitors, like the upland sandpiper and Henslow's sparrow, continue to prospect Freshkills like gold miners, a process called informed dispersal, in which individual birds search for and gather information on suitable breeding habitat. Both species are a high priority for grassland conservation in North America.

The vision for the park also remains elastic. You might ask: What would a road and recreational fields on the East Mound do to species of concern like grasshopper sparrows? The answer seems obvious: Needing large tracts of grasslands and relatively few disturbances, they would likely disappear. Based on the conversations I had, those plans appear to be on hold because of these sensitive birds. "This is something of much more than local significance," Veit told me.

Waiting plaintively for any sign of a sedge wren, a bird I'd never seen in New York, it struck me that at the heart of Freshkills lies a paradox: 50 years of garbage dumping saved this huge piece of land from the sprawl that today afflicts Staten Island and indeed the whole city. I wasn't alone in thinking this. Landscape architect James Corner, the head of Field Operations, argued in an interview with the author Elizabeth Barlow—rather, he said you *could* argue—"that the Fresh Kills landfill is the best thing that has happened to Staten Island." Four square miles of land, he said, "will never be subjected to overdevelopment like the rest of the island." But looking below the East Mound, I thought about those who had lived next to the landfill in the neighborhoods of Heartland Village and New Springville. Was there anyone still alive in those vinyl-sided houses who swam in or canoed Fresh Kills before the first trash barge pulled in? They live next to what I think will one day be the most spectacular park in the city, but they lived for too long with the broken promises of an environmental disaster.

This paradox was again made clear to me on a boat ride I took to Freshkills a month later. Cait Field, having left her job there some months earlier, was the captain and guide on the Classic Harbor Line's teak-paneled yacht called the *Manhattan*. I was handed a glass of champagne as we left Chelsea Piers under a cobalt sky and followed the same route as a barge of trash once had.

The harbor flexed its industrial might as we sailed south. The behind-the-scenes workings of the city—cruise-ship terminals and ports and dry docks and recycling piers—all seemed to intersect in these sparkling waters. Following Staten Island's north shore, we passed a container ship leaving the Port of Newark that was led by a tugboat like a chihuahua leading a bullmastiff, and then we swept under the Bayonne Bridge, the Arthur Kill Vertical Lift railroad bridge, and the Goethals Bridge.

On the Arthur Kill, the differences between the New Jersey and Staten Island shores were stark. The Jersey side, a Superfund site, was grimly lined with big-box Amazon warehouses, smokestacks, oil storage depots, and a power plant and petroleum refinery. Like Fresh Kills, it had once been marshes. Had Robert Moses kept his promise, Staten Island would have looked the same today.

Instead, gliding east into the park, we passed the West Mound. It was long, wide, and plateau-like, the flattest hill you've ever seen, and it was verdant. There was no trace of its previous life. Annoyed ospreys complained around us, sitting with their helpless chicks in messy stick nests on docks and telephone poles and wooden platforms. Several great blue herons floated across our path. Great egrets, cormorants, and a belted kingfisher rested on pilings as if they were a fish-catching guard of honor. We slipped under the West Shore Expressway, and I remembered how as a kid I'd hold my nose in the back seat of our family station wagon as we drove past the dump on trips to see relatives. Then we turned around where the Fresh Kill meets Richmond Creek.

It was a mile back to the Arthur Kill. On our right, Cait Field pointed out a large blue-sided warehouse. It was the Staten Island transfer station, where municipal garbage has been collected since 2006. Every day, 750 tons of Staten Island's trash is trucked to that station, compacted, tightly sealed in three or four orange containers, and loaded onto railcars. The railcars travel eight miles to the vertical lift bridge we'd passed, then they turn west to connect with the national rail network. The trash travels south, a seven-day, 666-mile trip, to Lee County Landfill in Bishopville, South Carolina. Landfills were once cheap for New York City. This is costly; the city pays more than $30 million each year to send away Staten Island's trash, and close to $400 million in total to export all of it. Other boroughs send theirs to landfills or incineration plants in Virginia, upstate New York, Pennsylvania, and New Jersey. One thing remains the same: Nobody wants it in their backyard.

CHAPTER 9

# Piping Plovers

In early March 2023, a five-year-old male piping plover got ready to leave the salt flats of Joulter Cays in the Bahamas. For the thousand-mile trip ahead, his internal clock told him to pack onto his seven-inch frame a couple more grams of fat from the marine-worm buffet. Many of the birds around him were also piping plovers, up to as many as 400. His coat was fresh, his back the color of the tide-washed sand, his forehead and neck daubed black. And he wore another thing: four tiny metal bands, two on each upper leg—yellow over red, light blue over green. Where he was going—a cold beach on the Rockaway Peninsula—people would identify him by those.

Wildlife scientists had cuffed him with the bands in 2018, six days after he hatched on the Jersey Shore roughly 60 miles south of New York City. For shorthand, they named him Clark Kent; the others in his brood were called Tony Stark and Diana Prince. Anyone who saw the birds could report their bands to the US Fish and Wildlife Service and add new locations to their official record. But only Clark Kent was ever seen again.

He was spotted in 2019 around Island Beach, NJ, as well as Fort Tilden in the Rockaways. He probably never found a mate that year, which is not unusual for a one-year-old male; like a beachcomber, he collected bits of information for the next season. But that didn't go well either. In 2020, he tried and failed to nest at Fort Tilden, on part of the beach that was closed to the public to carve out space for piping plovers like him. In 2021, Clark Kent found a mate, but, according to the US Park Police, a person stole their eggs right before they were about to hatch—perhaps as an angry response to those access restrictions. And in 2022, his chicks disappeared some hours after they hatched, preyed upon most likely by feral cats, gulls, or ghost crabs. The human backlash to the birds' protection that summer—and the beach closures they brought with them—was extreme: In addition to eggs being stolen, nests were vandalized and two plover chicks accidentally were trampled. Of the 58 pairs that bred in the Rockaways that year, only 12 of their chicks made it out alive.

So why leave Joulter Cays, a paradise for the birds as well as the tourists who flock there for sportfishing? Piping plovers have the run of those islands, part of an enormous national park that covers about 150 square miles of sand flats, mangrove reefs, and turquoise waters. Their ancestors once had the run of wind-raked beaches farther north, like Fort Tilden's. But in evolutionary terms, they lost it in a New York minute. Around the turn of the 20th century, hunters plundered all kinds of shorebirds, piping plovers included, and before they could stage much of a recovery, beachfront housing claimed their nesting sites. Where once there were tens of thousands, now around 4,000 piping plovers squeeze into state and federal beaches on the Atlantic coast of the US. Because of the species' federally endangered status, those beaches are usually closed to people between March and August. Another couple thousand piping plovers breed on alkali flats or along rivers of the Great Plains as well as on the Great Lakes. Federal officials tasked with their recovery pursue a goal of 1.5 fledglings per nest. But in 2022 in the Rockaways, they fell staggeringly short—at 0.2 per nest.

Around 90 percent of piping plovers nest within a mile and a half of their previous breeding site, so despite Clark Kent's lack of success, he left the Bahamas in 2023 for another shot at Fort Tilden. He arrived on a bracing St. Patrick's Day weekend. While he scouted the familiar dunes, about 20 people were marking a barrier around them with small metal poles and string tagged with neon-pink flags. They called it "symbolic fencing," because anyone wanting to step over it could easily do so. Besides a few park rangers, the group was made up of volunteers from the NYC Plover Project. They were excited to see Clark again, a bird whose story they knew well. During the summer, they would be asking beachgoers to mind the fencing and respect the plovers.

In the following weeks, Clark Kent defended his small plot of barrier beach from other male piping plovers. He crouched, and then charged them like a bull. Unlike in the Bahamas, they no longer tolerated each other. The females watched on. In one courtship flight, he glided like a crop duster low over the dune grass, announcing his desire with a sweet bell-like whistle of one or two syllables, *Peep* or *Peep-lo*. Eluding off-leash dogs, he scurried across the sand, legs whirring. At the water's edge, he tapped the wet sand with a vibrating foot as if it were a metal detector, bringing invertebrates to the surface. And when he found a mate, a one-year-old who had been banded on Fire Island, he sealed the deal with a "tattoo dance."

Standing tall, he high-kicked sand onto her and then landed several light kicks on her side and back as he drew near. She inched away but eventually accepted; he hopped on top of her and stayed there for a good 30 seconds. They separated and went their own ways. Later, he scraped a little divot in the sand and beach grass and lined it with shell bits. His mate was vigilant in fending off American oystercatchers—large shorebirds with long red-orange bills like daggers—which also nest in the dunes. In May, she laid four quarter-sized speckled eggs.

She and Clark Kent took turns incubating them for about a month. Shortly after hatching, their chicks would need to reach the shore to feed themselves. The water's edge is where the most nutritious marine food lies, and because the flightless chicks must move between shoreline and upland dunes, they need unpeopled beaches. Even then, more chicks usually die than fledge.

Through no fault of his own, Clark Kent faced enormous odds. But instinct drove him. The lives of piping plovers are much shorter than most other shorebirds, and so this was his prime age to reproduce—to replace himself, as it were—and add to his endangered tribe.

Hundreds of New Yorkers picked up birding when the pandemic gripped the city in 2020, and Chris Allieri, the founder of the NYC Plover Project, was one of them. He liked visiting Fort Tilden, since it reminded him of the Jersey Shore, where he'd spent his childhood summers, but on those biting early spring days, he found a crowded beach. And dodging off-leash dogs, kids climbing dunes, and people flying kites was a piping plover, the first one Allieri had seen in almost 40 years—this time, up close. As a boy, he'd watched a piping plover through the scope of a park ranger outside his family's house. There, plovers and other at-risk birds had three miles of off-limits beach. Allieri had learned how important that was for them, though he would later hear locals grumble about the restrictions.

Allieri didn't realize that piping plovers nest on New York's beaches too. But how were they able to succeed with all those disturbances? As he found out, they weren't. Having picked up photography, Allieri sent photos of the scene to higher-ups at Gateway National Recreation Area, the park that includes Fort Tilden. He submitted public records requests to see their management plan. And when he again looked closely at his photos of that piping plover, he noticed colored bands on the bird's legs: yellow over red, light blue over green. Finding out it was Clark Kent, a plover that had hatched on a beach not far from his family's house in New Jersey, stirred in Allieri a profound concern for the bird's plight.

Allieri returned to Tilden the following spring, and there Clark Kent was again. That day, Allieri watched a black poodle nearly snatch another piping plover out of the air like a Frisbee. He asked the dog's owners to leash their pet, explaining the gravity of the situation for the birds. They told him, "You need to calm down." In that moment, all the environmental loss in the world condensed into this small bird that had to fend for itself on the big city's beaches. He'd had enough.

That night, Allieri started the NYC Plover Project. He wrote to Gateway's chief ranger, asking: Would the National Park Service partner with his citizen-led effort to protect plovers? The ranger said yes. By Memorial Day 2021, he had 35 volunteers on the beach. They wore T-shirts with a stick-figure piping plover on them, a uniform designed by a Queens artist. Allieri, who holds a graduate degree in international relations from Columbia University, chose the powder-blue color of UN peacekeepers.

Over a short period of time, with grants from Patagonia and the New York Community Trust, the young nonprofit hired four paid staffers, who work on education, community outreach, and organizing volunteers. Allieri, who runs a PR firm that works with climate tech startups, remains the unpaid executive director. The organization has won recognition for its work, including an award from the National Park Service. But the group still butts up against entrenched feelings on beach access. In the 1990s, the federal government twice sued Breezy Point Cooperative, a private residential community, for failing to safeguard nesting piping plovers. And in 2022, the year piping plovers had one of their worst seasons in the Rockaways, a civic association located at the other end of the peninsula began calling for the repeal of a seasonal closure of 20 blocks of city beach.

At an NYC Plover Project orientation in June 2023, which I sat in on, Allieri told recruits, "We're not just going to set up a table and tell people to share the shore. This is hands-on work. We're an army of plover protectors." A park ranger then shared his techniques for conflict de-escalation. He recommended using the SLOW method: Stay cool. Listen. Offer validation/validate emotions. Walk away.

Looking around the room, I watched unease creeping onto faces. It was sinking in that the volunteers would be the ones defending the symbolic fence boundaries. What if beachgoers were angry or upset?

"If you feel unsafe," the ranger said, "the best thing you can do is walk away."

WALKING AWAY DOESN'T come easily to Chris Allieri. After the orientation, I went with him to Jacob Riis Park, the popular beach next to Fort Tilden. Riis is also part of Gateway National Recreation Area, and the National Park Service had invited Allieri to set up the Plover Project's summer headquarters inside a red-brick booth on the faded art deco promenade. A sandwich board with a chalk drawing of a piping plover and an invitation—COME ON PLOVER—pointed to their open window.

The air was soft, and the mood was light. Riis is still sometimes called the People's Beach, and though its concessions are no longer a bargain, it retains an air of egalitarianism and inclusivity, in part because of the gay beach at its east end. As I stood there with my notebook out, a leathery old man ran past us. "Don't support him!" he snarled.

I recoiled, but Allieri didn't.

He said he'd been heckled the day before by a man who shouted, "Plovers are a fucking myth!"

"Come to think of it"—Allieri laughed—"I think it was the same guy, only yesterday he was riding a bike."

Allieri felt he could handle it. But he fumed when it came to his young staff and volunteers. One had recently been told, "Kill the plovers!" as she walked off the beach.

"I'm seen as someone who's bringing volunteers from all over the city," Allieri, who lives in Brooklyn Heights, said. "The majority might not be from the Rockaways, but why is it a bad thing that people are showing up to your community to make this place better? Some are traveling an hour and a half or two hours to get here. This is a federal beach. It belongs to everybody."

He shrugged it off, but he was familiar with heartbreak. In the Plover Project's first two seasons, the number of fledglings on the federal beaches the group staffed hadn't broken single digits. But two dozen volunteers had been on beach duty the day before, and Allieri felt optimistic about the third season. Piping plovers at the tip of Breezy Point were getting a head start, and Clark Kent's nest was one of three at Fort Tilden.

Like a radio-dispatch office, the language of the team's mobilization bounced around the group's booth: "There's a new nest at seven…" "When Clark's chicks hatch, we can close the beach from forty-seven to fifty-three…" "The nest at two is close."

Three beachgoers in their early twenties walked up to the booth, their interest sparked by the pamphlets, leaflets, stickers, buttons, oversized photographs, and nest diorama.

"Can I tell you about piping plovers?" asked Ciara Fagan, the group's education director.

"Yes!" they replied.

A little later, Fagan told me she comes from a line of piping plover monitors—her grandmother staffed beach closures at Sandy Hook in the 1980s and 1990s. Like Allieri, who started an environmental club in his high school, she had been a youth activist. In fifth grade, she dressed as a climate protester for Halloween, carrying a sign that read

ONE EARTH, SAVE IT and wearing a crown made of water bottles. She volunteered for the Sierra Club. Her classmates called her Eco Freako, Green Girl, and Treehugger. While studying at the University of Vermont, she found her calling with birds, but it was in New York, she said, where she found the greatest biodiversity.

We looked toward the shore and saw two worlds roughly coexisting on the beach: an American oystercatcher colony surrounded by people sitting on chairs and blankets, under beach umbrellas. Oystercatchers are odd-looking; their red-ringed yellow eyes stand out from their black heads like planets in space. Several chicks hid from the bright sun under little wooden A-frames placed there for them. Unlike piping plovers, adult oystercatchers feed their young, which means the chicks can survive without access to the water's edge. I remarked to Fagan and Allieri that a beach like Riis could never support piping plovers.

Allieri smiled. "I have to show you something at bay seven," he said.

He and I set off down the promenade. But we couldn't go very far before Allieri spotted a future crime, like some avian version of *Minority Report*. He flagged a bike cop to pedal after a person who was leading their dog toward Fort Tilden. Then he stopped a group of four and kindly told them they couldn't bring their dog on the beach. Deflated, they turned around. Then we saw two teenage boys throwing rocks at some adult oystercatchers. Allieri sprinted after them, shouting, "Yo! Yo!"

I expected an altercation, but their conversation appeared surprisingly diplomatic. Allieri, breathing hard, returned a few minutes later.

"Did I employ the SLOW method?" he asked.

We both laughed.

Once we finally reached bay seven, a metal fence blocked stairs leading onto the beach. Allieri pointed to a 30-foot square of symbolic fencing about 25 yards away. In the middle of that lonely square, well camouflaged, was a male piping plover sitting on one egg.

Allieri believed the nest was a first for Riis, and he thought the pair was a young couple that had been forced off the dunes at Tilden or Breezy. It was competitive on the peninsula, and the beach at Tilden had eroded over the winter, leaving fewer places to safely lay eggs.

The beach here was raked every day, so I couldn't even see a wrack line, the nutritious belt of high-tide marine debris in which the chicks could feed. The walk to the shore looked to be a quarter of a mile. I doubted they could safely make it that far. Park rangers would have to section off a large swath of the beach, one in which thousands of people gathered on hot summer weekends, a scenario that Allieri feared would create a lot of enemies for them and the birds.

For now, rangers had hung two small signs on the metal fence—DO NOT ENTER and PIPING PLOVER BREEDING AREA—and a large one with a stock photo of a piping plover sitting on eggs. It began: "Hidden within the dunes before you dwells one of Gateway National Recreation Area's most treasured animals—the piping plover." There were no dunes, and to Allieri, string and signs weren't enough to support plovers; personnel needed to actively enforce off-limit areas.

I wasn't sure if Allieri was going to get his wish. But as we spoke, a young father strolled by, hand in hand with his toddler daughter. He pointed to the large sign, and said to her slowly, "There's a very special bird that lives here. It's called a plover. They have their babies on this beach." A smile spread across Allieri's face.

But it passed quickly. Soon his gaze fixed on two girls clumsily kicking an inflatable beach ball well beyond the nest, a pastime as old as plastic. Allieri turned to a summer intern standing by the fence and asked him to tell the girls to move farther away.

Watching the intern trudge over the sand, Allieri looked a little rueful. "It's like we're killjoys," he said, then sighed. "We're still working on it."

THE ROCKAWAYS IS a complex place, and the rather Byzantine control of beach access bears this out: from west to east, federal at the Breezy Point tip, private at Breezy Point Cooperative, federal at Fort Tilden and Jacob Riis Park, and then city for some dozen neighborhoods. Around 130,000 people cram into the 11-mile-long, three-quarters-of-a-mile-wide peninsula. Though almost evenly split between white, Black, and Latino, the population is, like the rest of New York, extremely segregated. Breezy Point, the whitest neighborhood in the city, where families go back three or four generations, was once known as the Irish Riviera. Of its roughly 4,000 year-round residents, 92 percent are white. The neighborhood of Edgemere, seven miles to the east, has a population of about 8,000, of whom 85 percent are Black or Latino.

Breezy Point Cooperative doesn't allow uninvited guests, has its own security force, and is predominantly gated, and the only way to access the ostensibly public beach at the tip is from the small permit-only parking lot I'd been to with Peter Dorosh and Doug Gochfeld. Park rangers don't restrict access to that wide beach; they just fence off the dunes for piping plovers and other beach-nesting birds like common terns and least terns, American oystercatchers, and black skimmers. Fort Tilden, as previously noted, sees large sections closed to foot traffic. In Edgemere, though, each summer the city closes a swath of beach about one mile long called the Rockaway Beach Endangered Species Nesting Area, or RBESNA. This seasonal closure dates back to 1996, but as I chatted with Allieri, an Edgemere civic association was calling for its removal, claiming that it was an act of environmental and economic racism targeted at a neighborhood of predominantly Black and brown residents. A couple hundred people had signed a petition that said that piping plovers had "taken over our beach for far too long!" Fearing a growing local backlash against the birds, Allieri had asked Mel Julien, a mid-thirties Plover Project volunteer, to lead the organization's response as its first director of community engagement.

Julien, who is Black and the child of Trinidadian immigrants, lives in Edgemere. She grew up in the adjacent neighborhood of Arverne, in a large complex of mismatched concrete apartment towers called Ocean Village. Many of the nearly 1,100 low-income units were filled by Caribbean families like hers; her mother's family settled there after the complex opened in 1974. Julien lived in an apartment with her parents and grandparents until she was 10, at which time they moved "uptown," meaning up the peninsula. Julien thought nothing of the beach that was closed in the summer right outside her door.

It was only many years later, after she found the NYC Plover Project on Instagram and signed up to join, that she realized these small birds were a big story. Assigned to guard beach closures at Fort Tilden, the normally reserved Julien was forced to open up and explain the restrictions to lots of unhappy people. "I had to remind myself that I wasn't doing it for me—I was doing it for the birds," she said. She works as a marketing consultant, but the Plover Project came to feed her soul. "Growing up, I didn't think birding was for someone who is young and Black," she told me. "That perception changed so much once I joined."

Representing the Plover Project in her community, however, posed a thornier challenge. As Clark Kent and other plovers returned in the spring of 2023, she began attending community board meetings and local events to talk about the group's efforts. In past meetings, Allieri had been told, "I don't care about those damned birds." Though Julien's goal was to share information, not to argue, she regularly encountered an uninterested or irritated audience. She heard people whisper, "The bird people are back," or "Another plover conversation." One community board member asked why the plovers at RBESNA couldn't be relocated. Another time, one asked, "What do plovers taste like?" And in June, four plover eggs were stolen from two nests at the east end of the peninsula. The penalty for stealing a plover egg is a fine of $25,000 and up to six months in prison; federal authorities announced a $5,000 reward for any tips leading to those responsible for the crime.

Several elected officials and the Edgemere civic association held a press conference the next month on the Rockaway boardwalk to call for changes to RBESNA. Why the uproar now? I had some ideas. A complex of affordable housing and retail called Edgemere Commons had just broken ground in the neighborhood. And Arverne East, a megadevelopment of 1,650 apartments, an urban farm, and a boutique hotel, was planned close to the east end of RBESNA. A beach that hotel guests and residents couldn't go on in the summer wasn't going to end up in its sales pitch.

But as I began to dig into RBESNA's history, I learned that it had in fact sprung from the very economic underinvestment the civic association alluded to in its petition. In 1996, city officials decided to cope with a lifeguard shortage by staffing the beaches with the most swimmers, which wasn't Edgemere or Arverne. There was a time when it was a popular resort area. In the 1930s, as many as a million people packed in on summer weekends, but by 1965, it was designated an "urban renewal" zone. Poor families and individuals displaced from elsewhere in the city lived in run-down bungalows and endured slum-like conditions—"as bad as in the worst ghettos," reported the Department of City Planning. Over 300 acres of Arverne and Edgemere were cleared in 1969. The city promised residents affordable housing and "year-round regional and local recreation," but they never came.

Instead, huge vacant lots, weedy and overrun by feral dogs, sat empty for at least 35 years. When the city prohibited swimming at Edgemere and Arverne's beaches in 1996, it sent Parks Department rangers to enforce the ban. The lack of foot traffic gave piping plovers additional space for their nests, and rangers began to monitor and manage the beach for them, paving the way for RBESNA.

The controversy appeared to be coming to a head when I met Mel Julien on the boardwalk next to the beach on a humid July day. She wore sunglasses and the Plover Project's powder-blue T-shirt. Runners from a half-marathon toiled by us, their expressions pained. Every so often, an airplane out of Kennedy roared overhead. According to the city's wildlife unit, there were 17 piping plover nests hidden out in the dunes. Common terns and least terns, carrying in their bills fish to feed the chicks in their colony, breezed overhead. Crisp white with black caps, they differed in size like siblings born several years apart. They flew by with effortless elegance; their long wings and forked tails were built for long journeys—these birds fly to and from the coast of South America twice a year.

On the upland side of the boardwalk, I was struck by a beautiful new nature preserve of coastal scrub. Looking at a map, I could see it stretched across 25 city blocks. I was mystified that such a large piece of beachfront land had been available, but then I quickly realized it was one of the deep scars left by urban renewal. Julien remembered the stray dogs and ring-necked pheasants that once convened there; for half a century, the land remained overgrown, a perpetual reminder for the community of the promise of "renewal." The Arverne East development was going to abut the preserve on another vacant lot.

I asked Julien about the fight over RBESNA, and she sighed. "It's picking up steam," she said. "Edgemere is a Black neighborhood. We're not on the higher economic end of things." Like her neighbors, she wanted to see more development, but, she argued, "this beach closure is not what's keeping the community from flourishing." The neighborhood remains a food desert, meaning it has few grocery stores, though a new one is on the way; it has only a playground or two; and it is near the very end of the A train. Edgemere is a long way from the halls of power—over an hour on the subway from Lower Manhattan. Residents still live with the extreme challenges of segregation, concentrated poverty, and health inequalities.

For a pilot project with the Parks Department, Julien was conducting short surveys on the boardwalk to get local opinions on RBESNA. I eyed question six: *Which one is a piping plover? Circle your answer.* Thumbnail photos showed a piping plover, an American oystercatcher, a ring-billed gull, an American robin, and a common tern.

"How many get that right?" I asked.

"Only one so far." She laughed.

Though residents couldn't pick a plover out of a lineup, Julien still believed they supported protections for endangered species. (That was another question.) Her own schooling in the Rockaways, she said, never put her in touch with the rich maritime ecosystem in her backyard. "Most residents don't know how much wildlife is out here," she said.

If she was going to bridge that gap, though, doing so one survey at a time seemed challenging.

I WANTED TO follow the news on Clark Kent and the unusual nest at Riis Park, so I kept in touch with Chris Allieri and Ciara Fagan. The birds carried hopes of a better season after previous disappointments. Fagan was concerned for the chicks at Riis, though. They were going to hatch so far from the shore, and having watched their parents for weeks, she saw signs that the adult birds were novices at this too. To her, they fit right into Riis's live-and-let-live culture. "Their incubation was spotty," she told me. "And they were copulating more than any piping plover couple I've ever seen—as often as five times a day. I was like, 'Guys, I get it. You're young. You're at Riis.'"

Fagan received Gateway's plan to create a walk-through passage at Riis—not a full closure—to allow room for people and emergency vehicles to cross from one half of the beach to the other. I read it as a compromise, a way not to provoke too much ire. The deck was already stacked against the plover pair. And their chicks came a few days early. But there were enough volunteers on hand to set up and guard the corridor that first day, and Fagan asked every volunteer who was free to come to the beach the next day, a Sunday. Thirty people showed up, three times as many as on an average weekend.

Shortly after eight in the morning, Fagan got a call from a volunteer on the beach. She was panicky. The parents were leading their three chicks west, toward Fort Tilden, she was told. It made sense—three-quarters of Tilden's mile-long beach was closed to the public because of its three nests, and the parents must have realized their young could feed on the shore there with far less interference. But the passage was extremely risky. Fagan closed the booth and sprinted to the closure.

At first, she couldn't find the chicks, and she grew frantic, like a mother who's lost her child in a crowd. Two beachgoers called out, "Look at that baby bird! It's cute."

Fagan spun around, but it wasn't a baby at all. It was one of the parents. That's how large *they* are. The babies are much smaller, Fagan told them. And they had vanished. She crouched low, looking through a tangle of legs for the chicks. Minutes passed, and then, in the shade of a walkway, she found them. They weren't left alone for the rest of the day.

For the next two days, it felt to Fagan like the whole of Riis was rallying behind the new family. Everywhere she went around the promenade, people asked about the birds. Employees at the concession stands who knew the Plover Project's work peppered her with questions. She provided hourly updates to her volunteers. And after a night of rain kept morning beachgoers away, she let herself believe that things might go their way. But once the chicks crossed into the American oystercatcher colony at Riis, things went south. An adult oystercatcher pecked one chick to death; the other two disappeared. Fagan theorized that the parents, seeing the impossibility of the situation, abandoned them. Short of one week old, the chicks were declared lost, and the beach was reopened.

As for Clark Kent, it also didn't look very good. Three of his and his mate's four chicks quickly disappeared. Cat tracks were found in the area, but there was nothing the birds or the volunteers could do about it. Still, by the time I made my way to Fort Tilden to see them, their last chick was two weeks old, almost halfway to fledging.

When I found them, the chick was sitting in the shade of a BEACH CLOSED sign. The sky was the color of beige paint, the air felt thick from wildfire smoke, and it was strangely quiet. I watched with binoculars from behind the dunes. The chick stood up and began picking through seaweed bits in the wrack line. Its bill was adult-sized, but it had the gangly look of a teenager entering a growth spurt.

Two ghost crabs faced off on a mound of sand. I grew alert, and so did Clark Kent. As his chick fed beyond the string line, he dashed onto a knee-high rock and peeped once. After watching for a couple minutes, he switched to another rock, as if to remind his chick of its boundaries. The chick retreated and, after a few more pecks at the wrack line, plopped down again in the shade.

Even the hardest hearts, I thought, would be softened by seeing piping plovers raise their young. I witnessed a fierce courage in the birds that summer. Once, with a friend at Breezy Point, I watched a pair of adults stand quietly between their two young chicks, feeding in the wrack line, and a group of great black-backed gulls, lazing on the sand. Gray, tailless puffballs, the chicks looked like an easy snack for the gulls. I'd seen those thick-necked beasts kill and eat small ducks before. But the parents didn't budge, and the gulls didn't get up. After I turned away and then looked back, the chicks had dissolved into the landscape. That was their camouflage.

Leaving the beach that afternoon, my friend nearly walked on three sand-colored eggs sitting well outside the symbolic fencing. Thankfully, he was watching his step. The eggs sat in a shallow depression lined with shell bits, and two adult piping plovers quickly appeared and scuttled toward him, showing whom the eggs belonged to. After we retreated, I wrote Allieri about the nest—just as dark clouds billowed over Manhattan's skyscrapers. He thanked me for the information and said he would ask some people to surround the new nest with string and poles to give them at least some additional safety. The rain started as we reached the car, and by the time we hit Flatbush Avenue it was like a monsoon. Wildlife technicians got to the beach after the storm, but by then there was no trace of the nest.

IN OUR LAST conversation, I asked Ciara Fagan why she thought people were so invested in the fate of piping plovers. I struggled to think of many volunteer groups that could rally over a hundred people to commit to three months of often-confrontational work, in all weather and in the summer, no less. Was there more to it than their endangered status?

"Have you seen that bird?" she said, smiling wryly. "It's a cute bird."

She paused a long moment, then went on. "I took a class in college called Sense of Place in the Anthropocene, and I reflect on it a lot. I thought about it on the days that the wildfire smoke was really bad here and volunteers would ask, 'How are the birds doing?' And I thought about it on rainy days when folks were still out there. Our sense of place is changing as the climate changes. Some people have gotten involved because this is a place they have come to for a long time. And some people have gotten involved because they wanted a place to go to, and this bird has provided that."

Many were new birders, like Mel Julien and Chris Allieri himself, or people who wouldn't even call themselves birders. Yet in a world gone mad, they had found meaning through this cute bird and the community that coalesced to protect it. Why the deep commitment? It's not like piping plovers are a keystone species that balances this coastal ecosystem; if they were gone tomorrow, I doubt the habitat would change in any discernible way. There aren't that many of them. The other animals that prey on them or their eggs—gulls, crows, cats, raccoons—would find something else to eat. And the marine invertebrates they feed on are also consumed by several other species. But this line of thinking, of judging the importance of a species by what we determine is useful, says something about us, not them. The fact is, there's a place for them here, and that in itself is valuable, even if we can't quantify it. For me, the beauty of hearing their sweet whistle over the dunes, of watching parents shield their young from danger, of seeing a chick stretch its wings for the first time, was enough.

Fagan was looking ahead to teaching local students about piping plovers. One idea was to pair elementary schools in the Rockaways with ones in the Bahamas, a pen-pal program between kids who lived at either pole of these birds' lives. But if such a program developed, I thought, the news exchanged in those letters would likely be bittersweet. The birds face enormous challenges, and their survival depends on our conservation efforts.

I could tell, though, that the Plover Project's commitment was making a difference. By the end of the summer, 25 chicks had fledged, about double the previous year, and 17 of them flew off beaches the group staffed. And the next year would be even better. In 2024, the federal beaches and RBESNA sent a total of 37 chicks on their way, a rate of one per pair. Twelve came from RBESNA, which the city agreed to open partially to beachgoers for the first time. The increase could be mere luck, a statistical one-off. Or, given the renewed attention on the site, perhaps it was the result of the Parks Department monitoring it more closely than before. It could also be circumstantial—Allieri thought more birds were moving down the peninsula, given the competition for space at Breezy Point and Fort Tilden. I was happy to learn that Clark Kent's chick was one of the 25 fledglings of 2023. His genes had finally entered the piping plover pool.

But nobody knew at the time that Clark Kent wouldn't return to Tilden—he hasn't been seen since that summer.

In late July, I went to Breezy Point on an overcast morning to get a last look at plovers before they left the city and flew south, many to the Bahamas. After the long walk from the parking lot, a very vocal least tern mother made several strafing passes at me below the dunes. I carefully stayed in the middle of the trail, on either side of the signs marking the terns' colony. But the little spitfire had reason to be aggressive. Her two helpless chicks stooped in a scrape near some seabeach amaranth, a plant that receives federal protection. After a few more sorties, she landed near them. One chick flapped its butterfly-sized wings with all its might to scoot underneath her. It was late in the season, and I wasn't sure if they'd ultimately make it.

Down at the shore, so many sanderlings chased the waves that the wet sand looked to be rolling. Given their size they're frequently mistaken for piping plovers, but most of these shorebirds still wore a deep rufous on their faces and chests from their Arctic breeding grounds, a color like the red bricks at Riis. When hundreds of them flushed, a cloud took shape above the surf, shifting and traveling as one, growing with more arrivals. Their molted feathers drifted across the sand.

I didn't see any piping plovers by the shore, but once I turned back to face the dunes, I couldn't miss them. Slightly camouflaged against the dry sand, there was a group of 10 behind some string. Six were juveniles, all plain gray and without the black slashes the adults sported on their neck and forehead. Then I noticed another six juveniles. Another flew into the beach party as if to test those long wings for the coming journey. One adult male, laying a marker for next season, broke the calm by running off three others.

Swinging around to the bay side, I counted at least 45 piping plovers in all, and about three-quarters were fresh young. I delighted at the numbers. They couldn't all be New York City birds. They were staging for migration, and this quiet corner of the Rockaways was an important place for their whole population. Some had probably come from Long Island or New Jersey beaches, just like Clark Kent had in his first year. I'd never seen so many together in such large, relatively peaceful groups. I figured this was as close to Joulter Cays as I'd get without traveling there.

Close to the jetty, I watched two adults scurry after a chick into the dune grass. Looking around, I realized I was standing right by the nest that had washed out after my previous visit. Allieri told me the pair had scraped a new nest inside the string line but again suffered the same fate. With the window rapidly closing on their breeding season, they'd tried a third time, laying only one egg, he said.

I told myself this was the pair I was looking at now, and this was its chick. Allieri had seen piping plovers make as many as four attempts to rear young in one summer. *This is what they do*, I thought. *They keep going.* But they also need us to let them.

CHAPTER 10

# The Guardian

The A train to Jamaica Bay is my favorite subway ride. I board it underground in downtown Brooklyn, then rise to daylight in central Queens as it traces the parks and cemeteries of the terminal moraine. Once it turns south, it cuts across glacial outflow to the Rockaways. The cars empty along the way, and few people remain after the stop at Howard Beach, which connects to Kennedy Airport. Jamaica Bay's northernmost creeks and marshes begin here, which you can guess by the houses outside the window that tilt like stubborn but worn-down crutches. The next part is the best: a three-and-a-half-mile run through the heart of the bay to Broad Channel, the longest distance between two stations in the subway system. It's like entering a shimmering new world.

The bay's intense human engineering can be read in how its half-circle shape has been hard-lined with reinforced concrete, asphalt, and masonry. Roughly 18,000 acres in size (two-thirds of which is part of the Jamaica Bay Wildlife Refuge), the bay lost almost 5,000 acres of marshland to Kennedy Airport, which opened in 1948. It's an estuary, an ecosystem of shallow coves and tidal creeks, where fresh water and salty seawater mix. The rich environment is the nursery ground of a host of fish and invertebrates; those, in turn, attract all kinds of birds on their seasonal migrations.

These days, most of the fresh water comes from stormwater runoff—which rushes across impervious city roads and sidewalks, picking up pollutants along the way—and treated effluent from four sewage treatment plants. The only natural sources left are a few creeks out past the airport. The tides that flow in and out of the bay from Rockaway Inlet filter the ocean-bound runoff, but the water quality can be poor. The limited exchange of water flow means the bay's flushing rate, or the circulation of the heavier saltwater under the fresh (or not-so-fresh) surface water, takes 33 days, according to one estimate. Of critical importance to the bay are its approximately 15 salt marsh islands. After the last ice age, salt marshes grew in the calm waters behind the Rockaway Peninsula as westward ocean currents piled up sand over thousands of years to create that barrier beach.

On a June afternoon, I rode out to tour the bay with Don Riepe. At Broad Channel, the least-used subway station in the entire system, I sprang out all by myself. Red-winged blackbirds loudly staked their territories from every tree, wire, and house. Broad Channel, which sits on the bay's largest island, called Rulers Bar Hassock, is, like Breezy Point, an enclave of mostly Irish families going back multiple generations. But the humans are vastly outnumbered by the birds.

Don lives a short walk from the station. His hundred-year-old white clapboard house sits on pilings over the water, and it's connected to the sidewalk by a narrow boardwalk. When I arrived, the front door was open, and I was greeted by a dozen small ceramic statues of Hindu gods. Most depicted half-human, half-animal many-limbed figures, some riding a swan, a tiger, or a chariot. Don collects them from religious ceremonies held on the bay's shoreline.

I walked in and entered a dark front room packed from floor to ceiling with maritime paraphernalia: decoys, taxidermy, wildlife carvings, horseshoe crab shells, bird toys, binders, books, news articles, certificates, maps, photographs, posters, and paintings. I couldn't decide where to look first. While I lingered on a Boy Scouts sash tacked to the wall, Don walked in from the direction of the kitchen.

"Sandy wiped out a lot of stuff," he said.

During that 2012 superstorm, the surge of water almost reached the six-foot-six ceiling. It took Don nearly five months to rebuild. Mormon missionaries who came to Broad Channel helped him gut the house. Sanitation workers picked up 10-foot piles of debris. He purchased a new boiler, new appliances, a new electrical system, new plywood floors, new furniture, and a new dock. He laid 24 new pilings beneath the house. And like all Broad Channel residents, he received a $600 debit card from a Buddhist group to spend however he wanted. Sikhs cooked meals for everyone at the neighborhood's American Legion hall.

Don picked up a beautiful wood carving of a least bittern and admired it. A few of these small, secretive herons still breed in the city's remaining freshwater marshes, and occasionally up the road at the Jamaica Bay Wildlife Refuge, where Don was a ranger for about 25 years.

"I bought it in Chincoteague from a well-known carver named William Bailey," he told me. "How much do you think I paid for it?"

Boy, was I the wrong person to ask. I had never watched a single episode of *Antiques Roadshow*, and still carry the trauma of being dragged to flea markets as a child. I rarely shop for anything, old or new. It was undeniably handsome, but as I glanced around the room, I didn't see much proof of expensive taste. Don was proud of it... but was he asking me because he thought he got a good deal?

"A hundred?" I guessed.

"Sixteen hundred!" he exclaimed. "I figured, why not. I'm eighty-three. I need to start spending money."

Don has lived for all but a few of those years on or around the bay. Growing up in Ozone Park, he and his pals explored its woods and marshes before the airport paved over them. They collected frogs, snakes, and black widow spiders; the spiders, they thought they could sell to the military for the silk used in crosshairs. Don lived by Aqueduct Racetrack and a hundred-acre farm, one of the last farms in Queens. He and his friends would steal radishes and potatoes and wash them under a sprinkler, while Dominick, the mean-looking watchman, would stumble, half drunk, after them. "We always thought that if Dominick caught you, he'd kill you," Don said. In the woods, where they had tree forts, they'd cook the potatoes over campfires, and Don would salt them with the shaker he kept hooked to his belt. His crew was led by Tommy Sheppard, a boy so nasty Don said you could only look at him sideways. In Don's accent, Tommy's last name comes out "Sheppud." Nicknamed Rabbit, Don was the fastest on his block. His father, a German immigrant who died when Don was 17, owned a butcher shop, and his neighbors were German, Irish, Italian, and Jewish. (Today, many of Ozone Park's immigrants are South Asian, Indo-Caribbean, and Latino.) His mother was Irish Catholic, and her seven children—Don was the second oldest—all attended Catholic school. But Don said he never bought into religion. He questioned too much.

We walked to the kitchen, where a sliding door led to his deck. Windows looked out on two marsh islands that were near enough to swim to. Beyond them was the western half of the bay and the hazy outline of the Manhattan skyline. Instinctively, I scanned for more curiosities in this part of the house. Six horseshoe crab shells hung on the wall, including one signed by Don's friends for his 80th birthday. Wood carvings of a redhead duck and of dunlins, one of the several sandpiper species found around the bay, sat on the microwave and the refrigerator. A taxidermy peregrine falcon watched over his desk. Next to it was an old framed photograph of Don. Dressed in a dark suit, he wore sunglasses, a polka-dot scarf, and thick-heeled black leather shoes. One hand held his hip, and the other a panama hat.

"You were a flamenco dancer?" I asked.

He clapped his hands and snapped his fingers, then stomped a few steps. As a child, he'd wanted to be like Fred Astaire—this never reached Tommy Sheppard—until the day he saw José Greco perform flamenco on *The Ed Sullivan Show*. In the summer of 1986, Don organized and danced in 22 outdoor shows at Lincoln Center. I told him he looked fit enough to bring them back. He said he lifts weights and doesn't take medicine or wear glasses or hearing aids. Besides prostate cancer, he'd had no other diseases. His calendar was full, and his cell phone rang every 10 or 15 minutes.

Don bounced through stories small and large, eclectic as the treasures in his house. But in learning about Don, I learned a great deal about Jamaica Bay. It was his life's work—he had not only witnessed but shaped its marked and rapid changes. After Kennedy Airport, the next big thing to happen to the bay was the making of a wildlife refuge. In 1950, the Long Island Rail Road quit its irregular service through the bay and to the Rockaways after its wooden trestle caught fire. The New York City Transit Authority bought the train line to add to its subway system, but it had to dredge sand to create an embankment for the cars to safely cross. Robert Moses, then the parks commissioner, would only allow it if his department got something in return. He wanted a refuge. The assistant director of the US Fish and Wildlife Service suggested that he build two dikes to impound fresh water; then it would become a goose factory—perfect for the agency's focus on hunting and fishing. In 1954, the Jamaica Bay Bird Sanctuary opened, but a lot more than geese moved into the East and West Ponds—ducks in the winter, shorebirds on mudflats in the summer, songbirds in the spring and fall in the perimeter gardens, nearly all of them migratory. A small and passionate staff led by a horticulturist named Herbert Johnson created one of the country's most important bird preserves, with records of over 330 species. And it sits on fill.

During a fiscal crisis in 1972, the city gave the sanctuary to the National Park Service to become the shining star of the new Gateway National Recreation Area. Local conservationists and birding groups quickly saw signs of the feds' overemphasis on human visitors at the expense of the refuge's flora and fauna. Johnson, who supported the takeover but wasn't immediately replaced as superintendent, was quoted in a *New York Times* article in 1974, saying the place was falling apart. "I thought the Government would have more money to keep it up properly. They can run the Grand Canyon; you'd think they can run this." A photo ran with the article that showed two rangers raking a shoreline; the one on the left, wearing jeans and a denim jacket, is Don.

Having taught English literature in high school for five years, it was his first season as a part-time ranger. After graduate school at the University of New Hampshire—the only three years he's lived outside Queens—he returned for a full-time job. The chance to join his fellow New Yorkers hoping to live up to Johnson's legacy was too good to pass up. He cemented his place on the bay when he and another ranger bought his current house for $10,000. Don became the sole owner after his friend left in the early 1990s, and by then he'd been elevated to the refuge's manager.

The job was nothing if not exciting. The Gambino crime family boss John Gotti, who lived in nearby Howard Beach, ruled at that time, and on several occasions Don fished gunshot victims out of the reeds near Cross Bay Boulevard. Don organized weekly presentations at the visitor center, where the most popular was given by his fortune-teller girlfriend. He almost felt guilty at how much he loved the work. But he retired in 2003, and while leaving to head up the American Littoral Society's Northeast Chapter, the state appointed him the first "Jamaica Bay guardian" and bought him a 22-foot motorboat.

Don still holds the title, which is like that of a citizen protector, and it lets him speak frankly about the state of the bay. Like Johnson a half century before, he feared the wildlife refuge was falling apart. Before I visited, he had been told by Gateway's management that its official policy was to keep it "natural," that the National Park Service was hands-off; it didn't manage natural areas.

"Hands-off?" he said incredulously. "Maybe that works in the Grand Canyon, but you're standing on fill. It's not natural. It needs to be managed."

"How *is* the bay doing today?" I asked.

"It's viable," he said. "But it all comes down to the marshes. If you lose them, you lose the lifeblood of the bay."

Like forests, salt marshes are fragmenting, and their defenses are weakening. Since the mid-20th century, they've shrunk significantly in Jamaica Bay, from around 2,500 acres to 700 acres today, mainly due to sea level rise and excess nitrogen, coming primarily from sewage. The Littoral Society has worked with the National Park Service and the Army Corps of Engineers to restore at least four marshes. The work is simple but backbreaking: Smooth cordgrass (*Spartina alterniflora*), the dominant plant of the region's low-lying tidal marshes, is planted one plug at a time.

"We're trying to bring them back little by little, but they'll never be the same," Don said.

I looked out the window and wondered how many plugs of cordgrass it would take to cover the nearest island. I'd be getting a closer look soon; Don had promised to show me the bay from his boat. My gaze drifted with my thoughts, then stumbled upon a stuffed animal toy of a barn owl on his desk. Noticing me, Don looked over at its heart-shaped face. "My favorite bird," he said. In 1980, he put up the refuge's first nest box for barn owls. "As a kid, I'd found one, so I knew they were around the bay."

"Is that why it's your favorite?" I asked.

"I'll tell you on the boat," he said, cracking a grin. "Let's go. The tide is coming in."

I SAT AT the front of the boat with Don. He kept a tattered Peterson Field Guide and binoculars beside the wheel and an eight-foot ladder in the back. He decided we'd first check barn owl boxes he had placed on several islands in the bay. If the boxes had families in them, the owlets would be around eight weeks old, old enough perhaps to fly short distances. As we pulled away from his dock, Don told me how he had found his first barn owl.

"I was eleven at the time, and there was an old incinerator out by Idlewild Airport. It had a large tower with big windows on both sides, like a belfry. My little gang, we called ourselves the Rawhides—we had our own T-shirts, green with yellow lettering—were riding our bikes past it at dusk, probably after some expedition. I saw this white thing fly out of the incinerator, and something told me it was an owl, even though I'd never seen one. I called out, 'Owl!' but nobody believed me. They thought it was a seagull. So I said we should go on an expedition the next day, and we did."

They brought a burlap sack, a net, a broom, and a grappling hook. "I have no idea where we got them." He chuckled, the madness of youth washing over him. "Somehow, we were able to get up to the first story, and then we threw the grappling hook over the top until it held. We climbed inside to reach the incinerator. There were two owls in there. One flew out a window, but we threw a net over the other one. Since we were all afraid of this thing, we drew straws to see who was gonna go down to get it. I think it was Tommy Sheppard, since he was the leader. He went down and pulled it out of the net and put it in the burlap sack. We carried it back to my friend's house and put chicken wire over half the garage. 'What an expedition,' we thought. 'We brought this thing back alive.'"

"But then we had to feed it," he went on. "We didn't know what it ate. We found a pigeon, a small pigeon, and put that in. The pigeon walked over to the owl, and kids are bloodthirsty, you know—we were cheering. But nothing happened. The next day, we found a small cat, larger than a kitten but not full-grown. We put it in there and figured this was going to be a fight to the death! But the cat stayed at one end and the owl at the other, and they didn't bother with each other. So we let the owl go."

The incinerator was gone by the time Don became a ranger, but he sought to return the owls to the bay by siting predator-proof boxes on its islands that had dry uplands. Between 1993 and 2022, he helped band 372 owlets. Few New Yorkers might imagine barn owls living here, but their range is more widespread than most people realize. From churches to caves, they're found on every continent except Antarctica, and their exceptional hearing allows them to hunt even in complete darkness. A hundred years ago in New York, they lived in a Flushing church belfry, a coal elevator in the Bronx, and a crumbling ivy-covered mansion in Pelham Bay Park. More recently, they moved into the ruins of old hospitals on deserted islands in the harbor. Once, in 1984, a pair bred in Yankee Stadium. In the late 1980s, almost 20 were found during the city's various Christmas Bird Counts, but now only a few turn up. Don thinks they still nest in six or seven places on Staten Island. But these days they're harder to find. Don told me that one year, planes struck eight owls as they flew over the runways at Kennedy.

We headed in that direction. But what started out as a calm day had changed. Drawing up out of the south, the wind blew whitecaps across the bay. The tide was coming in, which is the right time to travel to the east side of the bay. With an average depth of 13 feet and an average tidal range of five feet, it's easy to run aground—hence, Don's rush to leave the house. Despite the chop, he throttled it. We took the spray, and narrowly cleared a shallow channel as we sped toward the first of two bridges. Under the bridge, Don pointed out a peregrine falcon roosting on a ledge. The peregrine had been banded as a chick on the Bayonne Bridge nine years earlier.

We shot into sunlight at 35 miles per hour. To our right was the Rockaways and up ahead was the airport. From the water, its gray concrete sprawl felt dead. Beside it was JoCo Marsh, the bay's largest marsh, and its spartina grass twinkled like an emerald in the afternoon sun. An hour after we left Don's house, we dropped anchor at Subway Island and jumped into a few feet of water.

I'd borrowed waders from Don, and he wore his usual summer attire, a T-shirt tucked into shorts. Four American oystercatchers flew around us, peeping maniacally. Clearly agitated, they probably had nests on the island. Farther along the shore, a willet picked for crabs on the wet sand while double-crested cormorants and laughing gulls sunbathed there like old Russians on the Brighton Beach boardwalk. All of these birds nest on marshes in the bay.

Subway Island is artificial: In the early 1950s it was created at the same time as Moses's bird sanctuary, out of 40 acres of dredged sand, to carry the new subway trains to the Rockaways. With a dry center, it had Jamaica Bay's largest colony of black-crowned night herons, great and snowy egrets, and glossy ibises. These wading birds, or waders, have long and thin legs, long and specialized bills, and long and powerful necks. You could see them from the train in the summer, crowded into shrubs like so many rush-hour commuters. Before we had left Don's house, I saw in his bathroom a large photo from Subway Island of 25 great egrets bunched together, their heads emerging from a mass of white feathers like one of the many-limbed statues adorning his front door.

From the shore, I looked to the scruffy interior of the island, but there wasn't a feather in sight. Where was the colony? I asked Don. He pointed to paw prints in the sand.

"They're all gone," he said sadly. "The raccoons got to it."

He had made the discovery a few months earlier. He'd expected to find 200 pairs building stick nests and flashing their beautiful plumes, but instead he pulled up to an empty island. He still looked devastated. "It was once full of birds," he lamented. As the guardian, Don felt a certain responsibility, I gathered, for anything that went wrong in the bay.

If raccoons were the guilty party, they would have come on land at night. The birds, unwilling to chance laying eggs, would have left in the morning. It had happened to other islands in the bay. The birds still hadn't returned to them, even more than a decade later.

A glossy ibis cruised overhead. Its maroon head and metallic green wings gleamed, and its long sickle-shaped bill cut through the gusts. "They also nested here," Don remarked. The glossy ibis was the early poster bird for the urban refuge; in 1961, Herbert Johnson, Peter Post, and Paul Buckley found three nests with eggs in them, marking the state's first known breeding record of a species that in two decades had pushed its range dramatically northward.

Under the hot sun, we climbed over plastic chairs and rusted car parts, through a field of beach grass. A single juniper rose in the center, as a holdover from the spread of invasives that included ailanthus trees, phragmites, and bittersweet. Two A trains rumbled past each other, and I wondered what the riders on it would have thought of us wading into the chest-high vegetation.

"Those shrubs used to be full of egrets," Don said, gesturing toward a line of them near the tracks.

I grew pessimistic. Raccoons had a history of snatching eggs from barn owl boxes too. All of a sudden, I doubted we'd see any.

The passage to the box was blanketed with poison ivy, so Don pulled on waders. We carried the ladder together. I held it as he climbed up and peered into the box. He then looked down at me, poker-faced.

"There are three babies," he whispered.

A split second later, one flew out of the box and over my head. My heart skipped a beat, and I wasn't sure if I felt ecstatic or scared.

Don and I swapped places. Though he'd said "babies," the two in the box appeared as large as adults. I found it hard to imagine a family of five living inside. They were strangely beautiful and soft-looking, ghostly pale and otherworldly. Within their heart-shaped faces were deep-brown eyes, and pinprick speckling dusted their backs. Their sleeping quarters, however, were furnished with a dark, smelly, flattened mattress of regurgitated fur and bones. One crouched and bobbed side to side like a bantamweight. The other, half asleep, pulled back into a corner.

That behavior is called toe dusting, Don said as I quickly climbed down seconds later. It's a kind of stress response. "It's as if the bird is saying, 'You wanna mess with me?'"

I smiled to myself as we walked back to the boat. No wonder it was his favorite bird.

"Are four decades of recovery efforts your penance for your original sin?" I asked.

Don laughed. "Remember, I never bought into religion," he said.

"Then how about all those Hindu statues at your front door?"

"I'm hedging my bets," he said.

THE TIDE WAS still coming in, so we continued east toward the airport and JoCo Marsh. On the way, we pulled alongside its sister marsh, East High Meadow, but it was too choppy to enter the tight channels or to drop anchor. So we bobbed there for a few minutes. A female osprey gave a shrill whimper and watched us warily from a wooden platform on which her chick crouched inside a cylindrical nest of sticks. Ospreys add to their nests each year, and this top-heavy construction looked ready to tip over. Don said once they left in the fall, he'd tear down the nest so they'd be forced to rebuild it next year.

Ospreys are a major success story for Jamaica Bay. The pesticide DDT not only devastated peregrine falcons but also ospreys and bald eagles, and these fish-catching hawks only resumed breeding in the bay about 20 years after DDT's federal ban. The first successful nest, in 1991, was atop a tall platform Don had erected for them. Roughly 30 pairs now populate the bay in the breeding season, and the birds aren't choosy. They make their nests on abandoned boats, trees, telephone poles, old docks and piers—even on the sand on a few islands. They rarely need to leave the bay to fish.

Furthering the osprey's comeback is the recovery of the menhaden, a staple Atlantic fish that spawns in the bay and has benefited from fishery protections. Don thought there were more ospreys now than before DDT's rise. Most of those that breed in the bay migrate to South America each year, and Don had just received a report of one found dead in Colombia over the winter, a bird he'd banded as a chick on JoCo Marsh 25 years earlier. He has helped band nearly 350 osprey chicks.

In terms of restoration of natural riches, ospreys are a microcosm of the bay, and the bay is a microcosm of New York City. But some things are forever lost. As we swung around to JoCo Marsh, I tried to imagine the marshland gobbled up by Kennedy Airport. On an aerial map you can see remnants amid the neat outline of the airport—a few marshes and creeks squeezed between pavement. The Port Authority of New York and New Jersey, which runs the airport, is constantly seeking to expand deeper into the marshes, but wetlands have been federally protected under the Clean Water Act since 1972.

From the outside, JoCo Marsh looked navigable, but the inside is like a labyrinth, with a mosaic of narrow channels running through. Though eroding at two ends, the marsh remains the healthiest in the bay, Don said. We idled along the edge and spoke about the many birds that rely on its 200 acres.

On its high ground was a pair of American oystercatchers. In 1980, Don found the bay's first nest at Floyd Bennett Field. Once a southern-coast bird, it now lays claim to Jamaica Bay's marshes and islands and, as I knew from my time with piping plovers, the bayside and oceanfront beaches in the Rockaways. But the signature bird of JoCo Marsh is the laughing gull. Hundreds of these black-hooded gulls elegantly wheeled around above us now, and their high-pitched *Ha!* call was so constant I almost tuned it out, like the hum of traffic. Roughly 2,000 pairs nest here, about two-thirds of the bay's breeding population. In the high and dry areas, they build nests made from marsh grasses and vegetation.

When Don and Peter Post found upward of 15 pairs of laughing gulls nesting in JoCo Marsh in 1979, it was the first breeding recorded in New York state in almost 100 years; 19th-century hunting for the millinery trade had decimated their numbers, as was the case with egrets and herons. But by 1990, there were 7,600 nesting pairs in the bay, and airport officials grew concerned about collisions. So the next year, marksmen from the US Department of Agriculture shot down more than 14,000 laughing gulls over the airport.

Don pointed to a rock jetty at the rear of the marsh that was wrapped in razor wire, like the Berlin Wall. We couldn't see them, but gunners were stationed behind it. As a member of Kennedy Airport's Wildlife Hazard Task Force, Don sees the numbers, and he said the most common victims are geese, herring gulls, and great black-backed gulls. Ospreys are also shot, though the agency supposedly runs a trap-and-relocate program for raptors. It created that after public outcry one winter over the shooting of three snowy owls. As for laughing gulls, the airport has learned to live with a small colony. About 3,000 are still shot each year between their arrival in April and their departure in November, Don said. But he believes the Port Authority is overdoing it.

"I feed laughing gulls off my dock, and they can turn on a dime to catch fish in the air," he said. "If any bird's going to get out of the way of a plane, it's a laughing gull."

But birds aren't the only reason Don holds a soft spot for JoCo Marsh. Many years ago, he liked to pull his boat inside and wait for the Concorde to rocket overhead. Then he'd stand up, and the force would knock him back. "I know I'm not supposed to, but I love the Concorde," he said. "Standing out in that marsh, when that comes over your head at a hundred feet, it's better than drugs. It's a rush, man!"

He laughed. "I don't do drugs. I do planes."

Don turned the boat around, and we sped back toward his house through a volley of spray. In the west, a feeding frenzy caught our eye. Bluefish were chasing after menhaden, tipping off hundreds of gulls and terns, which swirled around the water like an ill-shaped tornado. Don pointed out Canarsie Pol in the distance, a long, narrow island with vegetation that rises from the shoreline like terraces: beach grass, taller shrubs, and taller-still deciduous trees. Wading birds abandoned their colony on that island in 2013, he said, but he hoped it would one day return.

"There's more life in this bay than you'll find in the woods upstate," he said to me. "You have more diversity here. You have the ocean, you have the estuary, you have the upland, you have the marsh, you have the flyway. Here, you got all the migratory birds, going back and forth year-round. You got all the marine life—diamondback terrapins, seals, seahorses, dolphins, humpback whales out by the Marine Parkway Bridge—and you got over a hundred species of fish."

Pointing to Canarsie Pol, he said, "If I transported somebody to the middle of that island and asked, 'Where do you think you are?' if they didn't see the cityscape, they'd say, 'City? This isn't a city.'" He smiled. "Oh, yes it is."

It was almost high tide as we eased up to his dock. A few feet higher, and his house would have been flooded. And this was a normal day. New-moon and full-moon tides routinely soak his plywood floors. From the water, the house wasn't much to look at—a tad ramshackle, weather-beaten, charmingly modest.

As if reading my mind, Don laughed. "Can you believe my house is now assessed at seven hundred thousand dollars?" Its value is in the view, he said, even though he knows it'll eventually be underwater.

WAITING FOR US on the deck was Edgar, the great egret I'd heard about on New Year's Day. "Look who's here," Don said.

Edgar waited by the open door as Don stepped inside. The deck was a workshop for Don's—and the Littoral Society's—many projects. On a wooden picnic table was a metal shovel, a posthole digger, and a barn owl box. On a red bench, small boxes for tree swallows sat in a row like parishioners in a pew. A wheelbarrow was used to shuttle spartina bricks to the boat. A green kiddie pool was a birdbath.

Inside the house, I found Don slicing a salmon fillet. Like Don and his wood carvings, Edgar's taste was also growing finer. Don used to feed him silversides. "Edgar's costing me a fortune," he cracked. Edgar followed me and stood on a welcome mat next to a wood cutout of Egor, his predecessor. Don handed him several pieces of salmon in quick succession. With each one, I expected Edgar to take a chunk out of Don's hand. But they were old pros. Edgar then went outside and drank from the kiddie pool.

Don and I sat at his dining table. On the table was a faded paperback about purple martins (he had put a house for them on his deck), a plastic watering can, a washcloth, a ball cap, and his calendar. We spoke more about the bay, which really is never far from Don's mind. When he flies out of Kennedy in the winter, he told me, he chooses a seat behind the left wing so that he can get photos of the bay as the plane ascends. The scenes he likes to capture on the ground often dramatize the urban backdrop—the Concorde rising above an osprey sitting on a nest, subway cars racing behind egret-filled shrubs, hundreds of snow geese landing in front of the blurry Manhattan skyline. Always, the birds are in focus.

"I like the city over there"—he gestured out the window—"where I can see it."

Only one of his siblings still lived in Queens. Another brother moved to Naples, Florida, where he lives in a gated retirement community that has its own gas station, restaurant, and swimming pool. "How can you live with so many old people?" Don said he asked him on one visit. His brother shot back: "You're older than most of the people here!" By the end of his trip, Don had come around to the amenities. "But I can't leave the city," he said. "I love the vitality and, of course, the bay."

But then he wondered aloud: Would it survive another hundred years? Was all his work worth it? He turned philosophical. He asked me if I believed in an afterlife. I said I didn't. He told me he was coming around to the Buddhist view of acceptance—he would do what he could in the here and now.

He stood up and walked over to the Boy Scouts sash hanging on the wall. His interest in nature began as a Scout, he said. He ticked off his merit badges. "Reading, cooking... I don't think we had ornithology. Reptiles and amphibians, swimming. I was so proud of getting swimming. But to become an Eagle Scout, I needed lifesaving. I could swim, but I couldn't pass that test. You had to jump in the pool with your clothes on, take off your dungarees, tie a knot and throw it over to someone, and paddle over and drag them in."

He took a big breath. "I loved Boy Scouts. We camped at the Ten Mile River Scout Camp in Rhode Island. Kids from working-class Queens weren't going anywhere. My father took us to Rockaway

Beach once in a while. He had seven kids to deal with, and he worked six days a week. There wasn't much time."

I walked over too, and above the sash I noticed a gaping hole in the foam-tile ceiling. I hadn't paid much attention to it earlier, I guess because it hadn't seemed out of place. On the wall, though, were muddy paw prints. A few were legible, and they matched the ones we'd seen on Subway Island.

One afternoon, Don explained, he and his colleague Alexandra Kanonik were working in the front room when they heard a crash in here. They rushed in and found a raccoon scrambling out to the deck. It had tried to cling on to the wall as it fell from the ceiling. In the attic, they found its mate. Don ultimately trapped six on the deck by leaving chicken scraps in cages.

"You're supposed to euthanize them," he said, lowering his voice, "but I couldn't bring myself to do it. I don't like killing animals." So he released them in an area he knew had several raccoons already, north of the bay. "I wanted to make sure there was water between them and me," he said.

AFTERWARD, ONE QUESTION nagged at me: Where did the wading birds of Subway Island end up? The former colony there joined a growing list of abandoned or sharply declined ones: Canarsie Pol and Elders Point East, on Jamaica Bay; Mill Rock, in the East River; Goose and Huckleberry Islands, in Long Island Sound. NYC Bird Alliance has annually surveyed the nesting wading birds on these and other islands in New York's harbor for the last 40 years. Up to 10 species of herons, egrets, and ibises move freely among the rubble of buildings, wrecked ships, and crumbling docks—a kind of urban wilderness amid the busy harbor traffic. The first great egret nests were found in the early 1970s on islands within Staten Island's toxic Arthur Kill, a surprising turn of events, even for a group of birds that had been enjoying a steady recovery since the Migratory Bird Treaty Act of 1918 ended their slaughter for women's hats.

Today, New York's waters are cleaner than they've been in a long time. But in a city that creates an average of 12,000 tons of trash per day, raccoons are seeking out new frontiers. Since 2000, the number of islands with wading birds has dropped from 15 to six. The number of wading-bird pairs has fallen by half too, an alarming trend largely driven by losses in two species: the black-crowned night heron and the glossy ibis. There are also climate-related reasons. Researchers believe that in response to warmer temperatures, great and snowy egrets are speeding up their egg laying, while black-crowned night herons are not. And recent surveys have found drowned great egret nestlings in low-lying marshes on Jamaica Bay, evidence that sea level rise isn't some far-off prospect.

Three colonies remain on Jamaica Bay, and a year after the exodus from Subway Island, I joined a six-person survey of the wading birds of Little Egg Marsh, a small, fluctuating colony, previously one-fifth the size of Subway Island's. We met at Don's house. Our leader was Shannon Curley, who coordinates NYC Bird Alliance's Harbor Herons program. José Ramírez-Garofalo also joined. Curley fretted. "I'm afraid of another Subway Island every time I go out now," she said.

As we pulled away for the five-minute boat ride to Little Egg, it was blue and bright on the water, but the skyline was draped with haze from the unhealthy mix of wildfire smoke and ozone pollution. Don dropped us off a quarter of a mile from the island. It was low tide, so we had to wade ashore. We all grabbed waders except Ramírez-Garofalo, who stuck with shorts and sandals. Jumping into the water, I felt the strange sensation of my waders vacuum-forming to my body. The shallows held all kinds of intrigue: kelp grass, whelk shells, and horseshoe crabs, including several males that had anchored onto the larger females. A week earlier on Little Egg, Don had seen hundreds of little semipalmated sandpipers gorging themselves on the crabs' pinhead-sized greenish eggs, fattening themselves up for the next leg of their Arctic-bound migration.

Reaching the mudflats, I shed my waders and laced up my boots. As I looked ahead, it hit me that we were invaders. In a Hitchcockian scene, hundreds of great black-backed gulls and herring gulls eyed us from a sandy ridge above the flats. The plan was for Ramírez-Garofalo to take half the group around the perimeter to count the gulls, while Curley, Angie, and I checked the interior thickets for wading-bird nests. Gulls lay their eggs on the sand, Curley reminded us, so we needed to watch our step.

As we walked forward, Curley in front, all the gulls picked up and started to swirl overhead like a gathering tornado, at least a thousand in all. Their cries sounded like wails and laughs. The great black-backed gulls let out a low *Heh heh heh*. Curley turned around. "Oh," she said, remembering another thing. "We're going to get pooped on."

Shadows raced across the ground as fluffy gray chicks trundled after their parents. One great black-backed chick stumbled toward us as if we were its parents before veering away. Watching my step, my eyes landed on a straw nest with a downy chick and a large speckled egg the color of chocolate milk. A tiny beak was pecking through a hole. The birds were upset by our arrival, and a bunch of adult great black-backed gulls locked their massive yellow bills in territorial scuffles. It was loud and disorienting. I followed Curley.

We made it to the first thicket, but there were no nests. The second thicket was also empty. It was easy to lose your bearings inside the tangle of branches, so we used a chalk spray to tag the trees we'd checked. Curley asked us to look for raccoon scat or prints. "I'm a little concerned," she said.

Working from west to east, we approached the next thicket. Suddenly, we saw 10 adult black-crowned night herons fly out the back, letting out an explosive *Krak!* Their call was raven-like; their genus name, *Nycticorax*, literally means "night raven." A big smile spread across Curley's face. "I'm so relieved," she said.

We bushwhacked into a dark tangle of sumac and poison ivy. Ducking under branches, Curley found 10 sling-shaped stick nests, matching the number of night herons that flew out. Hidden between branches roughly seven feet off the ground, their nests surprised me—they looked entirely too crude, too flimsy, to support a family of these large, stocky birds. But the young were coming; one nest held four teal eggs.

As we walked out, Curley explained the hierarchy of the canopy. For wading birds, which are colonial nesters, there is a safety-in-numbers arrangement. Great egrets tend to build their stick nests in the upper branches, a height that allows them more space to land and take off. Below them are snowy egrets and then black-crowned night herons, and then, closest to the ground, glossy ibises. Their nests look slightly different—snowy egrets make trim slings, and glossy ibises shape dense saucers—but all the nests are made of similar-sized twigs the birds have broken off whatever is growing around the island.

We began finding more nests, and, using a pickup truck mirror attached to a long pole, we saw some that were occupied. A squawking great egret chick was but a downy white ball, and black-crowned night heron chicks were gray and grumpy-looking, with a mop of wispy feathers, like old men. "They're the cutest," Curley said.

The beach grass was thick, and we couldn't walk far without accidentally flushing mallard hens sitting on their hidden nests. It jangled my nerves every time. One was so angry she charged Curley and pursued her even as she retreated. "I know, you're a very good mama. I'm leaving," she apologized. We hurried on.

Ramírez-Garofalo and Curley decided to quickly do a head count of the rest of the adult waders and flee the angry birds. We'd been on the island for an hour and a half. Little Egg had 40 nests the previous year, split almost evenly between great egrets and black-crowned night herons. We tallied more than triple that amount, including the nests of snowy egrets and glossy ibises that hadn't been there a year ago. "I think a lot of the Subway Island birds came here," a thankful Ramírez-Garofalo said. "Now let's get out."

Through the ruckus, we passed the two fresh great black-backed gull chicks I'd seen earlier near the shore. The one that had been pecking its way into the world was now slumped on its straw nest and weakly moving its neck.

"Happy today years old!" Ramírez-Garofalo said, taking a cellphone photo.

He strode to the water's edge, and I quickly followed. Don was anchored farther out than before. I inspected my clothes and backpack. I couldn't believe I was escaping poop-free. Curley turned to look back once more. She was smiling. "Isn't this wild?" she said.

CHAPTER 11

# The Bronx River

I first encountered the Bronx River as a kid visiting the Bronx Zoo, riding the Wild Asia Monorail over a flat ribbon of water toward Mongolian wild horses and red pandas. Like the animals I saw in enclosures there, I assumed the river wasn't exactly real—just a version of something wild modified for humans. It was only after living in New York for more than 15 years that I realized the placid surface I had gazed upon was the city's only freshwater river. I decided to get familiar with it.

The river begins 354 feet above sea level in the heights of Westchester County and flows south approximately 23 miles, about a third of it through the Bronx, to the tidal East River. On a humid June morning, I brought my bike on the subway and rode the train almost two hours from my home in central Brooklyn to Woodlawn, in the north of the Bronx. I was going to meet Emilio Tobón, a staff biologist at NYC Bird Alliance, who was surveying the wading birds on the river's city passage throughout the breeding months. After enduring centuries of the worst kinds of abuse, the river, thanks to several restoration projects, was seeing better days. But as with any ecosystem, the birds would tell us how much better.

I arrived early to our meeting point at the Woodlawn train station.

Catbirds, robins, starlings, and cedar waxwings fed on the dark fruit of a mulberry tree. It was peak mulberry season—sidewalks all over the city were turning purple with splatter. The river was not in sight, but a sign for Muskrat Cove—and an eastern kingbird twittering on a wire and a warbling vireo singing energetically up the paved bike path— suggested that it was near. Both those birds like to nest along water, so I walked toward the vireo and quickly entered a secluded path of white pines, beeches, and pin oaks. The river was there, about 30 feet across and flowing slowly. It wasn't the Colorado, but the sight of running fresh water in New York excited something elemental in me.

I turned back and waited for Tobón. When he pulled up, I was surprised at how light he traveled. He wasn't carrying water, food, or a bag—just a cell phone and small binoculars, which he could fit inside his cargo-shorts pockets. Tanned, with short gray hair and a thin white beard, he wore sandals and biking gloves. (I wished I had those.) He had biked from his home near Upper Manhattan's Inwood Hill Park; for each of these weekly surveys, he cycles a total of 30 miles round-trip. "I'm like a camel," he said. "Once I get home, I'll drink water like crazy."

Tobón, who grew up in Mexico City, moved to New York in 2008 after studying seabirds in New Zealand and on Pacific islands off the coast of Mexico. Now he lives on a much different island. "But there are a lot of birds here too, and many people don't realize this," he said. The harbor herons, he added, are one of the best examples.

In the East River was a colony of herons and egrets on South Brother Island, the second largest colony in the whole harbor, and it was birds from there that we hoped to see catching fish in the Bronx. But since it was still early in the breeding season, Tobón didn't expect to see very many. The adults would be staying close to their nests. Despite that, we still had to do the survey—even zero is a data point. By September, he told me, both the adults and their young would be making longer foraging trips up the river. I made a note to see this for myself.

We biked up to Muskrat Cove—the first of Tobón's 23 survey points—and then turned back south. Other stops would be less accessible. The Bronx River Parkway parallels the river from its source to the South Bronx. Our next stop was right beside the highway, and it was loud. We followed the river's east bank into the aptly named Shoelace Park, where the river was ruler-straight and narrow, squeezed between train tracks and the highway. Trash had been dumped on the bank in one area, but Tobón said the shallow river was much cleaner today than it had been on his first visit 13 years earlier. Large overhanging willows shaded it, and I lingered an extra moment to admire a triple-trunked silver maple, a wizened giant that bent over the river.

Shoelace Park is a mile and a half from north to south. At the south end, the river curves, and I lost my bearings as we whipped around a winding path underneath a pair of stone bridges that carry the parkway overhead—two of over 75 bridges that span the river. I presumed the bend was part of the river's natural course; its stretch through Shoelace Park was clearly artificial. Only humans make rivers that straight. The bike path turned diabolical, covered in half a foot of sediment from historic flooding two years earlier. Nearly eight inches of rain had fallen that day, and the river had submerged the Bronx River Parkway.

On the border of a dark forest, we stopped at the Burke Bridge. A dead pigeon floated by, and a sense of foreboding pervaded the scene. The riverbanks were thick and lush. We headed downslope on a cruddy trail. Boardwalks and footbridges that were new when Tobón first surveyed the river's wading birds in 2010 were now falling apart. We emerged at weedy, overgrown ballfields, and I grasped a borough's natural beauty allowed to wither, a land carved by highways and plagued by garbage, pollution, and noise.

At our next stop, we found two e-scooters and e-bikes in the water. "I've been finding them all over the river this season," Tobón noted grimly.

The ride smoothed out as we approached the New York Botanical Garden, which, like the Bronx Zoo and the forest Tobón and I had just passed through, sits within Bronx Park. Surrounded by great expanses of concrete, it acts as the Bronx's lungs. Having locked our bikes at the garden's entrance, I felt my breath settle while walking into the Thain Family Forest, 50 acres of old growth that was spared from the sawmills that once dotted the river. Here the river ran through a gorge carved by the Wisconsin ice sheet. Climbing steep, rocky slopes, we passed giant tulip trees, oaks older than the Revolutionary War, and the relics of a once-famous hemlock grove. Like they do now at Pelham Bay Park's Hunter Island, birders used to convene there to find wintering owls. A northern flicker flashed its yellow underwings as it led us toward a bridge where the river cascaded over dark rocks. Soothed by the waterfall's song, I didn't want to leave.

But there were more places to survey. And Tobón's prediction was right—we hadn't seen a single wading bird yet. We biked around the outside of the Bronx Zoo, and then over to River Park, where an osprey glided over a waterfall dam. Some blocks away, the river snakes under a terrifying intersection of highways that I would have never biked alone. We sprinted across the Cross Bronx Expressway, to the newly finished final section of the Bronx River Greenway, and into Starlight Park. Barn swallows traced figures over the river, their nest likely below a steel bridge. The river fanned into a wide basin, and as we pulled along its west side, a great egret—finally!—flew up from the bank and toward South Brother Island.

Moments later, from a dock down to my right, I heard chanting. "Protect the egrets! Protect the egrets! Protect the egrets!"

I walked over and found 25 children and about that many adults cheering them on. The kids held up posters with marker-drawn great egrets (or at least egret-like shapes) and messages like THE RIVER NEEDS TO BE CLEAN!, NO GARBAGE IN THE WATER!, and THE EGRETS NEED CLEAN WATER! One boy hoisted up a life-sized papier-mâché egret. The kids marched in a loose circle, some shaking tambourines and maracas.

Tobón was kind enough to wait as I explored further. One parent told me the students were first graders at a nearby bilingual community school. They were learning about watersheds, and the students had been split into three groups and each assigned a different creature that lived in or around the Bronx River: oysters, beavers, and egrets. The egret group's final assignment was organizing this rally, and they had gathered outside the Bronx River House, home of the Bronx River Alliance, a community organization that works on the very things the kids were asking for. "Today is our day of action," the parent told me.

I stood back and watched.

"Who wants to give a speech?" their teacher shouted through a bullhorn. In English and Spanish, the kids talked about the need for cleaning the water and making sure there was no trash in it. "Do not destroy the habitat!" one boy said.

"You know! You know!" the teacher cried.

"What do we say?" the teacher prompted them.

They resumed marching. "Protect the egrets! Protect the egrets! Protect the egrets!"

"¡Salve la garza! ¡Salve la garza! ¡Salve la garza!"

I returned to the bridge energized. The river was a community treasure, and it looked to be in good hands. As Tobón and I resumed our ride, two miles short of the mouth, with the toughest parts behind us, the last thing I heard from the park was a sparky girl leading her classmates in unison: "We are the water protectors! We are the water protectors! We are the water protectors!"

IN THE SPRING of 1974, *New York Times* editor Allan M. Siegal visited a month-old cleanup effort where the Cross Bronx Expressway tears through the river. "An alien growth is poking out of the banks of the Bronx River near West Farms Square," he wrote. "It is grass."

What had prevented it from growing? "Six wrecked cars, two rusted horse trailers, 50 to 60 refrigerators, one discarded 25-foot lamppost, five rotted sofa beds, a mimeograph machine, two boiler tanks and the remains of an upright piano," Siegal wrote. "And—oh, yes—a wine press."

Thousands of tires also choked the Bronx River, with more dumped nearly every day. Raw sewage emptied into it from two open pipes by the Woodlawn train station. From the other end, tides carried polluted East River waters as far north as Starlight Park. The water's bacteria count sometimes climbed to 40 times above the maximum acceptable level. Within the Bronx, the river was declared unsuitable for bathing, swimming, or other recreational purposes.

Ruth Anderberg, a brisk woman with the gift of gab, was leading the new cleanup effort. A secretary at Fordham University, Anderberg strolled along the river once a week inside the New York Botanical Garden. Unlike at West Farms, it was sylvan there. It was also clean and tree-lined in the Westchester suburbs. But in the South Bronx, it was a "yellow sewer," the NYPD's Bronx borough commander said at the time, hidden beneath all the trash. "You could practically walk across it," said Anderberg. And it was rendered inaccessible by scrapyards, parking lots, and warehouses.

Anderberg wanted to do more than clean up the mess. She wanted to see the river restored. Finding no government agency willing to tackle either, she quit her job and, with a few other residents, formed the Bronx River Restoration Project.

The first step was dismantling the junk bridge near West Farms Square. Anderberg recruited seventh graders from a nearby intermediate school, and, with borrowed garden tools, they got to work dragging out trash that was, in some instances, 150 years old. The city sent a bucket crane to help with the heavy items. Additional help came from Bronx units of the National Guard, local tow-truck owners, and scrap dealers eyeing an easy buck. Anderberg's youth brigade cleaned that segment in three months, but the rest would take years. Access to the river was—and still is—made difficult by no fewer than three highways.

Much has been written about the South Bronx in the 1970s—the decade the Bronx burned. Eighty percent of its housing was set on fire then, and 250,000 people displaced, as landlords paid to have their own buildings torched so they could collect insurance money. New York City was broke. Soon after Anderberg started the Bronx River Restoration Project, President Gerald Ford denied the city federal assistance to spare it from bankruptcy, leading to the famous *Daily News* cover: FORD TO CITY: DROP DEAD. While the river was a dumping ground, so were the neighborhoods that surrounded it. Fed up by that treatment, Anderberg's work was one of several community-led uprisings.

It had been 300 years since the first two mills opened on the river around that very spot. In even older times, the river meandered, flowing swiftly around bends and oxbows, through forests of oaks, hickories, chestnuts, and tulip trees. The Lenape people, who fished and hunted its banks, carved dugout canoes from the tulip trees. They called the river Aquehung (or Aquahung), which is often translated "river of high bluffs." Bronx River historian Stephen Paul DeVillo suggests the name may have referred to a specific place, or was possibly derived from the Munsee word *akawaltung*, meaning "that which is protected from the wind," a description that could have applied to its run through the gorge inside the present-day botanical garden. Either way, it was a special waterway. Alewife, a type of herring about a foot in length, swam up from the ocean to spawn in fresh water, while American eels passed them on their trip in reverse to the Sargasso Sea. Beavers shaped the river, and the ponds that formed behind their dams became the millponds of colonial times. Middens of oyster shells near the mouth, at today's Clason Point and Hunts Point, marked Indigenous settlements.

In 1639, a Swede named Jonas Bronck, employed as a merchant ship captain by the Dutch West India Company, became the first European to live near the river. Following his death shortly after, his 500-acre property, which Bronck had "purchased" for a barrel of cider, shirts, and tools, became known as Bronck's Land. Though his property never touched the river, his name was extended to it too. Two decades later, English farmers took control of the river, calling their first settlement West Farms. Colonists coveted it as a power source, and their water-powered mills churned out grain, timber, paper, and snuff through the end of the 18th century.

The byproducts they released into the Bronx River were natural, though, and New York City assessed it as a possible source of its drinking supply. According to a 1799 report, the river was "a collection of innumerable springs, issuing from a rocky and gravelly country, and running, with a rapid current, over a bed of the same materials." It was also said to have "a constant supply of water" that was "never failing." But this rapid flow also made the Bronx different from all the tidal waterways around—it could be harnessed to power heavier manufacturing. And fail it did.

Through the 1800s, paint, pottery, and textile mills flushed it with chemicals, dyes, and lead. A gas-light company buried metals in the soil, and a clothing factory stacked giant scrap heaps of wool and leather on its banks. Even so, some sections remained picturesque. In the late 1840s, Edgar Allan Poe wandered its passage through the river gorge on land owned by the Lorillards, a family whose riches came from tobacco. Having left the gorge almost entirely uncut, the city acquired it in the late 1880s, as part of a forest lying on both sides of the river. John Mullaly, a former newspaper reporter and editor and a city-government appointee, led the effort to turn 640 acres into Bronx Park, a large city park like Manhattan and Brooklyn had. His 1887 book-cum-sales pitch *The New Parks Beyond the Harlem* paints a vivid picture of the tract's "wooded slopes, rocky ravines, sequestered glades, banks carpeted with vines, [and] miniature mountains crowned with trees." The ink was hardly dry on the agreement to create Bronx Park before the city offered the park's loveliest bits to the institutions that would turn them into the New York Botanical Garden and the Bronx Zoo.

Mullaly noted one concern about the river: In 1885, its spring-fed headwaters in the town of Kensico had been impounded by a new dam and tapped for an aqueduct. With its flow cut by perhaps a quarter, Mullaly feared it becoming stagnant. (A fun aside: The headwaters still bubble away in the Kensico Reservoir, a "balancing" site that receives water for New York's drinking supply from reservoirs in the Catskills and Delaware River watersheds before it heads downslope to the city; so as the historian DeVillo writes, "In every glass a New Yorker draws from the tap, there are a few drops of the Bronx River.") And Mullaly was proved right. Hotels, breweries, and factories fixed sewers to the river. People built outhouses on its banks. Barnyards dumped into it. In 1899, the Bronx borough president said: "It is a quiet, dead little stream, except after heavy storms." And though a sewer system was quickly in the works, another remedy was proposed: a vegetated buffer and a 15-mile highway running beside its banks.

Factories, farms, and houses were cleared out, sometimes using eminent domain, and the Bronx River Parkway opened in 1925, one of America's earliest limited-access roadways (commercial vehicles weren't allowed). With a speed limit of 35 miles per hour plus two lanes in either direction, the parkway was intended for pleasure drives along the winding river. But while preservation of the river was the public goal, as a sign of things to come, a parkway engineer readily acknowledged that another was to encourage suburban development. In the northern Bronx, relatively few residents owned cars, and they were now cut off by the parkway from reaching the river on foot.

Though raw sewage became less of a problem, oil and gas now flowed into the river, and air pollution concentrated in the Bronx, not Westchester. Scenic though it was, the road quickly became a congested commuter route. Regardless, work soon began on other highways. Robert Moses pursued a highway-building spree that ripped apart the borough, and when he set his sights on the Bronx River Parkway, he widened it to six lanes and extended it to the South Bronx. Moses wasn't interested in protecting the river's twists and turns. In Shoelace and Starlight Parks, it was forced into rock-walled channels.

Moses also plotted the extension through Bronx Park's lowland forest, taking chunks out from the botanical garden and the zoo—important migratory stopovers for woodland birds. Much of the floodplain was paved over. Roger Tory Peterson, a regular on Bronx Christmas Bird Counts in the 1930s and 1940s, lamented the loss of freshwater marshes that gave sanctuary to Virginia rails and Wilson's snipes.

Moses rammed three highways through Van Cortlandt Park. Robert Caro, in his titanic biography on Moses, *The Power Broker*, writes of him chuckling over the failure of the "bird lovers" to stop him from running the Major Deegan Expressway through the park's large freshwater swamp. They pursued an injunction, Moses said, "but we just filled in a little faster."

As has been well documented by Caro and many others, the purpose of these highways was to smooth the flight of white people from the multiethnic and multiracial Bronx to the suburbs—people who could, in turn, purchase houses backed by federal programs like the Home Owners' Loan Corporation, or HOLC. Designed to help Americans recover from the Depression, the HOLC mapped neighborhoods in more than 200 cities and graded them from A to D, based on the quality of their housing stock and their residents' race, ethnicity, and income. Most Bronx neighborhoods along the river received the lowest grade and were redlined on maps, leaving no banks to issue mortgages there. Majority-white suburbs over the city limits had no such problem.

Almost a century later, studies show that nearly three-quarters of redlined neighborhoods are still struggling. And redlining devastated not only the financial health of these communities but also their ecological health. The Bronx River suffered from the same neglect as the people living within its watershed. These were the ruins Ruth Anderberg and others walked through in the 1970s. They knew that some damage, like the river's channelization, could probably never be undone, but over the next two decades, a new generation of local activists embraced its reclamation as part of a broad push for environmental justice. In 1997, community groups joined with government agencies and businesses to form the Bronx River Working Group, and they won $120 million in public funding for a greenway and restoration projects. Out of this group sprang the Bronx River Alliance. By the time Anderberg died in 2016, she had seen industrial sites transformed into waterfront parks, from West Farms to Hunts Point—integral links on the greenway I biked.

ON A STICKY early August morning, I followed sidewalk chalk drawings of sunfish to the Burke Bridge for the Bronx River Alliance's Water and Woodlands Festival. Just north of the botanical garden, the bridge was one of my early stops with Emilio Tobón—it was where a dead pigeon floated past. The original Bronx River Parkway had ended nearby. Staff were still setting up when I arrived. The shallow river crept under the bridge's single arch. Christian Murphy, the late-twenties ecology manager of the Bronx River Alliance, corrected a colleague who was hanging signs on plants. "That's not a box elder," he said, pulling down a saw-toothed leaf. "That's a slippery elm."

Besides my ride with Tobón, I had done very little birding in the Bronx, and I was curious to see what I might find along the river itself. I also wanted to learn more about the river's health today, so I introduced myself to Murphy. But before he could talk, he said he had to first rustle up some macroscopic invertebrates for his informational table at the festival. He pulled waders over his jeans and picked up a seine and slid down the steep bank to the river. A red-tailed hawk screamed and soared high above, catching thermals from the parkway. Another responded from deeper inside the forest; perhaps there was a nest around. I went to investigate.

I had visited here briefly on my bike ride, but the potholed path had rattled me good, and Tobón and I had moved quickly. It was clear to me now that it was one of the few segments where a natural floodplain survived. American sycamores, packed like matchsticks, rose ramrod-straight out of the wet soil. I'd never seen them growing wild in the city; their strong roots protect riverbanks and stream banks. On terraces above the sycamores loomed massive beeches, red oaks, white oaks, and tulip trees. It seemed to be a snapshot of the north-meets-south plant communities that grew in postglacial New York. As I walked south, the river split, forming an island, then reunited as it flowed into the botanical garden. A belted kingfisher flew past me heading upriver, announcing its territory with a long, harsh rattle. With their oversized dimensions—blocky head, big bill, and shaggy crest—kingfishers strike me as cartoon birds. This bird's dark-blue back, I thought, was a match for a cleaner river. Moments later, a second followed, the female of the pair, which I could tell by her rust-orange belly band. I guessed they had a nest in an earthen burrow on the riverbank.

The stretch felt like a relic of the river that once was. I remembered it was part of the forest that John Mullaly, the 19th-century newspaper reporter, had called on the city to preserve. "Scenes as romantic as any in the Adirondack wilderness," he wrote. I squinted and could see it. But I couldn't ignore the motor roar from the parkway, nor the trashed forest floor. A boardwalk was split in half. Two metal garbage cans, one rusted and disintegrating, slumped on their sides, disgorging their contents. An interpretive display about the floodplain restoration was so faded and begrimed that it was unreadable. What kind of city lets a place this special languish? Unlike Central Park and Prospect Park, no private fundraising arm specifically supports its maintenance. That work falls to the Bronx River Alliance.

I returned to the event, where staff at one table were handing out cups of a punch made of chokeberry and elderberry. I found the tart juice refreshing, especially when I learned that the fruit came from a food forest at Concrete Plant Park, in the South Bronx, the only New York City park where foraging is legal; the idea for the food forest there was born out of a public art project that floated outside on a barge in the river to skirt the ban.

By now, Christian Murphy was back from the river. He had caught two crayfish locked in an embrace—it was mating season for arthropods. He had been looking for caddisflies and mayflies, two groups of insects that spend most of their lives as larvae in fresh water, feeding the rest of the food chain. "For a dirty and polluted river, they're able to live in it," Murphy commented, sounding a little surprised himself. I glanced at those minute crayfish, now beneath glass in a plastic tray of water, then scanned the rest of the table for other specimens. "As a kid I loved this stuff," Murphy said with a grin.

Growing up in Manhattan, Murphy was a difficult kid, he told me, prone to end up in detention. But the outdoors provided relief. A project on birds when he was about the same age as the Protect the Egrets cadre had him and a classmate studying the eastern kingbird. They drew a large cardboard cutout of it. Then they went birding in Central Park, and he loved the experience. Murphy's nature education deepened on trips to visit his maternal family in England. (His mother had left England to work as a nurse in New York City during the AIDS crisis, and she met his father, who had fled civil unrest in Jamaica, in the admitting department of the hospital where they both worked.) His grandfather, a career forester who worked in southwest England, would take Murphy and his younger sister on long walks in the countryside. They would roll over rocks and logs to see what was crawling underneath, and he would describe the relationships between living things that made up ecosystems.

The lessons never left Murphy. In 2018, he found an apprenticeship a year out of college on the Bronx River Alliance's conservation crew, a group that restores the riparian habitat and softens the hard edges that previous engineers imposed on the river. The river was new to him too; he had seen it in the zoo and the botanical garden but thought it was an artificial feature. In 2020, he was hired for his current role.

Murphy spends most of his time in the South Bronx. Since the Bronx River drains into the East River, what happens to it impacts the entire New York City ecosystem, from the fish to the birds that eat them, like belted kingfishers, egrets, and ospreys. Murphy told me that a report some years ago discovered that 80 to 90 percent of the plastic pollution in the harbor pours in from the Bronx River. Much of it flows down from Westchester County. Sewage, though, remains the greatest problem. In the city's pipes, stormwater and wastewater travel together to a treatment plant, where they are, in theory, purified and discharged into an adjacent body of water. But those pipes were built a century ago, and not for a city of its current size. They can't handle the volume of water that now washes into them during heavy rainstorms. In those events, the pipes are overwhelmed—raw sewage and runoff combine, bypass the treatment plant, and flow together into our waterways. Five combined sewer overflows, or CSOs, empty into the Bronx River.

All this pollution leads to algal blooms and fish die-offs, like a recent one at the botanical garden. "We need to reduce the volume of water going down to the river," Murphy said. One major attempt is working with municipalities in Westchester County to restructure their century-old sewer systems. They're worse than New York City's, but most towns find it too expensive to repair them. "I don't think we'll ever see a day where there's no sewage on the river," Murphy said, but he didn't sound defeated. "But if we fix those pipes, we can cut it down and make the river safer for wildlife and humans."

For us, Murphy said, the river has generally been safe to paddle in kayaks or canoes for the last 25 years. But we can't swim in it or safely eat fish and crabs from it—though people try. But he dreams of the day the Bronx River Alliance can demonstrate the old lifeways of subsistence fishing on the river, something missing for at least two centuries. Though the river is damaged, it's filled with wildlife. Menhaden enter the estuary to spawn. The first beaver returned in 2007 outside the Bronx Zoo, having likely paddled down from Westchester. People catch Atlantic blue crabs in it. Two dolphins were spotted outside Starlight Park in 2023. And alewives, the fish that had their spawning grounds obstructed by the river's first dam, have been reintroduced. They're helped by a fish ladder on the dam, a series of low steps the fish swim and leap up. Once the fish returned, so did the birds. Ospreys, a familiar sight in Bronx Park during its early years, again breed on the river. Bald eagles have been spotted catching American eels. And, of course, herons and egrets ply its banks.

"I think building more habitat has been more impactful than trying to stop all the pollution from entering the river," Murphy reasoned.

I asked him if there was an event on the river that stuck in his mind. Mine was easy: the Protect the Egrets rally earlier in the summer. He recalled that while canoeing down the river during a Bronx River Alliance outing, he'd watched a 15-year-old boy hook a striped bass below the centuries-old dam. "A big game fish like that—in the middle of the Bronx, in the middle of this urban metropolis," Murphy said.

The boy reeled up the fish, and it swung like a pendulum in front of Murphy's face. "I asked him to hold it there for a second, so I could take a photo," he said. "Then he caught a couple of sunfish. It was not hard for him to catch fish from an industrial part of the river."

He pondered that for a moment. "If that's not a testament to what restoration can do," he said, "I don't know what is."

EMILIO TOBÓN HAD encouraged me to return to the river later in the season. If it was indeed healthy enough, he'd said, there should be plenty of wading birds coming up from the harbor islands. I figured the best way to find out was to get out on the water.

But the rest of the month was extremely rainy, and CSOs poured untreated sewage into the river at unhealthy levels. The Bronx River Alliance was forced to cancel multiple paddling outings. On those days, Christian Murphy was in the lab of the organization's solar-powered headquarters in Starlight Park, checking the bacteria counts of water samples. September was worse. One day, nine inches of rain fell on parts of the city. Inside Starlight Park, the river turned into an angry torrent, foaming with a fetid brown scum.

But I got my chance on Labor Day weekend to canoe its tidal strait, from Concrete Plant Park to the mouth. When I arrived, a mother and daughter were collecting nuts and berries in the shadow of two old concrete mixers in the park's food forest. Concrete making happened here from the mid-1940s through 1987, and after its cessation, dozens of cars and thousands of tires piled up on the mudflats until the NYC Parks Department acquired the abandoned property in 2000. The mixers looked like upside-down rocket ships, painted a pinkish peach. Pigeons seemed to like them. Flying in and out of a mixer's round base, their cooing echoed inside the hollow drum. I could hear them because the warehouses and highways and Amtrak tracks were only waking up.

I watched the river as I waited for others to show. A green heron did the same. Crouched on the end of a floating trash boom, the dark little heron peered into the murky water, looking for fish and other small prey in an oily slick. Murphy had mentioned that booms and sewer outfalls attract filter feeders like menhaden. Not the kind of food chain I'd want to partake in.

At 10, seven paddlers gathered in the sun around Nick Scaglione, the Bronx River Alliance's bearded young recreation coordinator. He ran through some safety protocols. "This is not a river you want to go swimming in," he warned. "Do not dip your hat in it to get water to cool down your head. You don't want this water in your scalp." I nodded seriously, though I was really watching a ruby-throated hummingbird hover behind him.

I got lucky and rode shotgun in Scaglione's canoe. The tide was going out. On the mudflats were a great blue heron and a yellow-crowned night heron. Already, my wader count matched my multi-hour survey with Tobón. We paddled under the Bruckner Expressway, and the sounds of the South Bronx fell away. Our oars splashed softly in the odd quiet. After gliding past an active concrete plant, we pulled alongside the dock of a large metal recycling facility. It was an outpost of Sims, the same company that had a Swainson's hawk at its Brooklyn complex. Three barges sat there. One overflowed with plastic trash bags, and it smelled acrid. Another held mounds of car parts; the other, metal scrap. A tugboat grumbled upriver, pushing an empty barge, and flushed a black-crowned night heron from the rock wall. It flew off with a loud *Krak!*

Suddenly, I saw several wading birds dotting the hard-edged banks on either side of us. Great egrets perched on exposed branches, and both black-crowned and yellow-crowned night herons hid within bushy willows. As we pushed ahead, more herons and egrets flew by, murmurs of surprise rising from our canoes to meet them. Most of the night herons were streaky mottled-brown juveniles. They had hatched around the time I first visited the river. Now they were foraging on it.

I noticed a bird bobbing on the rocks by a large opening in a concrete block. A spotted sandpiper! I pointed it out to Scaglione, and he identified the hole next to it as a combined sewer overflow pipe. I eyed the maw of raw sewage. The bird was picking bugs from its discharge on the mudbank. As we passed, I wondered, Was it just me or was the water more viscous, the soft oar splashes juicier? I noted plastic bottles and jugs, a car bumper, and one of those plastic toddler toys that looks like a standing vacuum attached to a space helmet filled with bouncing colored balls.

"There are fish here!" one guy yelled. A school of menhaden jumped in the greasy slick. A pair of kingfishers lifted off the bank, one swooped down to snatch a fish, and I wondered if they were the same birds I had seen a couple weeks earlier. Scaglione pointed to an osprey nest on a light tower on the grounds of the Hunts Point Produce Market.

The river was grungy, but birds foraged here. I wrapped my head around that. There was no perfect environment. Cities are real—if wildly imperfect—ecosystems. Even in its current state, the Bronx River had a lot to offer.

Scaglione had us stop at the mouth. Almost a dozen wading birds were tucked into the spindly willows that grew from the concrete bank. The trees had grown from seeds carried by the wind or dropped there by small birds or other animals. Though I'd gotten used to seeing wildness climbing through the cracks, I couldn't remember an image as perfect as this one. The great blue herons were so tall that their attempts to crouch in the willows made me think of adults playing with toddlers in a game of hide-and-seek. Only one or two pairs of great blue herons nest in the harbor, since they usually prefer quiet and remote areas, which suggested that these herons came from outside the city to this happy fishing ground.

Several planes came in hard and low from our left, rumbling toward LaGuardia Airport. Distant across Flushing Bay, the white roof of Arthur Ashe Stadium, home to the US Open, gleamed.

"It's so pretty here," said Scaglione. "I almost forget I'm in New York."

Nobody was in a rush to return. The air was salty, almost fresh, helped by a southerly breeze that carried a Mister Softee jingle. Buoyed by the Bronx waters, we floated there for 15 minutes, then turned and let the rising tide help carry us back.

# FALL

CHAPTER 12

# Tribute in Light

I woke up with a feeling of dread on September 11, 2023. The day felt heavier than normal, and I mulled over the reasons. The city's direction, for one. Mayor Eric Adams had just proposed slashing agency budgets, having said that migrant families seeking asylum in the city would "destroy" it. So much for "Give me your tired, your poor, your huddled masses yearning to breathe free"—this was Father Coughlin, not Lady Liberty. We were coming to the end of the hottest summer in the hottest year on record—a grievous milestone that would be surpassed the following year and potentially every successive year of my lifetime.

And then there were the birds. Later that night, the 9/11 memorial Tribute in Light was going to shoot two extremely powerful beams into the sky from a parking garage roof in Lower Manhattan. What would that do to them? Light pollution and glass are like a one-two punch: The first disorients nocturnal migrants, and then, weakened and confused, they crash into the glass surfaces they can't see. If it was a strong night of migration, tens of thousands of birds were going to get sucked into the beams.

I wasn't the only one feeling tense. Dustin Partridge, NYC Bird Alliance's conservation director, had been losing sleep over the weather forecast. Birds were beginning to return south, and in the fall, they usually wait for a night of colder winds from the north to propel them. There was a good chance of that happening tonight. The memorial would stay illuminated from eight that evening until six the following morning, and it would be Partridge's responsibility to ask its organizer to turn off the beams for a short period if at least a thousand birds were trapped. I had signed up as a volunteer to help count for most of those 10 hours. Partridge hoped for rain, to stop any migration. "If it's pouring and we're miserable, that's great, because that means birds aren't getting stuck," he told me. After my volunteer shift, I planned to meet Melissa Breyer to look for collision victims around the World Trade Center.

Project Safe Flight hadn't resumed for the season until September 1, but Melissa had been picking dead and injured birds off the hot pavement since early August. What we birders call fall migration is really a catch-all for southbound migration; July and August see the first departures of shorebirds and songbirds from their northern breeding grounds.

With a few cold fronts in August, Melissa had found 120 collision victims, about a fivefold increase over previous years. On her worst morning, she had found 41 dead birds, including nine Blackburnian warblers, their migrations to the highland forests or shade-coffee plantations of South America cut way too short. Melissa posted a photo on social media of them lying in her hands above a sidewalk littered with other warblers; their orange throats were like a beacon from a more humane world.

It was a devastating count. On the best migration days, I've seen at most four or five. We have our favorites, and the Blackburnian is mine. Some of my brightest memories feature it, from the pin oaks of Lookout Hill to the gardens at the Jamaica Bay Wildlife Refuge to several pine trees at Green-Wood.

Forty-one dead birds may sound like a lot, but for Melissa, it was nowhere near the worst she had seen. For collision monitors, the chance of trauma is much higher during fall migration, especially in September. And I knew Melissa was still haunted by her worst day—a massacre she'd walked into almost two years before, on September 14, 2021, in her first season at the World Trade Center.

"As I exited the subway that morning," she later wrote in *Audubon*, "I saw dark shapes in every direction from half a block away, as if someone had strewn sacks of birds across the sidewalks. I'm not easily rattled, but for the first 10 minutes, all I could do was murmur, 'Oh my god,' as my trembling hands scooped up carcasses."

Some birds had struck the WTC buildings before dawn, but more crashed into windows as Melissa gathered up the tiny bodies. She was only able to assess the total damage later, once she got home, but she collected 229 dead birds and 29 with injuries. When a custodian at One WTC told her he hadn't seen many dead birds, she invited him to look up—there were 40 birds lying prone on a glass awning above them. Shocked strangers dropped injured warblers in her lap. Others ran up asking for help. She handed two grocery bags packed with injured birds to the Wild Bird Fund's communications director, Catherine Quayle. Melissa told herself it was all too much for one person.

A warbler weighs less than half an ounce; Melissa's backpack weighed pounds. Back at her apartment, she locked herself in the bathroom and laid its contents on parchment paper. It took her an hour to sort through all the birds. Row after row of warblers: black-and-whites, ovenbirds, common yellowthroats, redstarts, parulas. Melissa got permission from NYC Bird Alliance to post about it on Twitter, and her story made headlines in news outlets around the world, from the *New York Post* and NPR to *The Guardian*.

Afterward, Project Safe Flight's volunteers more than quadrupled, and a local law was passed that required city-owned buildings to turn off their overnight lights during spring and fall migration. "A little trauma for me brought a lot of awareness to the issue," Melissa told me matter-of-factly. But privately owned buildings like the World Trade Center continued to be exempt.

Why had this massacre happened? In short, the answer was bad weather and light. Migration experts like Andrew Farnsworth, the director of BirdCast, believed that an overnight storm had forced birds to fly beneath a low cloud ceiling, and the downtown lights had lured them into the canyons of glass. Melissa had witnessed what was the latest in a long line of New York City mass-collision events, which dated all the way back to the opening of the Statue of Liberty, the country's first electric lighthouse, in 1886, only four years after Thomas Edison delivered electric light to Manhattan.

Lady Liberty's illuminated torch, reaching 305 feet above sea level, immediately caused havoc for migrating birds. One stormy night in late August 1887, more than 1,400 were found dead, slumped around the statue's base. In May 1904, the naturalist William Beebe spent a foggy night inside the torch, and he described it later: "As the fog increased and condensed in the warmth to almost rain, birds began to pass through the periphery of illumination, then to strike intermittently against railing and glass.... They came in waves, a few scattered birds, then a mob, swift and dense as a swarm of golden bees." Some slammed on their "feather brakes" in time and clung to his coat, Beebe wrote, painting quite the picture. Once the fog lifted, things calmed down. But when he descended, he discovered 271 dead birds scattered on the ground.

"Thanks to the protests of bird lovers and especially half-dazzled pilots of passing vessels," Beebe noted, "the light of the statue was diminished and rendered indirect." But it became merely one point of light in a vast illuminated landscape that scrambled the celestial cues that nocturnal migrants use to fly through the night sky. The

Empire State Building opened in 1931, and its searchlight, too, spelled mass death for migrating birds. On the night of September 10, 1948, a heavy fog settled on the Hudson north of the city, and the Empire State's illuminated upper floors pulled birds toward the skyscraper. Newspapers reported that hundreds crashed into it and plummeted to setbacks or sidewalks. Many that survived the fall were run over by passing cars. Pedestrians carried home injured birds or brought them to restaurants, where they thought they could be nursed and fed. Further reports of mass collisions at the Empire State followed in October 1954 and September 1970.

"Manhattan can be a haven for migrating birds; it can also be a menace," says the 1966 book *Enjoying Birds Around New York City*, "for on certain foggy nights in autumn, when a sudden lowering of the ceiling and following winds combine, our tallest buildings take a toll of landbirds by the hundreds."

Looking back on them, what all these events had in common were bright lights, bad weather, and low clouds during a large pulse of migration.

Scientists still aren't sure why nocturnal migrants are attracted to artificial light, but they are, and the effect seems to be like what can happen to a person walking through Times Square: sensory overload. And today, there's no escape. During fall migration, birds flying south out of the forests of New England and southern Canada can see New York City from about 125 miles away, according to research by a team led by the University of Delaware's Jeff Buler, who noted that essentially "there is no place in the northeastern United States where they can't see the sky glow of a city." While the top 125 US cities account for about 2 percent of the country's land area, they emit more than 35 percent of its total light radiance, per one recent study. Sky glow is growing too, at an annual rate of over 10 percent in North America.

If numbers are your thing, then fall migration in New York is the best time for birding. While around five million birds cross the city in spring, roughly four times more pass through in the fall. Scientists point to at least two reasons for this. In the spring, the jet stream that flows up from the Gulf of Mexico supports an incredible movement of birds up the center of the country, but in the fall, the continent's prevailing winds shift easterly, so birds returning south compensate by tacking that direction, often lending a clockwise loop to their migrations. Another reason is that the mass of migrants now swells with the fresh young embarking on their first migration; for most species, the juveniles go solo, led south by their genes alone. For New York City, the Atlantic coast acts as a geographic barrier too, and birds tend to pile up and wait for a proper tailwind to continue going. Blackpoll warblers, for instance, which can arrive from as far west as Alaska, will fly out over the ocean and not rest until they reach South America three days later.

But artificial light is changing these ancient pathways. "Were you to look at barriers to movement, you might think an ocean or the Gulf of Mexico are ecological barriers, but, no, birds fly over them all the time, though there are conditions where they can't," Farnsworth told me. "But human-created barriers like light pollution may be a more challenging and more complex barrier to bird movement than anything ecological."

And where's the most light pollution? Cities, of course. According to the latest radar ornithology, sky glow is a top predictor of the density of birds at migration stopovers. They're being pulled toward the light—and thus cities—like moths to a flame. It's a reminder that the hard work of protecting and restoring urban parks is of the utmost importance; those stopovers are like gas stations along a continental highway for the billions of birds traveling between their breeding and wintering grounds. Without them, cities covered in glass and concrete have the potential to become—if they aren't already—what scientists call "ecological traps."

And as for traps, well, I was about to encounter one of the strongest.

TRIBUTE IN LIGHT debuted on the six-month anniversary of 9/11. Eighty-eight 7,000-watt xenon light bulbs were arranged in two 48-foot squares that, according to its organizer, the Municipal Art Society, echoed "the shape and orientation of the Twin Towers." Visible from 60 miles away, the shafts of light were the strongest ever projected into the night sky, and they stayed on for a week. Much of downtown was fenced off that March, so Andrew Farnsworth, Project Safe Flight founder Rebekah Creshkoff, and a few others from NYC Bird Alliance watched from afar, looking for any sign of birds in trouble.

When the display returned for the one-year anniversary, in September 2002, they were allowed onto the parking garage at the beams' base to observe. Since the tribute fell during the peak of fall songbird migration, they didn't know what to expect. "For all we knew, birds could've started falling from the sky and needed rescuing," Creshkoff told me. She expressed her concern to the organizers, but as she recalled, the event's producer, Michael Ahern, mockingly asked her, "So where are all the dead birds?" Shunted to the corner of the garage, Creshkoff said she could feel the hostility from members of the Municipal Art Society and Ahern's production company.

In a conversation about how to honor the dead, there was no place for birds. Afterward, an impasse set in. In 2004, northerly winds brought a wave of migration, the first to fall during Tribute in Light. While visiting friends in Greenwich Village, Creshkoff gazed downtown and saw what looked to be thousands of birds swirling in the beams. She felt ill, and had to bite her tongue when she overheard an onlooker say, "It's so pretty. These are the spirits of the dead souls."

In 2007, Creshkoff urged Glenn Phillips, NYC Bird Alliance's new executive director, to convince the organizers to change the protocols. They needed to turn off the beams on nights like that, Creshkoff said. Phillips agreed. But when? How often? What rules should be in place?

With radar ornithology in its early days, understanding the effects of artificial light on bird migration was still something of a mystery. So Phillips sought feedback from the likes of Andrew Farnsworth and Susan Elbin and presented a protocol to the Municipal Art Society and Michael Ahern. It went like this: When a thousand birds were observed in the beams, or some number of them were clearly in danger, they would request a 20-minute shutoff. To his surprise, Phillips received no pushback. By then, emotions had cooled.

Later, researchers—including Farnsworth, Elbin, Kyle Horton, and Benjamin Van Doren—used radar to study the impact of Tribute in Light. And it was extreme. The peak densities of birds were sometimes 150 times higher than normal, they found. Between 2010 and 2016, 1.1 million birds, mainly passerines, changed their flight paths because of the lights. The radar highlighted a major point, though: Once the beams were shut off, the birds scattered.

AROUND SIX ON the night of September 11, 2023, I watched from my apartment as sinister gray clouds let loose a downpour that turned streets into rivers. I thought Dustin Partridge's wish was about to come true. But the rain passed quickly, and as night fell, the winds shifted to the north. The radar showed birds arrowing our way.

I exited the subway in Manhattan at Trinity Place and Rector Street a little before 10. Clouds hung low like a drop ceiling. I looked for the Tribute in Light beams. They pierced the mist above the parking garage and formed a shelf of light beneath the clouds. Circling in them, twinkling, flying erratically, were lots of insects. Hundreds, maybe a thousand of them. A biker gang roared north on Trinity toward the World Trade Center—was this part of the tribute?—as dozens of tourists took selfies in a little triangular park. An ice cream truck idled there.

When I reached the garage, the atmosphere was tense. People crisscrossed the roof, spoke hurriedly, and wore fraught expressions. I saw Partridge pacing, the color drained from his face. "We have to turn off the beams," I overheard him say.

Then it hit me: *Those aren't insects. They're birds.*

They were flying erratically, like insects, because they were confused. Forced low by the clouds, they didn't know which way to go. Most were warblers—or specks of warblers, to my naked eye—and they called to each other like soft rain falling on a roof. Some dropped within the beams, visibly tiring, and their calls grew louder and more frequent as the pileup grew.

Partridge went to speak to the tribute's director. Word began to spread that the beams were going to be shut off. From what I could gather, the director asked Partridge if he *really* thought they should turn off the lights when close to a million people were watching. Partridge said he wasn't making the request lightly. At 9:56, they began going dark one block at a time, a process that took five minutes. The birds quit calling. It was the earliest shutoff in the 22-year history of Tribute in Light, and it wouldn't be the last.

My volunteer shift was about to start, but for the moment there were no birds visible enough to tally. I rolled out a picnic blanket in the corner of the roof beneath the north beam and prepared for a long night. A colleague of Partridge's named Katherine Chen, who works closely on Project Safe Flight, walked by holding a brown paper bag. Inside was an early victim: a black-and-white warbler, concussed but alive, that Farnsworth had scooped up after it crashed into an 80-story curved-glass tower. That luxury apartment building at 50 West Street practically touched the north beam.

At 10:12, the lights began to return one by one, short of the full 20-minute shutoff. Several hundred songbirds were instantly drawn in, and while calling loudly they flew at cross-purposes, like shooting stars. I saw several birds crash into 50 West as they attempted to land on its windows.

"It looks like it's going to happen again," an anxious Partridge said to me and my volunteer partner for the next two hours, actor and birder Lili Taylor. She'd done this shift in the past, but it had never been this bad, she said.

We did our count—of birds visible near the beams—and it came close to the thousand-bird threshold. Our next count would be in 20 minutes; that was part of the protocol.

Flight calls rained down, and I wondered why. I later found out from Farnsworth that birds were seeking information on how to find a path through the traffic, like honking at a driver encroaching on your lane. Calling begat more calling, which pulled in more birds, and added to their extreme agitation. I watched a succession of small birds drop inside a beam, finally claw their way out, then return to the trap. It felt like watching a horror film, I said, with the slasher hiding behind the bedroom door.

Until the next count, I decided to focus on individual birds as they tried to escape. It was nearly impossible for me to identify their species only with my binoculars. Unlike others on the roof, I didn't have a camera, nor did I possess anything like the identification chops of Andrew Farnsworth or Doug Gochfeld. Their expertise drew from years of watching morning flight, using shape and tail pattern and flight calls to make split-second IDs. There were exceptions, however. I followed one tiny bird, spotlit in its descent through the beam, and could tell it was a magnolia warbler because of its yellow body and its white tail with a black tip. No other warbler looks like that from below. I watched as it flew out of the beam and almost brushed the side of 50 West, then turned north toward the World Trade Center. I cheered inside, but I knew more danger waited around the corner. How cruel that these birds had all but safely made it off Manhattan. This was the southern tip.

I'd been focused on the birds, but my attention turned to insects when a beautiful brown moth landed beside my blanket. A cabbage looper, according to iNaturalist. Like the monarch butterfly, it migrates in groups from Canada to Mexico. "Fly away, will you?" I whispered.

When I looked back up, I now saw moths plunging to their death and clouds of spotted lanternflies exploding like starbursts on the smoking-hot glass of the xenon light bulbs that produce the beams. A short, mustachioed man in a denim jacket circled the bulbs and wiped the glass with a small bristle brush.

I looked around for sympathetic faces. Five members of the event crew were sitting in plastic chairs in the center of the roof, surrounded by American flags. They wore leather jackets with FDNY logos on them. Had the Dead Bug Sweeper, I wondered, drawn the short straw? I wanted to ask these men what they thought of all this.

In that moment, the whole display felt deeply wrong to me, and totally unnecessary. Perhaps it's hard for some to understand, but I was in despair over what I took to be senseless harm to birds that were already facing enough hazards on their journeys.

Then the lights went off for a second time. Again, the birds flew off, their calls evaporating into the night. It was only 10:40. I stood up and walked around. Jupiter shone brightly in the southern sky. Raising my binoculars, I could see four of its moons. I also noticed all the light spilling out of empty office buildings. I marveled at its power; I didn't even need a flashlight to read my notebook. The Tribute in Light was essentially a one-off—though the beams are tested in the days leading up to it—but the city's vast field of light every night pulls in birds, and many collide with buildings then or the next day.

Others I'd gotten to know over the past year began to arrive for their volunteer shift or simply to watch: Shannon Curley, José Ramírez-Garofalo, Junko Suzuki. Curley had placed a thermal camera on the roof to film how birds responded to the lights going dark. She knew they dispersed, but just how quickly?

I watched some of her footage later. In one clip, the preshutoff scene is patternless, with birds erratically swerving like they're bouncing off an invisible force field. A *normal* flight pattern would appear much slower and often unidirectional, Curley told me. As the shutoff begins, however, their flight paths straighten and they speed away. Their migration in the night sky, she said, should look like snowflakes drifting in the wind.

This was her third year on the roof. Her father, Michael Edward Curley, had spent 25 years as a firefighter in Brooklyn's Engine Company 204, and she was wearing his old FDNY sweater. Her feelings, I'd learned, were more complex than my simple anger.

"I understand the value of Tribute in Light, and it makes me feel emotionally connected to my father," she said. "But then I also feel this visceral reaction from seeing its impact on the birds."

Curley's father wasn't stationed at his firehouse when the Twin Towers were hit. His company rushed to the scene, and the crew took shelter in a nearby parking garage when the towers collapsed, destroying their truck. Though his company had been spared, 343 members of the New York City Fire Department died that day. Curley still remembers her father breaking down and weeping at their Long Island home that night. All he could say was, "I lost so many friends." It was the first time she'd seen her father cry.

A former US Army paratrooper, he was beloved by his fellow firefighters, and it was said that he could get his company water from the desert if it meant putting out a fire. In the weeks after 9/11, he picked through the rubble of Ground Zero and attended many funerals. He became withdrawn, less jovial, more solemn, Shannon Curley remembers. To her, he suffered in silence.

Like many 9/11 first responders, he developed chronic obstructive pulmonary disease (COPD) and dementia. In 2020, he died at the age of 71, a couple months after his daughter earned her PhD. Though his memory was failing, he'd greeted her as "Dr. Curley."

The lights came back on at 11:02, and again the beams filled with birds. Dustin Partridge walked by, and we watched the glass terror at 50 West Street. It made for painful viewing, because we knew the birds couldn't get relief until more were sucked in. Sitting on a yoga mat next to me, Lili Taylor said, "This *is* like a horror movie." Having featured in several, I figured she would know.

We noticed birds flying through a gap near the top of the tower, onto what we imagined was a rooftop observatory. We wondered if they were slumped with exhaustion up there or crashing into glass railings. "We have to shut it down again," Partridge said, walking off. It was now 11:30, and about 15 minutes later, they did, for the third time. Eight was the record, and it looked within reach.

We could feel the wind coming a little from the west now, which meant a new batch of migrants was picking up and would probably drift this way. I sagged on my blanket. But soon I noticed a change. Small groups were forcing their way out of the beams. Were they working together? Were they helped by a stronger tailwind? They were flying higher now, and I heard fewer flight calls.

And then the pizza arrived. Twenty people remained, and the speed with which that pizza was devoured was only matched by a peregrine falcon that a little later appeared in the beams like a spectral demon and made several high-speed passes at songbirds. I'd heard this happened at Tribute in Light, but seeing it was shocking.

After a lull, the number of birds in the beams again reached the danger zone. Some of the later migrants must have arrived, and I noticed Farnsworth and Partridge engaged in a tense conversation. At 2:59 in the morning, the beams went off for the fourth—and final—time.

I felt dazed. I'd seen close to 10,000 birds in five hours and gotten to watch nocturnal migration up close, which was extraordinary. But because of the extreme light, it was a twisted version of what it should have been. Birds are subjected to experiments in the lab all the time, but this was the real world. I didn't like it, but I recognized the importance of working with the memorial's organizers to monitor the effects of light on birds and allow them safe passage at critical times.

I soon packed my things and prepared to meet Melissa Breyer. People wished me luck. Farnsworth had been in touch with her the day before, and he spoke about her warmly, as did others. They valued her contribution and they knew how few people could handle its trauma.

Partridge's rough night was nearly over. Sitting in a beach chair now, he anticipated a morning of collisions. "We haven't had a strong migration like this so far this season..." His voice trailed off. The rest I knew.

I left the garage a few minutes after 4:30. Dead spotted lanternflies carpeted the roof. I tried not to think about what was going to happen next. More death, that was for sure. *What kind of a city is this?* I thought. I didn't want to answer.

ONE WTC LOOKED like something out of *Blade Runner*. In the dark sky, its upper half was shrouded in fog, and light spilled out of most floors. While I looked around for Melissa, a security guard cleared the metal barricades still in place from the previous day's ceremony at

Ground Zero. That was the only sound for minutes: metal scraping on pavement.

A little after five, I saw someone hurrying to the east facade. It could only be one person. "Good *morning*," Melissa called over to me. I smiled. Given my trepidation that we were about to find lots of dead birds, her lightheartedness eased the tension.

As I reached her, Melissa was lifting a dead black-and-white warbler off the plaza. Its glass entrance was like a lighthouse, and my eyes burned while staring at it. The warbler looked so out of place among the glass and stone, like a prop left there.

We began Melissa's Project Safe Flight loop—past the new Perelman Performing Arts Center, a glowing cube of blue and pink lights, past Calatrava's wild Oculus, north to 7 WTC, south to 3 WTC and 4 WTC. Strangely, we found nothing, and it dawned on us that there wouldn't be a catastrophe today.

We sat on a bench outside the 9/11 memorial grove, and I took a moment to vent about what I'd witnessed at Tribute in Light. I asked, I suppose naïvely, why we honor the dead by killing things. Melissa's face tightened. "I used to think the tribute was lovely," she said. "Now I think it's a death trap."

She hadn't slept much, but I sensed a greater weariness. We were coming up on the second anniversary of the mass-collision event she'd become associated with, but today she didn't want to say much about it. She instead spoke about the legacy of capitalism and colonialism on the city, the way our building choices drive out nature, the fact that birds can't change their migration routes. "It's like it doesn't matter what was here before—we're going to take it over and use it for our own good," she said. "Birds have been flying through here for millennia. I get so many benefits from living in the city, but I ask myself, How can we benefit at such great expense to the natural world?"

The sky cleared just after six and suddenly a flock of warblers flitted past us through the grove's skinny oaks, too quick to focus on. "I guess they're coming in!" Melissa said. We followed them toward One WTC, passing a colleague from her day job on the way. Having been up almost 24 hours by then, I'd forgotten it was a workday. Melissa said hello to the woman, but her response was a puzzled look. Melissa shrugged back and said, "Birds."

Across from One WTC, we found a stunned ovenbird at the side of the road. It took Melissa about three minutes to catch the bird. It was awful watching this little warbler—too injured to manage its usual walk—muster only some scoots.

Then Melissa noticed, in her peripheral vision, a small body about 50 feet away. Even from that distance, she could tell it was a common yellowthroat: a female, pale yellow and brown, without the male's Zorro mask. She was dead. We found her splayed out in a puddle, and in the water was a reflection of One WTC's dark glass wall touching the blue sky. Melissa called the photo she took *Portrait of a dead bird and the building that killed it.*

Melissa kept circling those buildings, but I took the subway home and went right to bed. Closing my eyes, I saw specks of birds like stars in twin columns of light, and I fell asleep to the steady patter of flight calls.

THE DISASTER I had feared happened three weeks later. Only I didn't see it, nor did anyone else in New York. It happened in Chicago.

On an early October night, it was as if the northern forests emptied of their songbirds all at once. Making up for lost time, millions of them raced ahead of a cold front. Coming toward them from the other direction, however, was a heavy rainstorm, and they slammed into it, grounded. Even for nonbirders, the scenes around Chicago were impossible to miss.

Tens of thousands of birds *per hour*, most of them warblers, poured through the city's waterfront parks and into its leafy neighborhoods. The river was so thick that the best strategy to approximate a count was to estimate the rate of passage—in some places it was 2,000 birds a minute. Anywhere would do for a short break for these birds—lawns, alleyways, street trees, telephone wires. Birders reached for words to describe a spectacle they had never seen before and expected never to see again: *incredible, overwhelming, utter madness, chaos, mind-blowing.*

Many birds angled toward downtown, and everyone knew what that meant. The worst scene was at Chicago's convention center, the McCormick Place Lakeside Center. As monitors scooped up hundreds of bodies, still more crashed into the low facades above them. It was as if the birds were still on a kind of autopilot, one observer recalled; they were still taking advantage of the excellent tailwind. More than a thousand birds of some 40 species were collected there, and half were palm warblers and yellow-rumped warblers, two species that breed in Canada's bogs and conifer forests. This made international news—something Melissa Breyer was familiar with.

I happened to be on the phone with Andrew Farnsworth that morning, and he apologized for having to cut short our conversation. That afternoon, he and his colleague Benjamin Van Doren published a story on BirdCast's website, using observations, radar, and weather maps to describe what had happened in Chicago. Their post began and ended with a plea to turn off nonessential lights during migration and to treat windows with bird-friendly materials. McCormick Place hadn't done either.

In a 2019 study, Farnsworth and colleagues ranked Chicago as the country's most dangerous city for migrating birds. (Houston and Dallas were next; New York was ranked fifth for fall migration.) Location is the main reason, since the middle of the country witnesses the greatest number of migrants. On top of that, in downtown

Chicago there's a staggering concentration of glass buildings on Lake Michigan, which is a bottleneck for migrating birds. In 2020, Chicago approved an ordinance to encourage bird-friendly design, but compliance was voluntary.

McCormick Place was probably the deadliest building in North America for birds. Prior to the events of that October 2023 morning, scientists from the Field Museum of Natural History had picked up well over 40,000 dead birds there since 1978. And the convention center had, like Tribute in Light, been used to study the effects of artificial light on migratory birds. Using decades of records on both its collisions and its lighting, researchers found that turning off the lights there would reduce deaths by about 60 percent. In other words, what had happened that morning was entirely predictable—and avoidable.

Melissa saw parallels between the McCormick Center and One WTC, a building whose management, she thought, dug their heels in after being shamed in the press. The more publicity they got, the faster they tried to sweep the dead birds on their sidewalks away. She was emphasizing the need for a citywide lights-out bill in New York. Though horrifying, I wondered whether the tragedy in Chicago was so visible that it could be a turning point for the cause in New York City, and maybe all over the US.

Indeed, soon after, Dustin Partridge secured a pledge from the management of Brookfield Place in Lower Manhattan—one of Project Safe Flight's original monitoring locations—to install bird-friendly film on its large glass atrium. And then Circa, the apartment building on Central Park that years ago pulled Melissa into Project Safe Flight, paid $60,000 to retrofit its interior courtyard—the site of 90 percent of its collisions. Given the bad publicity Circa had received, residents had started to worry that their apartments would lose value. Circa's condo board worked with Partridge and architect Dan Piselli on the retrofit, and when I spoke with Piselli, he told me he hoped they would expand coverage to the rest of the building, including its park-facing front. Around the same time, the first apartment buildings under Local Law 15, New York's bird-safe requirement, were finally going on the market.

*Some things are no longer easily swept up*, I thought. But the biggest surprise would follow. Less than a year later, McCormick Place installed at a cost of $1.2 million bird-safe film on its glass and automatic shades that could help curb its nighttime glow. We went from despair to elation: I couldn't remember a better piece of news in all my years of birding.

The next fall, when monitors made their normal rounds of the convention center, they found only 18 dead birds.

CHAPTER 13

# Hawk Watch

The first morning of fall started with a bang. Thunder rumbled, lightning split several trees on my block, and wind sent the rain sideways. Summer didn't want to go quietly. But the storm left quickly, like the memory of a dream upon waking. By the afternoon, it felt like an entirely different day. The wind swung out of the northwest and swept the sky clear, sucking out the humidity and bringing clarity to the newly crisp air. A cold front brings birds into New York, so I knew anything was possible.

I went to Green-Wood with two friends I wanted to introduce to birding. They were eager to see what the fuss was about, so I'd brought them binoculars. The cemetery was deserted when we arrived. We crossed the damp, blustery ground to the crest of Ocean Hill. I found great pleasure in picking out my apartment from the rows of brick buildings beyond the cemetery gates. Home for me and thousands of other people—but for birds it was a great gray chasm to cross, with little refuge.

"What are those?" one friend asked, pointing to a group of five long-winged silhouettes flying erratically toward us.

"Common nighthawks!" I yelled.

Nighthawks aren't hawks at all, but part of a family of insect eaters known as nightjars. They also typically appear at dusk or dawn;

at least that's been my experience. But sunset was an hour and a half away. I looked to my right, to the base of the hill, and framed by a backdrop of sparse but active clouds, a stream of them flowed south. I wasn't used to seeing them in such sharp focus. Their flight was stiff but smooth, punctuated by quick and unpredictable turns, like boomerangs carving the sky. Behind the bend of their long wings was a white slash. They looked ancient and mysterious, like winged messengers out of Tolkien, with mothlike patterning and small bills that opened to bizarrely large mouths. Indeed, fossils of common nighthawks close to 400,000 years old have been unearthed across the continent.

The most nighthawks I'd seen before were a few dozen in late August or early September hawking insects in the twilight of Prospect Park's Nethermead. This end-of-summer storm followed by northwest winds seemed to be telling the stragglers to get moving. And they had a long trip ahead, to South America, one of the longest migrations of any bird that breeds this side of the equator.

For another half hour, the surge continued, with at least 50 common nighthawks coming across. When the pace slowed, we hurried down the hill. An evening concert was about to take place there, in the cemetery's catacombs, but I stood around for another few minutes. Dodging equipment vans, I watched 15 more nighthawks slip overhead, low enough to see their white throats and the very fine barring on their bodies and underwings. The females, more buffy than the males, glimmered in the golden light.

Walking out, I gleefully rambled to my friends about the rareness of what we had just seen. I used to hear stories from older birders about the nighthawks that swarmed over the cemetery on nights like this—one of the city's migration spectacles. I didn't think it still happened. Chance was the drug of birding, I said, bringing the ecstasy of the unexpected encounter.

Leaving behind Green-Wood's grand Gothic entrance, we

went to a nearby tavern called Sea Witch. It felt like walking into a submarine—there was a fish tank behind the bar, and the low-ceilinged space was five times as long as it was wide. This felt appropriate as we went into the tree-lined backyard. The wind had picked up again, shaking paper-thin leaves turned yellow after a dry summer. I pulled on a jacket and wondered what the weather might surprise us with tomorrow.

I WOKE UP early the next morning, unable to sleep well. The nighthawks were still on my mind, as was the chance of witnessing another special migration event. I walked into Prospect Park around seven, the sun barely visible in the eastern sky, wind raking the treetops. A lonely chimney swift twittered overhead. For a while, I listened to the whole scene: Drivers honking needlessly on Parkside Avenue. Cyclists carrying on conversations in high-speed pelotons around the park drive. The engine roar of airplanes every few minutes. Then I shut it out without much effort and began looking for small things moving.

Great gusts hid the warblers in my midst. I heard their high-pitched calls, but it was only when the wind calmed for a fleeting second that I could see a flock of five or 10 at a time shoot from one tree into another, like straphangers racing into a subway car as the doors close. I watched a yellow warbler flatten itself on a branch and puff out its feathers for warmth. Every moment like this was a lost chance to rebuild its fat reserves after an overnight flight. I was on the south side of the park, meaning these birds were probably overshoots. They had found themselves blown south of here at daybreak and had quickly doubled back to the park.

I looked for a sunny patch, for me and the birds, and ran into three birding friends. We found, halfway up a large oak, a sunlit clump of pale-green leaves. Warblers fed feverishly in that tiny patch, catching insects stirred up by the warmth, challenging our identifications with the muted, variable plumages they had molted into after the breeding season. A black-throated green warbler, its black throat nearly complete, popped its yellow face out of the foliage. But a second one appeared showing only a five-o'clock shadow. Blackpoll warblers, streaky and greenish, looked nothing like they do in the spring, when the black cap of the males sits low over their eyes. Northern parulas, smaller still, with much less distance to cover in migration than the blackpolls, darted through the canopy. The wind whistled around us. "Fall came in not playing!" shouted my friend Chaz Faxton, a longtime bartender and Brooklyn native.

We sat on a bench as the sun worked more of its magic. We zeroed in on a black cherry tree and watched several warbler flocks rush through. A blue-headed vireo pulled up the rear and looked around for a few seconds, as vireos do, like a wise elder surrounded by hyperactive kids. I have a soft spot for this bird—it was the first I was able to identify on my own, flipping through my Peterson Field Guide until I found its white spectacles on a steel-blue head. "You could shoot a basketball through that eye-ring," Chaz observed.

Briefly, the talk turned away from birds. Chaz told me his idea for a science-fiction novel called *Catharsis*. The premise is that at 18 you enter "catharsis" and live in a state suspended from aging for the next 32 years. At 50, your teenage body reenters the flow of time, and you live out the rest of your life buoyed by the wisdom you gained during that period of carefree experimentation.

I remembered that Chaz was two years short of 50. I told him the question that birders would ask: Do you get to keep the birds you saw in catharsis on your life list?

AT THE SAME time, Junko Suzuki, whom I first met on Central Park's Christmas Bird Count in 2022, waited for the bus at the crowded intersection of 125th Street and Lexington Avenue to take her across the Harlem River to Randall's Island. She had already spent an hour in Central Park and planned to return there in the afternoon, where she would hawk-watch from the stone terraces of Belvedere Castle, one of the park's famous landmarks. It was a custom of hers on fall migration days like this. But first, she was going to spend time at Randall's Island, studying a bird she had found two days earlier—a discovery that still struck her as unbelievable and which had drawn over a hundred birders to the island in pursuit of her quarry.

The bird was a buff-breasted sandpiper, and it was the first record in Manhattan (or New York County). There aren't many left in the world—estimates are under 60,000—from a population that once numbered in the hundreds of thousands or millions. Until the early 20th century, that is, when they were hunted to near extinction, often on their migration from the high Arctic tundra to the grasslands of Argentina.

While Junko waited, she thought back to her good luck the morning she'd found it. She had arrived early to Randall's Island for a Linnaean Society outing led by Andrew Farnsworth. She scouted the empty baseball fields at one corner of the island, watching double-crested cormorants circle overhead and a flock of starlings foraging in the dirt by home plate. Nothing unusual there. As she was about to walk onto the infield, she noticed out of the corner of her right eye a bird quietly feeding at the edge of the outfield grass. A small shorebird. But what kind? she asked herself.

She had tried to identify it as a common and familiar species, but she knew instantly it wasn't. She felt her heart beating. The so-called grasspipers, shorebirds that you might find foraging on a ballfield, were easy to tell apart. This one had delicate features: a dovelike round head and an innocent-looking face... a short bill... gold-yellow legs... tawny-buff scales on its crown and back... and, yes, a buffy front. If she was right, she would alert the various Manhattan birding networks, so she double-checked her field guide against all those field marks. But she already knew it was a buff-breasted sandpiper.

Afraid of flushing the bird, Junko had barely moved. As she typed out a message to the Manhattan rare bird alert GroupMe, the bird flew north toward the Bronx Kill, the narrow strait that separates Randall's Island from the South Bronx, and she lost sight of it in the bright morning sun. Two other birders hurried over. They looked around and relocated the bird one ballfield over, but it took off again and circled, landing on the exact same spot where Junko had first spotted it.

One by one, other participants in the Linnaean Society group had arrived at the field. Danger momentarily showed itself in the form of a peregrine falcon soaring high above. The sandpiper froze on the ground, becoming almost invisible. Farnsworth had said this was typical behavior for an open-ground specialist; flying out would make it an easy target for the peregrine. Three hours later, when the group returned after birding the rest of Randall's Island, the sandpiper was still foraging in the same area, with plenty of other birders watching and photographing it.

The bird had stuck around the next day, and now Junko was hoping it would stay a third. She was a thoughtful birder who liked to spend extra time with a bird she had already seen—a beautiful specimen, no doubt, like a buff-breasted sandpiper—so she could etch in her memory the finer details of its plumage and its behavior. There was only one problem: There was still no sign of the bus.

Junko had already waited 20 minutes, and it dawned on her that at this rate—it was now about 10:15—she might not make it back to Central Park until around one in the afternoon. She decided to turn away from Randall's Island and get a start on her hawk watch at the park.

ONCE SHE WAS back in Central Park, Junko felt a sense of reassurance. A cluster of 20 hawks flew low over the Ramble, and even before she reached higher ground to get a better view, she could tell they were broad-winged hawks, by their size and the way they grouped together. She walked quickly to Belvedere Castle to begin her count. On the way, she bumped into two birders who told her they were off to see the buff-breasted sandpiper. She laughed about it later. "Good luck," she wished them. As it happened, it was the sandpiper's final day on Randall's Island.

Broad-winged hawks are practically synonymous with hawk-watching in the eastern US, from Vermont's forested peaks to the coastal plain of Texas. Small, compact, and crow-sized, broad-wings are in the family of soaring hawks known as buteos—masters of wind and thermals, the uprising currents of warm air. In late August, broad-winged hawks clear out of eastern forests and migrate down the continent in astounding numbers: 10,000 in a single day at mountaintops across New England, 50,000 in a day at Great Lakes hawk-watch sites, 300,000 to 500,000 in a couple hours on the narrow plains of Corpus Christi or Veracruz. Save for a small wintertime population in southern Florida, the rest empty out of North America.

Big groups of broad-wings normally bypass New York City, since the birds steer clear of large bodies of water, which lack thermals. Instead, they stick to inland mountain ranges like the Appalachians, where updrafts provide an added lift. Occasionally, though, a wind that drives hard out of the northwest on select days in September will push them to the Atlantic coast, and the city's birding records show a handful of flights between 1,500 and 5,000 hawks, and once over 15,000.

In other words, a day like this one.

Hawk identification had always held a certain allure for Junko. When she was a relatively new birder, she joined veteran hawk-watchers at Belvedere Castle on an autumn day in 2003 or 2004. She had been a quick study in birding, but hawk-watching was mystifying to her. The others could identify specks in the sky as broad-wings or other hawks. *How could they possibly tell?* she'd asked herself. Rather than feeling discouraged, though, she grew fascinated. She was taken by one watcher's evocation of a sky full of broad-winged hawks, hundreds or thousands of them circling together in a kettle—called that because of its likeness to water boiling up in a pot. She bought books on identifying hawks in flight, studied their shapes and behaviors, and eagerly returned to Belvedere Castle during fall migration to apply what she had read and learned.

But her timing never seemed quite right. When large broad-winged hawk flights did occur, they seemed to always happen when she was at work. She would still race up to Central Park's Sheep Meadow on a lunch break and look to the sky, but that was never very successful. And once—a year before this, in fact—she and a few others had gone to Hook Mountain, a Palisades overlook a short distance up the Hudson. They'd expected to witness a great passage of broad-wings. They saw four. Meanwhile, she began to get reports from those who had stayed at Belvedere Castle of hundreds of them there. She kicked herself. She had missed her chance again. By the time her group made it back to Central Park, the migration was all but over; they saw 30 hawks bringing up the rear. She let others joke about it. To her, it was painful. After two decades, it started to feel like she might never witness a sky full of hawks.

Once Junko reached the castle this time, however, shortly after 11 in the morning, she could sense a much larger episode taking shape. Broad-wings are relatively late risers; they wait for the earth to warm so thermals can give them a lift. The first hawks she had seen over the Ramble were low, buffeted by the wind. It was still early; she knew more had to be coming.

She sat on the stone steps of the castle, facing north. Her view was panoramic, and she lined up her markers. The gray tower of Mount Sinai Hospital on the Upper East Side was the main one, since it sat on the southwesterly path that hawks often took flying over Manhattan in the fall. The Great Lawn stretched out below her. Whether or not you were a fan of cities, it was a spectacular view, she thought, but an unlikely place to watch hawks. Turning around to look above the tree line, she noted the tops of the supertall towers of Billionaires' Row that loom over the park.

Minutes later, several broad-wings came from south of the castle and banked past her right shoulder. That was an unusual path, she thought. Her guess was that the strong winds had pushed them east into Queens or to southern Manhattan, and they were struggling now to head west over the island. Inside the park, the wind dragged them closer to the ground than she had ever seen broad-winged hawks. They weren't specks. She marveled at their variable marking, the mix of adults and juveniles; in general, they were mostly clean and white below, like a fresh canvas.

Another 25 followed, then 30. She alerted other birders in the same chat where she had posted the buff-breasted sandpiper. Just before noon, over a hundred broad-wings emerged east of the castle, turned west, and formed a kettle, swirling up an invisible thermal. Several long lines appeared and gathered into still another kettle, and together they rose like a tornado.

The sky above her filled with hawks. "For the next four hours, they just kept coming and coming and coming," Junko told me later. Hearing her describe it, there was no mistaking the awe in her voice.

AS THE HAWKS continued to find each other and the thermals they needed to cross the landscape, birders sent messages of their own across the city and beyond. About 35 miles northeast of Belvedere Castle, in Greenwich, Connecticut, the official hawk counter at

Quaker Ridge cursed his luck. Sitting in an Adirondack chair in a grassy field, Harry Wales, a recent college graduate, could tell that the gusts were driving broad-wings away from his location and toward Long Island Sound, barely 10 miles away. Face to face with a large body of water, the hawks would hug the coast of the sound on its southward curve toward New York City. Wales sent a message to Rich Aracil, a Bronx birder who was the counter at Chestnut Ridge, six miles north of Greenwich, and told him it had been relatively slow for broad-wings at Quaker Ridge because of the strength of the wind. At this rate, Wales said, the hawks would continue to bypass them to the coast.

In his fourth season at Chestnut Ridge, Aracil knew there was some luck involved in predicting the flight path of broad-winged hawks—but once the birds have made their choice, they follow each other down that line as a kind of cohesive group in search of thermals. When Wales wrote to him, Aracil had already seen about 600 broad-wings pass Chestnut Ridge through the morning, but he knew a lot more were aiming toward the city. The night before, as I'd watched the trees shake in the back of that Brooklyn bar, Aracil was warning his fellow Bronx birders of the scenario that was currently playing out. And so just as the first broad-winged hawks were reaching Junko's watch at Central Park, he sent out another alert to his Bronx network. Hawks were coming their way.

Picking up the signal, Patrick Horan scrambled over to the parking lot of Orchard Beach, right on the sound in Pelham Bay Park. There used to be an official hawk watch there, and one September day in 1990, a day like this one, with northwest winds close to 20 miles per hour, over 15,500 broad-wings passed by. As Horan stepped out of his car, he saw a few kettles made up of almost 400 broad-wings drifting overhead. Several dozen hawks flew so low that bystanders watched without binoculars. A local television crew happened to be there on an entirely different assignment, but Horan, a Bronx native, set the scene for them. The wind is the key thing, he said. If it dropped below 10 miles per hour, then the hawks would flee the coast to the interior ridges. Horan had seen flights stop cold there when the wind died down.

There was no sign of that happening today. Back in Manhattan, the sky was dense with hawks—if you knew to look. Vicens Vila-Coury and Augie Kramer, two young scientists in the American Museum of Natural History's ornithology department, ate their lunch on the roof. They estimated 800 broad-winged hawks during their hour-long break by extrapolating the count of one bird-dense patch of sky to other bird-dense patches. Those were distant kettles—they also noticed hawks landing in the treetops of Central Park.

The pace was picking up. At Belvedere Castle, Junko was joined by several other birders, including Richard Lieberman, a friend and early mentor of hers. Lieberman had been there on Junko's first visit to a castle hawk watch. Though the experience had been intimidating, Lieberman himself was not. A longtime birder and native Upper East Sider, he had welcomed Junko and showed her around Central Park. Twenty years later, they now worked together to continue the effort Junko had started midmorning—to accurately count what was shaping up to be a once-in-a-decade event.

Standing on their overlook, they checked every direction, calling out groups of birds. Many hawks continued coming from the east, forming kettles and lines that tacked west toward the Watchung Mountains, the New Jersey ridges you can see from Battle Hill in Green-Wood Cemetery. Junko noted how the broad-wings would rise on bowed wings, higher and higher, after finding a thermal and then peel off together in long glides until the line of birds reached the next thermal. The formation reminded her of a very organized army. After her group had tallied more than 400 hawks in 30 minutes, Junko sent out her last alert at 1:42 p.m.

Shortly after, a Manhattan birder named Dale Dancis climbed to the roof of her apartment building at 70th Street and Broadway. Dancis saw that within the park, the line of hawks stretched about 20 blocks, from the castle south to 59th Street. Over the course of about 20 minutes, the line started moving west across the island and over the Hudson to New Jersey. Bundled in a coat and scarf, Dancis stayed up there for three hours. Having visited Pennsylvania's famous Hawk Mountain in the past, she still called this her best day of hawk-watching. "There, you have to schlep all the way up the hill and sit on those rocks," she said.

Seeing the reports, Andrew Farnsworth began to piece it all together at his East Side apartment. In fact, the hawks' flight path, he knew from past experience—coming from the east, going west to New Jersey—was the typical pattern on big days in Manhattan. Hawks were blown down to the Bronx and sometimes across Long Island Sound into Queens; fighting the wind, they worked hard to fly back into Manhattan, rather than risk drifting out to sea. Farnsworth pulled up the weather radar on his computer and noted large green and red blobs—those were kettles of birds in transit from 1,000 to 2,500 feet above the ground. Many were thus beyond our vision from down on the grass and asphalt.

At the time I was unaware of the wildlife drama unfolding around the city. Though I'd been in Prospect Park early that morning, I'd left to meet a friend for lunch in Manhattan and I hadn't checked any birding alerts. The wind being what it was, though, I decided on my trip home to get off the subway at Prospect Park. I had my binoculars with me.

I exited the station around three, and the open sky of the park felt like a godsend. Looking up, I noticed two red-tailed hawks soaring and, above them, several smaller buteos—broad-winged hawks! Unlike the red-tails, the broad-wings had to rely on quick, stiff wing-beats to stay aloft. I hurried over to the south end of the Nethermead and planted myself there, with a wide view of the sky. Over the next hour, about 35 hawks managed the fierce wind by all manner of tucks, dives, glides, and soars. And when I raised my binoculars to what seemed like empty sky, I noticed numerous dots, at least 50 of them, spinning higher and higher, like a cyclone.

Brooklyn birders were now sending alerts on their own WhatsApp group: "Seeing a huge kettle, going over Prospect Park viewed from my roof." "There is currently a kettle of at least 100 high up over Green-Wood, almost certainly more. Wherever you are, get outside and look at the sky!"

The first broad-wings I'd seen on the Nethermead were almost all adults, but as sunset approached, the makeup had changed to almost all juveniles. The soft light streamed through the tops of their flight feathers, lending a translucent appearance from below. Though perhaps hundreds of hawks were still drifting southwest, I could tell that the thermals were beginning to taper off. Everywhere I turned, hawks were coursing low over the trees, looking for nighttime roosts. Challenged by the wind, landing in an urban park—this was a major test of migration, I thought, and it brought home why even for birds of prey, most juveniles don't survive their first year.

The smell of charcoal from a few barbecues hung in the air as I made my way out of the park. But I couldn't let go. Standing on the sidewalk, I continued raising my binoculars to the sky every few seconds, hoping to find more dots. I wanted to get a true sense of the scale—the urge to count was always there. I caught several double takes from people who must have wondered what I was watching. To them, the sky was empty. I doubt they would've believed me if I said you could see hundreds or thousands of hawks in New York City. Hard as it was to pull myself away, I reminded myself that the hawks would leave their roosts tomorrow. I would see them again.

Junko left Central Park at five. She hadn't eaten anything all afternoon. A sky full of hawks had proved to be more overwhelming than she'd imagined. She was spent. Hers was the longest hawk watch anywhere in the city, and alone in her apartment, she totaled her numbers: 3,256. But she believed this was an undercount. Farnsworth, for his part, estimated from the radar that perhaps as many as 6,000 hawks had passed through.

*There is still mystery in this city,* I thought, *even if it is in the sky.*

CHAPTER 14

# Rarities

If New York has taught me anything, it's that you can witness migration from almost anywhere here. Just look up, as Andrew Farnsworth once told me.

I biked to Green-Wood the morning after the great broad-winged hawk flight. In the dawn light, I pedaled quickly uphill, and above me, following the same path, were dozens of warblers flying barely higher than a six-story building. They were redirecting north to the cemetery; morning flight, the phenomenon that had captivated me in the spring, was happening right outside my apartment. The birds must've passed the cemetery's tall trees a short while earlier and now, seeing only asphalt and concrete, decided to backtrack.

When I pulled up to the cemetery, at least 10 warblers were clinging to the first tree inside its wrought-iron fence. Outside it was the concrete lip of the neighborhood. I thought of the scarlet tanager I'd seen at Breezy Point in May, clinging to almost the westernmost shrub in all of Long Island. I felt I could relate. After a summer of fire, I was also seeking a grip on this unstable planet. I sought reassurance in the presence of bigness. Junko's experience reminded me that, despite it all, there are still large numbers of birds out there. But they need our help.

The world may be coming unstuck, but I want to believe its natural processes are still working. If I feel encouragement, it is in the ability of birds to adapt to upheaval—to live, however dangerously, alongside humans. I saw it in Flaco, and I see it in peregrine falcons, ravens, red-tailed hawks, and, yes, starlings and house sparrows, which make their nests on buildings, bridges, and churches—an environment we built. (A diet of rats and pigeons may be satisfactory for those birds of prey, but the least we can do is make that diet not toxic for them.) I see it in the migrating birds that sweep across the city, searching out green islands, driving—against the odds—to keep up with spring. I see it in the grassland specialists and wading birds that move into restored or reclaimed landscapes, like capped landfills, marsh islands, and a less-polluted river. I also see how some people give so much of themselves to help—collision monitors, beach patrollers, habitat managers. We see New York as a bird city, and I hope one day more allies will materialize.

At times, I find it easy to slip into despondency. Then I think of Doug Gochfeld's approach, which is proactive. To him, finding migration stopovers, keeping records, and documenting changes in the abundance and ranges of different species are ways to sound the environmental alarm. Data matters. It was from the long-term records of hawk watches, after all, that Rachel Carson learned of steep declines in the populations of peregrines, ospreys, and bald eagles. I read a journal article Doug wrote, in which he asked New York birders to predict the newest species to be found in the state, and he began with a quote from Galadriel, Tolkien's long-memoried elf: "The world is changed. I feel it in the water. I feel it in the earth. I smell it in the air."

"Where the changed world is perhaps most evident is in nature, and this is one of the reasons that birding has a never-ending appeal," Doug wrote. "As things change, birds adapt in both behavior and distribution, and there are forever new layers to peel back, and new things to discover and contemplate."

I'm not one for fantasy, but perhaps Doug's reach for it is a way of processing all the alarming changes happening to the earth—to us, to birds, to everything in it. It's a reminder to broaden our imaginations. Though I tend to view the changes wrought by humans pessimistically, change is the vehicle of life. Nothing is static. In cities especially, a strange alchemy plays out between the very concrete designs of humans and the forces of nature.

SEARCHING FOR THAT alchemy brought me to the North Channel Bridge parking lot on Rulers Bar Hassock on Jamaica Bay. Right around sunrise, warblers started taking off from a line of stubby trees next to the asphalt pad. A tiny songbird shot over my head, followed by two flocks of five. I laughed, unsure where to look. Then another 10! They bunched together, rising and calling against the clear sky. The wind was strong. And they were flying *into* it, which I had learned from Doug was a key ingredient to navigational control. Pilots do the same thing—it allows the airplane to generate lift. Most were northern parulas, the sky-blue warblers. Some hesitated and dropped into a pair of gap-toothed ailanthus trees next to the lot, while several more circled back to their takeoff spot. Up ahead was water: roughly a mile of it across the shimmering bay.

I had fallen under the spell of morning flight in the spring, but I knew morning flight in the fall was of another magnitude, and I couldn't wait to experience it. I had gone through Doug's old records from this location, looking for the factors that had led to his big days, hoping I might be able to catch the same magic. There was a greater chance to witness something big in the fall, something rare, like the broad-winged hawk flight.

But the North Channel Bridge parking lot sure seemed like an unlikely setting for it. It sits beside the four-lane Cross Bay Boulevard, north of the Jamaica Bay Wildlife Refuge. South of the pavement is a patchy stretch of grass and dirt, and then the thicket the parulas flew out of that dead-ends at the refuge's East Pond. Brown rats live in the grass. Lanternflies crawl over the ailanthus trees. That morning, a rooster walked beside the road with a plastic bag stuck to its back. Halved coconuts and red roses littered the shoreline, offerings made by local Guyanese immigrants during religious ceremonies. For them it's a pilgrimage site, and it's also where Don Riepe gathered some of the little statues he keeps at his front door. Despite all that, large groups of birds—sometimes hundreds or even thousands of warblers—bottle up here after sunrise as they search for better habitat.

Doug discovered this morning flight site. Leaving the refuge and driving up Cross Bay Boulevard one day in 2019, he saw blue jays flying northbound. Blue jays are common, so few birders would think anything of that sight. But, as Doug knew, they prefer to migrate along the barrier beach of the Rockaways, rarely showing up over Jamaica Bay's islands. Doug swerved into the North Channel lot and opened a map on his phone. He could see he was parked at a choke point of land and water—the perfect situation for morning flight.

He and another birder checked it out the next year after a cold front in late August. Standing in that grassy circle next to the lot, Doug said it was "warbler mayhem" for the first hour or so, with 40 to 60 warblers per minute rocketing past them. Snapping photos and taking counts with a clicker, they estimated 3,000 warblers, more than a third of them American redstarts. They tried to explain the phenomenon. The southbound birds must have ridden tailwinds during their nocturnal flights. At dawn—perhaps after finding themselves offshore—they dropped into the vegetation south of the parking lot.

Very quickly not finding it suitable enough, they moved north until they had to fly up and over the bay to the next line of trees. Since the island is situated north-south, the birds could fly *into* the wind on a fall migration day like this one. Bingo. It reminded Doug of morning flight at Cape May's Higbee Beach, a place he knew well.

Future visits reinforced for Doug the optimal conditions. The wind had to be strong overnight to push birds to the coast, and then stay that way in the morning to keep them low. The sky had to be clear and sunny.

I visited several times—once with Doug, also on my own—before I witnessed the event. Once those parulas started flying out this time, I knew the conditions were just right.

A magnolia warbler landed in a bayberry by my feet next to the parking lot. It had to decide whether to return to the crappy habitat or keep going. The maggie continued. Then a northern waterthrush barreled overhead, and this streaky, sturdy-looking warbler was clearly not turning back. Another warbler cut through the wind as cleanly as a jet. I turned to a fellow birder there, a friendly evolutionary biologist I had met earlier, and asked, "Did you see that?" It had happened in a flash, but I thought that the bird—heavy-bodied and uniformly yellow underneath—was the strongest warbler to fly past so far. "Was that a Connecticut?" I asked. He thought so, but with so many warblers shooting around us, he hadn't been able to snap a photograph of it. Connecticut warblers, one of the rarest warblers we can see in the fall, ride the jet stream up the Great Plains in the spring, then loop back in the fall closer to the Atlantic coast, riding the wind all the way to the western Amazon basin.

Fractions of an inch made a huge aerodynamic difference when faced with strong winds. It was thrilling watching these birds navigate the environment. Each bird, I realized in that moment, is structured according to its life cycle: where it's going and what it takes to get there. A parula's fairly short, round wings only need to get it perhaps as far as Florida, whereas a blackpoll warbler's relatively long, pointy wings will take it all the way to Colombia. Everything they do is related to wind. It whips out of the poles, drives major weather patterns, and carries them great distances in the spring and fall.

Sometimes, though, it's too strong. Because of climate change, fall storms are growing more powerful. Days before, a hurricane had lashed the Northeast. Blown out to sea, some warblers ended up in the United Kingdom, several of them the first on record—a Canada warbler in Britain, a Blackburnian warbler in Ireland, a magnolia warbler in Wales. Hundreds of birders from across the region dropped everything to chase them. For all the singles that made it, though, a lot more undoubtedly perished at sea.

After the Connecticut flew by, I tallied the numbers. We'd seen more than a hundred warblers. One of the ailanthus trees filled up again with staging birds. First a magnolia landed, then a chestnut-sided warbler in its lime-green fall plumage, then a black-and-white warbler. They didn't stay long. Another 15 warblers climbed out of the last row of trees high over the bay, but two parulas hesitated, then circled back to the beginning. A minute passed. One took off again, followed by the other. They really had no other choice. The closest place to find food and shelter was Forest Park in Queens, roughly six miles to the north. Together, they flapped mightily into the wind.

I'D BEEN WATCHING one category of morning flight: the course correction of nocturnal migrants. But in the middle of October, I was drawn to Fort Tilden for the other category: the diurnal, or daytime, migration of birds toward their eventual destination. A few minutes after seven on a Sunday morning, I took the steps up to a graffitied wooden deck on top of a concrete gun battery. I wasn't the first to arrive. Three Queens birders had already been there an hour and a half, listening for the predawn voices of owls.

It was the Queens County Bird Club's 10th annual Big Sit, in which the goal was to count as many species as possible from this one spot. Corey Finger, the event's organizer, was one of the three. I greeted everyone and then took in the spectacular view from a hundred feet above sea level—the western Rockaways and Jamaica Bay, the Manhattan and Brooklyn skylines, the full sweep of the coastal plain. Low clouds blanketed the rising sun. Seaside goldenrod flared in the dunes. Had piping plovers and American oystercatchers really crowded onto that sand two months ago? Below the battery were the pines where the Owl Whisperer finds his saw-whets. The thought that those little owls would return in a month or two made me smile. The comings and goings of birds marked the passage of time for me.

Finger laid out some oceanside markers: the dead tree, the bunker straight ahead (the bunker), the bunker topped by a pine (the pine bunker). Right away, the dead tree had an American kestrel perched on it, eating a small bird. Minutes later, a darker falcon, roughly the same size—a merlin—took its place. Then the flight began. Sharp-shinned hawks, not much bigger than blue jays, flapped stiffly as the wind jostled them. Northern harriers, rangy and long-winged, coursed low over the dunes. After an hour, the sun broke through the cloud wrack and the sky turned the blue of a box of Snuggle dryer sheets. Skeins of Canada geese flew through the wind-torn clouds. These were the wild ones, not the golf-course pariahs, coming from breeding grounds in the Far North. Their honks trumpeted a new season for me. Sharpies and kestrels now crossed our platform in pairs or in groups of three and four.

"Short-eared owl!" someone shouted, pointing to the dunes to the west. The owl flapped mothlike out over the ocean, chased by two ravens. We followed them, holding our breath. "No! Leave him alone!" someone cried. A raven attacked from above, but the owl lowered its talons and spun around. As it got some space, each downbeat of its wings propelled it higher. Up and up it went, crossing the path of an airplane coming in off the ocean, becoming a speck in the clouds.

A restless energy was in the air. On the ocean, a parasitic jaeger chased gulls and terns. A peregrine falcon flew off the ocean and came right after a pigeon over the platform. "I'll bet five dollars on the pigeon," Finger called out. The pigeon zigzagged before dropping into the trees below us. A few seconds later, the peregrine flapped out, empty-taloned, and chased a sharpie for good measure. Merlins, ever pugnacious, harassed a raven, a sharpie, a bald eagle, and each other.

The platform was also an impassioned place. Any moment could bring a new species for the Big Sit. The single-day record was 93. Could we break it? Everyone pushed for more. "Shorebirds!" "High-flying duck!" "Ducks on the bay!" "Passerines coming this way!" A few people went down the stairs and flushed some small birds up to the platform. Several warblers and vireos went on the list.

There is a place for all different kinds of birding, I thought. But I felt torn between the need to compile—the birder's and, yes, the reporter's quest for accuracy—and the desire to just soak it in. I see the need for scientific data. Morning flight is perfect for that. Even if you can't identify all the species, you can do your best to count the total number of birds that fly past you and even separate them into orders like passerines and raptors. But being so focused on counting, I find, can set you apart from the raw emotion of the spectacle. Sometimes, I just want to feel the wonder of it.

I left the platform for a little while. In the shadow of the battery, I watched kestrels and sharpies float by. I couldn't hear the people up top, and there was nobody else around. I noted the colors in the dunes. The path of the sun. So many raptors had already passed that their shapes, flight styles, and behaviors appeared familiar to me. I tried feeling out the birds, tapping into an overall impression: The nervousness of a sharpie. The lightness of a kestrel. The directness of a merlin. The smoothness of a harrier. The rippling power of a peregrine. The faultlessness of a bald eagle. I watched the sky and felt unhurried, formed and formless like the clouds.

In previous years, I might have stayed all day. But I decided I didn't need to see *every* bird. I had seen enough to last me until the next morning flight. The Big Sit reached 92 species: one short of the record.

IT WAS NOW early November. Morning flight at the northern tip of Manhattan, from a pier at the west end of Dyckman Street, felt ancient. Perhaps it was the view of the sheer cliffs across the Hudson—tracing the rocks down was like looking back in time. I tried to imagine which crags on the Palisades were the old peregrine aeries. Behind me was Inwood Hill Park, a fiery red and orange. A cold wind blew down from the Great Lakes, sending the clouds south. It was the kind of autumn day where if you were in the right place, you could see something rare.

That was certainly on my mind. November is a great time to find birds that stray outside their normal range, called vagrants. As individuals, they travel far—farther than 90 percent of their population. New York's classic example in the fall is western birds ending up on our coast. Often they're juveniles. Researchers sometimes group them into two categories: disoriented and misoriented. Disoriented birds, having never inherited any means of navigation, tend to disperse in random directions. Misoriented, meanwhile, inherited faulty navigation systems, as if their internal compass swaps north for south or east for west.

Those errors, however, are seized upon by birders. Finding vagrants adds to the scientific record, but there's also the elation of finding a totally unexpected bird, especially when others then clamor to see "your" rare find. On this November day, I suffered for options. It would have made sense to return to Breezy Point or Fort Tilden. If you look at a map of the continent and trace your finger up the Atlantic coast, you'll find it takes a sharp right turn at Long Island. Migrating birds carried by strong westerly winds over the open ocean see those beaches—the land's end—as a haven. The upshot, as New York birders learn quickly, is the regular appearance of western vagrants. But I'd chosen instead to go to Upper Manhattan. The Dyckman Street pier, which I had never been to, had piqued my curiosity. Perhaps I'd see a golden eagle. There aren't many in the east, and every so often in late fall one drifts over from the mountains to the edge of the city.

The turkey vultures got up first. Almost 30 of them flapped out of Inwood Hill Park and floated lazily south toward the George Washington Bridge. It was half past seven; the earth was beginning to warm. They had probably spent the night roosting in the park's mighty old trees before picking up a cross-continental migration that could take them to South America. An adult bald eagle appeared from upriver, all white head and tail, and coasted on updrafts that climbed off the Palisades. Red-tailed hawks joined the flight, and then another bald eagle caught a fish and took it into the park. There was a resident pair of peregrines on our side of the Hudson, and all morning the two took swipes at any songbird that dared to cross the river.

It must have been close to nine when I saw something unusual. One birder on the pier called out a hawk well to the north. Its wings were long and rose in a slight dihedral, but its flight wasn't wobbly like a northern harrier's. Its proportions didn't fit a golden eagle's either. We were stumped. I was new to this morning flight crew, but I took a stab: "How about a rough-legged hawk?"

"If it's a rough-legged, it better come this way!" the original spotter said.

Like a golden eagle, a rough-legged hawk is rare in the city. They breed on tundra cliffs, and winter in grasslands where they can catch rodents. Rather than fly closer, though, the hawk we'd had our eye on disappeared below the tree line on the east side of the river. The observation slipped through our grasp.

*This happens*, I thought, comforting myself.

Clouds drifted over and cast shadows on the Palisades. The river lapped against the rocks below my feet. I felt my breath slow. I imagined the Lenape people who lived in settlements on the Inwood heights and how they must have appreciated the dance of light and dark on those cliffs. The peregrines and eagles would have been familiar to them.

As I prepared to leave, I decided to check my phone for rare bird alerts. Ash-throated flycatchers—a western species—had been spotted at a tiny park on Jamaica Bay and at a cemetery in Bushwick. Vagrants were prone to show up in odd places.

My phone buzzed as I entered the subway station: A gray kingbird had been spotted at Canarsie Park on the south coast of Brooklyn. I had to look up the species. The one and only record in Brooklyn was from 1930.

The gray kingbird, a type of flycatcher, is largely a Caribbean species, though small numbers of them breed along the southeast Gulf Coast. This was clearly a "reverse migrant," a misdirected bird whose compass was off 180 degrees; it had flown north rather than south. Canarsie Park is best known for its cricket grounds. Very few birders visit there, let alone on a weekday in November. The finder would have been looking for vagrants in pockets along the coast. You can probably guess who it was: Doug Gochfeld.

I DIDN'T TAKE the subway to the other end of the city later that same day hoping to see the kingbird in the fading daylight. I only occasionally chase vagrants. I rarely confess this to other birders—see, it only took me 14 chapters to do so. For most, the calculus is simple: Rare bird shows up, go see rare bird. British birders call it twitching. Once, talking to Junko Suzuki in a Starbucks near Central Park, I told her I didn't particularly enjoy chasing. If I had seen the bird already, for instance, in its typical range, I didn't feel an urgency to see it simply because it was an odd visitor in my town. And I didn't put much stock in my county or state lists. She furrowed her brow. After a pause, she said, "But this is the fun part of birding."

She was right, of course. What isn't fun about seeing an unexpected thing? I tried to explain my reasons. Viewing a vagrant that is far off course, a bird that likely isn't going to survive, always makes me feel a little uneasy. It can feel like disaster tourism. I remembered a secretive little rail called a corncrake that should have been on its way from northern Europe to southeast Africa but instead ended up on Long Island in a grassy median strip of a two-lane highway. Some birders flew in from out of state to see it, and more than a hundred birders crowded the blacktop with their scopes and cameras for two days. On the third, the corncrake was dead, hit by a speeding car. Remember those warblers carried across the Atlantic to the British Isles? They were also doomed.

But does this mean we shouldn't go see them? We didn't create the hurricane that blew them off course—well, not directly anyway. Some birds have faulty compasses. Weather adds unpredictability. Dick Veit has researched vagrancy, and he suggests that it's driven by population growth and a pressure to go travel farther in search of resources. He says vagrancy may also be healthy—not for every individual, of course, but for its species. For threatened species especially, it allows them to reach more habitat and broaden their gene pool. Early generations of American starlings did that, colonizing a new continent.

And birds that appear lost to us might not be so lost after all. As José Ramírez-Garofalo pointed out, waterbirds like brown pelicans are now regularly showing up north of their expected breeding range. As habitats change, a species can set out in search of its preferred one or expand its preferences. With freshwater wetlands drying up at southern latitudes, for instance, birds like anhingas, wood storks, and roseate spoonbills are looking to find ones to the north. "Not every vagrant manages to breed; indeed, most probably do not owing to the difficulty of finding a mate and/or suitable habitat," writes Veit. But when enough of them get together in a new place, they do.

Was Doug's gray kingbird a pioneer? It was hard to say. There's a long record of them being seen in the fall along the Atlantic Seaboard from the Carolinas to New England, but the frequency seems to be increasing. It was the third straight autumn with one in New York City—the first two were on Staten Island. I was also seeing more records of western vagrants this fall than in any of my previous years of birding (though I know this observation is extremely unscientific). Were they expanding their range, or was it just a successful breeding year for their species? I could be sure of one thing—there were a lot more birders than ever before searching for them.

At least 15 people hurried to Canarsie Park the afternoon of Doug's report. And when I heard the next morning that the kingbird was still there, I decided to chase it too. A vagrant in one place is usually a common bird elsewhere—in the Caribbean, gray kingbirds are roadside birds. But I had never seen one, nor was I planning a trip to its home range anytime soon. And I reassured myself that this large flycatcher was unlikely to be too disturbed by a bunch of enthusiastic birders.

CANARSIE PARK SITS on old Jamaica Bay marshland. It was quiet when I arrived. Several American pipits and a snow bunting were casting around for seeds on empty baseball diamonds. It was clear why Doug had come here. This was his kind of migration stopover: seldom visited, rarely surveyed, but full of potential for its mix of patchy woods, fields, and water. After finding the gray kingbird in some willows around a lagoon, he'd followed it through woods to the shoulder of the Belt Parkway. It was there again on day two.

I cut across the cricket grounds to a trail through the woods, listening for the sound of speeding cars. Inside, though, the trail disappeared underneath trash bags and beer bottles. I became convinced I was walking in circles. I debated if this bird was worth the trouble, but I still had to find an exit. I kicked my way through multiflora rose, which snagged my jeans, until I came to a clearing. The highway was above a short berm. I followed it north.

Up ahead was a group of five birders, separated only by a guardrail from onrushing cars. "Did you bring a machete?" one joked. Others were having even more trouble than I was. On the rare bird alert chat, somebody was asking for directions: *We are lost in the cricket field. Where do we go from here?* Doug responded—though I believe he was home at the time—with a map of the park on which he had drawn color-coded lines for the trails and color-coded circles for the bird's previous locations.

Some chases require extreme patience. I saw the kingbird instantly. It was perched on a bare branch against a golden backdrop of dried leaves. I was told the bird had just been catching dragonflies. "This is a good bird," someone said. That was the understatement of the year. In terms of rarity, it was a *great* bird.

But it occurred to me that nonbirders would look at it and say, "What's the big deal?"

Like all kingbirds, it had a crisp look. Its back was cool gray, and it had a smudgy black mask. But its feat was in how it had ended up here. Doug thought it was an immature female, and that made sense: Juveniles migrate later than adults in the fall, and, because they're new to this, they commit more navigational errors. The shortest distance the bird would have traveled was roughly 600 miles—in the wrong direction.

That's the thing about most vagrants: They become crowd-pleasers only outside their normal boundaries. In the West Indies, where gray kingbirds have profited from the clearing of native forests, they're so common that they've earned local nicknames. Most are a commentary on their twittering call or their rowdiness: *petchary, chinchary, pitirre, pitirre abejero, titirre, pestigre, pipirite, pick-peter, christomarie,* and *fighter*. They've adapted well to living among humans, taking up power-line and treetop perches from southern Florida to South America. In Canarsie Park, this gray kingbird had found a similar habitat.

I enjoyed watching the kingbird sally around. But the Belt Parkway was so loud that I was forced to lean in to have a conversation with others. Assaulted by the noise, I decided to leave after half an hour.

Fighting my way out of the woods, I ran into two friends hacking their way in. "Ryan, I didn't think you chased birds," one said in mock surprise.

Maybe it *was* time I got over my discomfort, expanded my own range. Everything is changing now. Maybe this bird was at the forefront of gray kingbirds inching up the Atlantic coast. Maybe it was scouting future breeding territory. Maybe in my lifetime, a gray kingbird will become a roadside bird in New York City.

I later heard from other birders that another 20 people showed up to see the kingbird that day. Wedged against the guardrail, their presence caused a rubbernecking slowdown on the highway. The driver of an SUV almost caused a pileup when he swung over to ask them what they were watching. Local news broadcasts had no explanation for the traffic delay.

MOST DAYS, THOUGH, I just enjoyed seeing what I could close to home.

On the morning after Thanksgiving, I joined Peter Dorosh's third annual Turkey Trot in Prospect Park. Details were scant on the Brooklyn Bird Club's calendar, other than the time and place to meet, and this description: "Celebrating the holiday weekend in the spirit of festivity—giving thanks for our winter birds!" Peter had hung the bird feeders in the park that week. On his blog, he wrote: "The Prospect Park feeders are now up! We give thanks to birds enriching our lives. A few reminders: please do not enter the feeding perimeter. I've given Ryan Goldberg permission to enter if necessary as he will be my backup. Email me if you see anything amiss."

I hadn't asked for the assignment, but I said I'd accept it.

I met Peter on the west side of the park. A murder of crows, about 25, passed us going in. Peter had been signing off his emails lately with a quote attributed to the author Sir Kristian Goldmund Aumann: "November; Crows are approaching, wounded leaves fall to the ground." Two other birders were waiting, Susie and Kiani. They said they were new to birding, and I watched Peter's face light up.

Well, he said, Prospect Park is one of the best hotspots in the city, maybe in the whole Northeast. "This is my zone," he added, pointing down the southwest perimeter to Lookout Hill. He talked about his restoration work—digging up Norway maples, planting a variety of native species, improving the habitat. "Insects host on native plants," he said. "That's the key. An oak tree can hold up to six hundred species."

Susie and Kiani nodded along. As we walked into the park, Susie said she hoped we would see some woodpeckers. Peter went through the possibilities. We probably wouldn't see red-headed woodpeckers, since at most one or two winter in the city. But the first red-headed woodpecker he'd ever seen was at the Gettysburg battlefield, he remembered. Wait, no, it was at Antietam. The bird flew past him as he stood on Bloody Lane, the farm road that during the Civil War battle turned the same color as the woodpecker's dark-crimson head. Then Peter explained why he was there in the first place: He's a history buff. His Scotch Irish ancestors served in the Civil War, he said. One was a drummer boy. "I'm Brooklyn all the way back. A lot of rich families paid poor people to take their places."

Then we came upon an equestrian walking ring where Peter recalled seeing a Virginia rail on the Christmas Bird Count. Did they know a Virginia rail? It's a funky bird that in New York seems to find itself in all kinds of weird situations: perched on cars in the neighborhood, hiding in a laundry basket in a laundromat, scurrying through a wedding party in Prospect Park.

"But it's not just about rare birds," he declared. "Common birds are beautiful." To make the point, he praised the red-bellied woodpecker above us. Two, in fact, scoping out a tree cavity. Clear out of nowhere, two starlings arrived and bullied them out of the hole. *It happens after all*, I thought.

I wondered what the new birders thought of Peter's free association. They seemed amused. I knew his stories well enough to recite many of them on my own. Because Peter reads lips, conversation is hard; storytelling is his primary mode of communication. But we hadn't gone a hundred yards; at this pace, I thought, we'd never cover a quarter of the park.

A merlin flew into a high snag, annoying an onlooking blue jay. Peter beamed. "The merlin is the one with the attitude. It chases larger birds. I told this story to Ryan many years ago..."

One day at the Jamaica Bay Wildlife Refuge, he'd watched a merlin fly straight toward him only a few feet above the ground. Peter didn't move. But rather than veer around him, the merlin flew up and over Peter, then continued straight on its way.

"I was just a bump in the road." He laughed. We all did.

"It's a good story," Kiani said.

"You get a lot of great memories when you're out birding," Peter said. "Things that stay with you forever."

I began to soften. The sky was pastel blue, and the clouds were loose, patternless. The sight lines were long and open. It struck me that the park always looks smaller this time of year, when the trees are bare. I had the feeling of coming to an end of something. Perhaps it was my reporter's instinct, making me want to follow every step of this birding world. It wasn't my birding education—no, that was never going to end.

I found myself telling Susie and Kiani about the Christmas Bird Count—it was coming up soon—and encouraging them to join a team. I was sliding into Peter's role of teacher. But it made me happy to think I was part of a long urban naturalist tradition, brought into it by him. And nothing made Peter happier than sharing his knowledge.

As we walked into the woods, there was a muffled crunching of yellow leaves underfoot. We heard a much louder racket in the distance. "I hear blue jays," Peter said. He remembered his mother pulling him to the window as a kid and catching sight of them in their backyard. This made me wonder if there was a bird sighting today that would change someone's life. Maybe the wood ducks we would see later, pretty as a painting, engaged in courtship rituals. Or the cedar waxwings by the feeders, quietly eating buckthorn berries, feathered in sleek, peachy bodysuits. Or the northern shovelers spinning circles around the lake, feeding cooperatively. They were all spark birds for people I knew.

After we'd been out two and a half hours, Peter checked on his audience. He still wanted to visit the compost pile, the Midwood, the Lullwater, the feeders, the lake. Susie had to leave.

"You're not in a rush, are you?" he eagerly asked Kiani.

"No," she said, "I can stay longer."

I said I could too.

A smile flickered across Peter's face. "Good," he said. "I'm a slow birder. I like to enjoy the environment, and everything in it."

I knew that look. It said: *Let's keep going.*

# ACKNOWLEDGMENTS

As a journalist, I'm always humbled by the willingness of people to tell me their stories, especially those who aren't that used to somebody writing down what they say in a notebook. I don't accept their trust lightly. I interviewed over 60 people for this book, and I'm grateful to all of them. My sincere apologies to those who do not appear by name, but please know that what I learned from our conversations still made its way into the book. And to those who spent many hours with me over the phone and in the field, patiently answering my endless questions, I offer my greatest thanks: Doug Gochfeld, Bruce Yolton, Andrew Farnsworth, Melissa Breyer, Calista McRae, Shannon Curley, José Ramírez-Garofalo, Chris Allieri, Ciara Fagan, Mel Julien, Christian Murphy, and Junko Suzuki. As for two others, Peter Dorosh and Don Riepe, I must admit the typical reporter-source relationship was less conventional. I became friends with them through birding well before I began thinking about this book. Getting to know them and their stories, however, was a major inspiration for wanting to write it. In our conversations, they remained as honest as ever. Both men have sparked a passion for nature and birds in countless New Yorkers.

The Brooklyn birding community I found in 2016 was the most unexpected thing. I didn't think it would change my life. Since then, my best memories in New York entail birding with the mentors I've met and the friends I've made—too many to name here. Their fingerprints are all over this book; for me, they make this city a richer place to live. I only wish that my friend Janet Schumacher were still alive to read it. Thanks to Ed Crowne, the most scholarly birder I know, for all the out-of-print nature books, and to Dennis Hrehowsik, the president of the Brooklyn Bird Club, who let me spin through the club's archives (three boxes in all, but they were stuffed with old newsletters, pamphlets, and a real gem, the 1951 guide *Birds of Prospect Park*), and for my 40th birthday gave me his copy of John Bull's *Birds of New York State*. I'm also thankful to Joe Charap and Sara Evans, the horticulturists at Green-Wood Cemetery, who provided me with invaluable research on the history of the cemetery and its cultural landscape. Their management of Green-Wood has made it a better place for birds.

I'm infinitely grateful to my agent, Elias Altman, who listened to my undercooked ideas for several years before I finally came to him with this one, which was hiding in plain sight. He helped craft the proposal that got the book sold and gave me the confidence to go out and write it. At every turn, his counsel was superb. And I'm lucky to have had editors at Algonquin—first, Amy Gash, and then Madeline Jones—whose support was firm despite a lot of reshuffling behind the scenes. They helped me find my voice within the New York narrative I wanted to tell. Thanks also to Elizabeth Johnson, whose copyediting of the book was fantastic. Aimee Lusty elevated the text with her magnificent black-and-white illustrations for each season. I feel proud to have my words graced by her artwork. I'm also immensely thankful to my fact-checker, Ismail Ibrahim, a great reporter who, lucky for me, is interested in birding, and to SK Winnicki, an evolutionary ecologist at the Ohio State University, who generously agreed to read my manuscript to ensure I was always on firm scientific ground and, as a bonus, offered many thoughtful comments in the process.

Major thanks to my friends who reviewed early chapters of the manuscript or the whole thing: Phil Guidry, Louie Lazar, Tyler Dorholt, and Karen O'Hearn. Their feedback was more valuable than they probably realize. Thanks as well to Tina Alleva for guidance on the artistic elements of the book, not to mention all our fun years of birding in Brooklyn. And much love to my parents, who always keep their bird feeders stocked, and to my brother, Scott, an excellent birder himself, who found time between caring for his patients to read several chapters and generally offer encouragement.

None of this would have happened were it not for Beth Goldberg, my aunt, an avid birder who introduced me and the rest of the family to this endeavor. While visiting her in New Jersey almost 10 years ago, she suggested we go birding in a park I had passed all the time as a kid. *Birding, really?* I thought. I was an urban animal, and I hadn't taken many walks in the woods before that day. But I was game. Trying to identify a falcon we found perched atop a dead tree—was it a merlin or a kestrel?—and flipping through the field guide left me desperate to learn more. Hours later, I didn't want to leave the woods. I still don't.

Lastly, if a book has many authors, here one stands above the rest: my wife, Angie. We went birding together my second time, and we haven't stopped since. It has changed her life as much as it has mine. She shaped this book from start to finish, from our first whiteboard sessions to my final revisions. She's my first reader and editor, and in that role, she is truly gifted—intelligent, honest, and compassionate. She lived through some of the events in the book and knows most of the people in it, and she has listened to me speak of little else the last three years. She has shown the patience of a saint. I love her dearly, and this book is dedicated to her. It is as much her achievement as it is mine.

# AUTHOR'S NOTE ON SOURCES

This book follows events that took place in New York between the summer of 2022 and the spring of 2024, though mostly in 2023. It is the product of more than five dozen interviews and my travels around the city, taking notes and watching birds. This makes up the foundation of the book. I tried to capture this moment in the bird life of New York—as the ranks of birders grow to never-before-seen levels—but it is a modest installment in an otherwise vast literature about the natural history of the city. I made great use of that literature, as I did with the many books, scientific papers, and magazine articles on bird migration. At the end of this book, I have included a bibliography of those sources. A little reporting from before these years—for a story I wrote about Peter Dorosh for *The Village Voice* in 2017 and another about Green-Wood Cemetery for *Popular Science* in 2021—also crept in. But in truth, the work really began once I started birding in 2016. I became a sponge for local bird lore shared by Peter and others, learning about the places, people, and birds that would inform my reporting for this book.

My most important day-to-day source was eBird, the Cornell Lab of Ornithology's global citizen-science platform. Most birders in New York submit their observations there, and like many of them, I subscribed to eBird's daily email digests of rare birds for the city's five counties (the same as the boroughs). Hundreds of local birders post their lists on eBird every day—more in the spring and fall—and they allowed me to stay informed of what was happening in all the places I couldn't visit at once. I gained a huge appreciation for the birders who tell a little story in their comments, like Junko Suzuki with the buff-breasted sandpiper she found at Randall's Island, and Doug Gochfeld on his gray kingbird discovery at Canarsie Park, and the many chronicles of the Swainson's hawk at the Sims recycling plant. On eBird, I was also able to find records of approximately 430 species in the city limits, the figure I cited in chapter 1.

To stay further in the loop, I subscribed to some of the borough-based rare bird alerts on WhatsApp and GroupMe, which have since been replaced by Discord channels. Providing real-time alerts, these online tools make birding a much different endeavor than the one I first joined, though admittedly, by the end of my reporting I was ready to return to pen and paper. Throughout, I visited Peter's blog as another source of Brooklyn birding news. For breaking news on the Eurasian eagle-owl Flaco, I depended on Bruce Yolton's blog. I also stayed glued to Twitter for updates on Flaco during his first few weeks outside captivity, especially the night he was nearly recaptured.

Within the natural history literature, I leaned on the various books about the birds of New York that have been published almost every twenty years since J. P. Giraud Jr.'s *The Birds of Long Island* in 1844. Scientific in nature, they include all kinds of encyclopedic information and records of birds seen in the city and the state. The books I referenced were written by, in chronological order, Frank Chapman, Elon Howard Eaton, Ludlow Griscom, Allan Cruickshank, John Bull, and, most recently, P. A. Buckley, Walter Sedwitz, William J. Norse, and John Kieran, the authors of *Urban Ornithology: 150 Years of Birds in New York City*. These books offered great local context on the species I wrote about, especially those whose ranges have changed over the last century and a half. Chapman's memoir, *Autobiography of a Bird-Lover*, was the source of the anecdote about his tallying the different kinds of birds that women wore on their hats. The archives of *Bird-Lore*, where Chapman put forward his new Christmas bird census, are available online. There are also plenty of general-interest guides about where to go birding in New York City, and I searched a few of the older ones. My favorite was *Enjoying Birds Around New York City*, published in 1966, whose authors artfully described the nature of migration in this urban landscape. For general New York City history, I looked no further than *The WPA Guide to New York City*, the 1939 classic, which I think every New Yorker should have in their library.

As for narrative accounts of New York City birding, readers will have noticed that I quoted from Roger Tory Peterson's *Birds Over America* more than any other. This is something of a forgotten classic on the bird life of this country, but since Peterson was a New Yorker for many years, he filled pages with urban anecdotes, from the enormous starling roosts that whitewashed the Met to the best garbage dumps for birdwatching. For particulars on the ecology of New York, I frequently referred to Eric Sanderson's towering *Mannahatta*. Writing about the geology of the city, including the terminal moraine, I learned a great deal from Sanderson, John Kieran's *A Natural History of New York City*, Robin Lynn and Francis Morrone's *Guide to New York City Urban Landscapes* (namely, its chapter on Green-Wood Cemetery), research by geologist Sidney Horenstein, and *The Forests and Wetlands of New York City* and *Green Metropolis* by Elizabeth (Betsy) Barlow Rogers. The two Barlow Rogers books were also excellent sources on Fresh Kills and Jamaica Bay. For the history of the Bronx River, I consulted three books—Maarten de Kadt's *The Bronx River: An Environmental & Social History*, Stephen Paul DeVillo's *The Bronx River in History & Folklore*, and John Mullaly's *The New Parks Beyond the Harlem*—as well as the outstanding online resources of the Bronx River Alliance.

There are a great many sources on conservation issues in New York, like bird collisions, artificial light, and habitat management.

The book *Natural History of New York City's Parks and Great Gull Island*, published by the Linnaean Society and available in full online, was especially helpful. Allison Sloan, a former coordinator of Project Safe Flight, wrote a chapter about the program's early years, leading up to 9/11. Another chapter about piping plovers at the Rockaway Beach Endangered Species Nesting Area, written by Theodore Boretti, Evelyn Fetridge, and Alexander R. Brash of the NYC Parks Department, addressed the history of that area.

For a view of the forests and wetlands of New York City today, I read several reports published by the Natural Areas Conservancy. Don Riepe was, of course, my primary source for Jamaica Bay, but he also directed me to several National Park Service management plans for the refuge and a 1981 report written by history professor Frederick R. Black, called *Jamaica Bay: A History*. *The Kingbird*, the quarterly journal of the New York State Ornithological Association, was another useful source. Doug Gochfeld's Galadriel quote came from the June 2023 issue. Several papers written by José Ramírez-Garofalo and Shannon Curley, such as about the sedge wrens at Freshkills, offered insight into New York City ecology. Their extensive research at the park, which they shared in the form of presentations, studies, and pamphlets, greatly enhanced my reporting.

I also used the exceptional research that has come out of NYC Bird Alliance over the years—annual reports, nesting surveys of the Harbor Herons project, and studies on collisions, the Javits Center, and Tribute in Light. The group's newsletter, *The Urban Bird Call* (formerly *The Urban Audubon*), provided timely updates on Project Safe Flight as I was writing. Articles Rebekah Creshkoff wrote for the newsletter in 1997 and 1998 documented the start of the monitoring program. Another newsletter, the Brooklyn Bird Club's *Clapper Rail*, was also an important source, and I say that not only because I have volunteered as its editor for the last eight years. In its back issues from

1998 to 2010, no writer was as prolific as Peter Dorosh, who wrote many columns about the joys found in every season of birding—even winter. We publish a recap of the Christmas Bird Count each year, and those stories confirmed my recollections of the event. Additionally, I pulled all numbers from the National Audubon Society's complete Christmas Bird Count dataset, which is searchable online.

On migration, which is where New York really makes a name for itself, Andrew Farnsworth and Doug Gochfeld were my primary contacts. Both know how the city fits into the continental web. For broad context, Scott Weidensaul's books *Living on the Wind* and its follow-up, *A World on the Wing*, were essential reading. My understanding and love of migration began years ago with the former title, and to my mind it is the gold standard on the subject. I wanted to situate what I was seeing on the ground within the latest research on this infinitely complex phenomenon, and so that brought me to the field of radar ornithology. Without listing all the scientists doing this work—see the bibliography—I got an education from their studies on how birds cross different landscapes, where they choose to stop, how artificial light is changing their ancient pathways, and how they're trying to keep up with climate change. On the evolution of migration, which I wrote about in chapter 7, I drew from a presentation that Benjamin Winger gave to the Linnaean Society in April 2024. For more background on collisions, such as reports on bird-friendly building design, I tapped the online resources of American Bird Conservancy's glass collisions program. I also watched several presentations by that organization's collisions expert, Christine Sheppard. Kaitlyn Parkins, the program's coordinator, previously studied collisions at NYC Bird Alliance and shared research she led during her tenure there.

Finally, for the life histories of the bird species I wrote about, I made regular use of the Cornell Lab of Ornithology's Birds of the World, an online platform that gathers scholarly content from celebrated works of ornithology, like *Birds of North America* and *Handbook of the Birds of the World*. I also referenced Audubon's online guide to North American birds, *The Sibley Guide to Bird Life & Behavior*, and, for my favorite family, *The Warbler Guide* by Tom Stephenson and Scott Whittle.

Additional research was necessary for some species or individual birds. For starlings, that included the work of Lauren Fugate and John MacNeill Miller on the Shakespeare myth, and the work of Natalie Hofmeister on their rapid evolution in America. For peregrines, a pre-DDT view was captured by a two-decade study of the birds around New York by Richard Herbert and Kathleen Green Skelton Herbert, published in 1965, while Tom Cade's preface to Saul Frank's book *City Peregrines* provided great details on their urban reintroduction. In addition to Bruce Yolton, Ed Shanahan of *The New York Times* produced some of the best coverage of Flaco; among Flaco's many obituaries, my favorite was written by *Defector*'s Barry Petchesky. On grasshopper sparrows, Alexander Wilson's observations from his nine-volume *American Ornithology* can be found online. On the lives of piping plovers, a major source was Anne Hecht, a National Park Service biologist who has studied them for 40 years and spoke with Chris Allieri for an NYC Plover Project webinar in December 2023. As for the piping plover Clark Kent, his background was shared with me by the New Jersey wildlife scientists who banded him. And *Hawks in Flight*, the hawk-watching classic written by Pete Dunne, David Allen Sibley, and Clay Sutton, added context to the migration of broad-winged hawks.

# BIBLIOGRAPHY

Arbib, Robert S., Jr., Olin Sewall Pettingill Jr., and Sally Hoyt Spofford, for the Laboratory of Ornithology, Cornell University. *Enjoying Birds Around New York City: An Aid to Recognizing, Watching, Finding, and Attracting Birds in New York City, Long Island, the Upstate Counties of Westchester, Putnam, Dutchess, Rockland, and Orange, and Nearby Points in New Jersey and Connecticut.* Houghton Mifflin, 1966.

Armistead, George L., and Marshall J. Iliff. "The Vagrancy of Gray Kingbird in North America." *North American Birds* 57, no. 2 (2003): 148–61.

Baker, J. A. *The Peregrine.* New York Review Books, 2004. First published in 1967 by Harper & Row.

Barlow, Elizabeth. *The Forests and Wetlands of New York City.* Little, Brown, 1971.

Beebe, William. *Unseen Life of New York: As a Naturalist Sees It.* Duell, Sloan and Pearce, 1953.

*Birds of Prospect Park.* Brooklyn Bird Club, 1951.

Breyer, Melissa. "Reflections of a Bird Collision Monitor." *Audubon,* Spring 2024. https://www.audubon.org/news/surprisingly-long-history-movement-make-buildings-safer-birds.

Buckley, P. A., Walter Sedwitz, William J. Norse, and John Kieran. *Urban Ornithology: 150 Years of Birds in New York City.* Cornell University Press, 2018.

Bull, John L. *Birds of New York State.* Doubleday, 1974.

Campbell, Anthony, Yeqiao Wang, Mark Christiano, and Sara Stevens. "Salt Marsh Monitoring in Jamaica Bay, New York from 2003 to 2013: A Decade of Change from Restoration to Hurricane Sandy." *Remote Sensing* 9, no. 2 (2017): 131. https://doi.org/10.3390/rs9020131.

Caro, Robert A. *The Power Broker: Robert Moses and the Fall of New York.* Alfred A. Knopf, 1974.

Carson, Rachel. "How About Citizenship Papers for the Starling?" *Nature* 32, no. 6 (1939): 317–19.

Carson, Rachel. *Silent Spring.* Houghton Mifflin, 1962.

Chapman, Frank M. *Autobiography of a Bird-Lover*. Appleton-Century, 1935.

Chapman, Frank M. *The Birds of the Vicinity of New York City*. American Museum of Natural History, 1906.

Chen, Katherine, Sara M. Kross, Kaitlyn Parkins, Chad Seewagen, Andrew Farnsworth, and Benjamin M. Van Doren. "Heavy Migration Traffic and Bad Weather Are a Dangerous Combination: Bird Collisions in New York City." *Journal of Applied Ecology* 61, no. 4 (2024): 784–96. https://doi.org/10.1111/1365-2664.14590.

Cruickshank, Allan D. *Birds Around New York City: Where and When to Find Them*. American Museum of Natural History, 1942.

Curley, Shannon, José Ramírez-Garofalo, and Cait Field. *The Birds of Freshkills Park*. Freshkills Park Alliance, July 2022.

Davis, William T. *Days Afield on Staten Island*. L. H. Bigelow, 1892.

Day, Leslie. *Field Guide to the Natural World of New York City*. Johns Hopkins University Press, 2007.

de Kadt, Maarten. *The Bronx River: An Environmental & Social History*. Arcadia, 2011.

DeVillo, Stephen Paul. *The Bronx River in History & Folklore*. Arcadia, 2015.

Dunne, Pete, David Sibley, and Clay Sutton. *Hawks in Flight: The Flight Identification of North American Raptors*, 2nd ed. Houghton Mifflin Harcourt, 2012.

Eaton, Elon Howard. *Birds of New York*, vol. 1. University of the State of New York, 1910.

Eaton, Elon Howard. *Birds of New York*, vol. 2. University of the State of New York, 1914.

Forbush, Edward Howe. *The Starling*. Massachusetts State Board of Agriculture, 1915.

Frank, Saul. *City Peregrines: A Ten-Year Saga of New York City Falcons*. Hancock House, 1994.

Fugate, Lauren, and John MacNeill Miller. "Shakespeare's Starlings: Literary History and the Fictions of Invasiveness." *Environmental Humanities* 13, no. 2 (2021): 301–22. https://doi.org/10.1215/22011919-9320167.

Gochfeld, Doug. "What's It Gonna Be? Predicting the Next New Additions to the Avifauna of New York—v. 6.0." *The Kingbird* 73, no. 2 (2023): 90–113.

Griscom, Ludlow. *Birds of the New York City Region*. American Museum of Natural History, 1923.

Guo, Fengyi, Jeffrey J. Buler, Jaclyn A. Smolinsky, and David S. Wilcove. "Autumn Stopover Hotspots and Multiscale Habitat Associations of Migratory Landbirds in the Eastern United States." *Proceedings of the National Academy of Sciences* 120, no. 3 (2023): 1–10. https://doi.org/10.1073/pnas.2203511120.

Guo, Fengyi, Jeffrey J. Buler, Jaclyn A. Smolinsky, and David S. Wilcove. "Seasonal Patterns and Protection Status of Stopover Hotspots for Migratory Landbirds in the Eastern United States." *Current Biology* 34, no. 2 (2024): 235–244.e3. https://doi.org/10.1016/j.cub.2023.11.033.

Herbert, Richard A., and Kathleen Green Skelton Herbert. "Behavior of Peregrine Falcons in the New York City Region." *The Auk* 82, no. 1 (January 1965): 62–94. https://doi.org/10.2307/4082795.

Hofmeister, Natalie R., Scott J. Werner, and Irby J. Lovette. "Environmental Correlates of Genetic Variation in the Invasive European Starling in North America." *Molecular Ecology* 30, no. 5 (2021): 1251–63. https://doi.org/10.1111/mec.15806.

Horton, Kyle G., Jeffrey J. Buler, Sharolyn J. Anderson et al. "Artificial Light at Night Is a Top Predictor of Bird Migration Stopover Density." *Nature Communications* 14, no. 1 (2023): 1–11. https://doi.org/10.1038/s41467-023-43046-z.

Kalm, Peter. *Travels into North America*. Translated by John Reinhold Forster. T. Lowndes, 1773.

Kaufman, Kenn. *Kingbird Highway: The Biggest Year in the Life of an Extreme Birder*. Houghton Mifflin, 2006.

Kieran, John. *A Natural History of New York City: A Personal Report After Fifty Years of Study & Enjoyment of Wildlife Within the Boundaries of Greater New York*. Houghton Mifflin, 1959.

La Sorte, Frank A., Myla F.J. Aronson, Christopher A. Lepczyk, and Kyle G. Horton. "Area Is the Primary Correlate of Annual and Seasonal Patterns of Avian Species Richness in Urban Green Spaces." *Landscape and Urban Planning* 203 (November 2020): 103892. https://doi.org/10.1016/j.landurbplan.2020.103892.

Leopold, Aldo. *A Sand County Almanac, with Essays on Conservation from Round River*. Oxford University Press, 1966.

Loss, Scott R., Tom Will, Sara S. Loss, and Peter P. Marra. "Bird–Building Collisions in the United States: Estimates of Annual Mortality and Species Vulnerability." *The Condor* 116, no. 1 (2014): 8–23. https://doi.org/10.1650/condor-13-090.1.

Lynn, Robin, and Francis Morrone. *Guide to New York City Urban Landscapes*. W. W. Norton, 2013.

Mehlman, David W., Sarah E. Mabey, David N. Ewert et al. "Conserving Stopover Sites for Forest-Dwelling Migratory Landbirds." *The Auk* 122, no. 4 (2005): 1281–90. https://doi.org/10.1093/auk/122.4.1281.

Melosi, Martin V. *Fresh Kills: A History of Consuming and Discarding in New York City*. Columbia University Press, 2020.

Mullaly, John. *The New Parks Beyond the Harlem*. Record & Guide, 1887.

*Natural History of New York City's Parks and Great Gull Island*. Linnaean Society of New York, 2007.

Parges, Meredith, and Viveca Morris. *Building Safer Cities for Birds—How Cities Are Leading the Way on Bird-Friendly Building Policy*, Yale Bird-Friendly Building Initiative, August 2023.

Peterson, Roger Tory. *Birds Over America*. Dodd, Mead, 1948.

Post, Peter W. "An Irruption of Tufted Titmice in the Northeast." *American Birds* 33, no. 3 (1979): 249–50.

Post, Peter W., and Don Riepe. "Laughing Gulls Colonize Jamaica Bay." *The Kingbird* 30, no. 1 (1980): 11–13.

Pregitzer, Clara C., Helen M. Forgione, Kristen L. King, Sarah Charlop-Powers, and Jennifer Greenfeld. *Forest Management Framework for New York City*. Natural Areas Conservancy, 2018.

Ramírez-Garofalo, José R., Shannon R. Curley, and Caitlin E. Field. "Breeding by Sedge Wrens at an Urban Reclaimed Landfill in New York." *Urban Naturalist* 46 (November 2021): 1–10.

Robertson, Ellen P., Frank A. La Sorte, Jonathan D. Mays et al. "Decoupling of Bird Migration from the Changing Phenology of Spring Green-Up." *Proceedings of the National Academy of Sciences* 121, no. 12 (2024). https://doi.org/10.1073/pnas.2308433121.

Rogers, Elizabeth Barlow. *Green Metropolis: The Extraordinary Landscapes of New York City as Nature, History, and Design*. Alfred A. Knopf, 2016.

Rosenberg, Kenneth V., Adriaan M. Dokter, Peter J. Blancher et al. "Decline of the North American Avifauna." *Science* 366, no. 6461 (2019): 120–24. https://doi.org/10.1126/science.aaw1313.

Sanderson, Eric W. *Mannahatta: A Natural History of New York City*. Abrams, 2009.

Seewagen, Chad L., Christine D. Sheppard, Eric J. Slayton, and Christopher G. Guglielmo. "Plasma Metabolites and Mass Changes of Migratory Landbirds Indicate Adequate Stopover Refueling in a Heavily Urbanized Landscape." *The Condor* 113, no. 2 (2011): 284–97. https://doi.org/10.1525/cond.2011.100136.

Sibley, David Allen, Chris Elphick, and John B. Dunning Jr. *The Sibley Guide to Bird Life & Behavior.* Alfred A. Knopf, 2013.

Stephenson, Tom, and Scott Whittle. *The Warbler Guide.* Princeton University Press, 2013.

Subramanian, Meera. "The World's Fastest Animal Takes New York." *Smithsonian,* December 2009. https://www.smithsonianmag.com/science-nature/the-worlds-fastest-animal-takes-new-york-12317871/.

Swadek, Rebecca K., Marit Larson, Georgina Cullman et al. *Wetlands Management Framework for New York City.* Natural Areas Conservancy and NYC Parks, 2021.

Todd, Kim. *Tinkering with Eden: A Natural History of Exotic Species in America.* W. W. Norton, 2002.

Van Doren, Benjamin M., Daniel Sheldon, Jeffrey Geevarghese, Wesley M. Hochachka, and Andrew Farnsworth. "Autumn Morning Flights of Migrant Songbirds in the Northeastern United States Are Linked to Nocturnal Migration and Winds Aloft." *The Auk* 132, no. 1 (2015): 105–18. https://doi.org/10.1642/auk-13-260.1.

Van Doren, Benjamin M., David E. Willard, Mary Hennen et al. "Drivers of Fatal Bird Collisions in an Urban Center." *Proceedings of the National Academy of Sciences* 118, no. 24 (2021). https://doi.org/10.1073/pnas.2101666118.

Van Doren, Benjamin M., Kyle G. Horton, Adriaan M. Dokter, Holger Klinck, Susan B. Elbin, and Andrew Farnsworth. "High-Intensity Urban Light Installation Dramatically Alters Nocturnal Bird Migration." *Proceedings of the National Academy of Sciences* 114, no. 42 (2017): 11175–80. https://doi.org/10.1073/pnas.1708574114.

Veit, Richard R. "Vagrants as the Expanding Fringe of a Growing Population." *The Auk* 117, no. 1 (2000): 242–46. https://doi.org/10.1093/auk/117.1.242.

Waters, Hannah. "The Waves of Migration." *Audubon,* Spring 2023. https://www.audubon.org/news/wave-theory-of-bird-migration.

Weidensaul, Scott. "A Matter of Timing: Can Birds Keep Up with Earlier and Earlier Springs?" *Audubon,* Spring 2022. https://www.audubon.org/magazine/spring-2022/a-matter-timing-can-birds-keep-earlier-and.

Weidensaul, Scott. *A World on the Wing: The Global Odyssey of Migratory Birds.* W. W. Norton, 2021.

Weidensaul, Scott. *Living on the Wind: Across the Hemisphere with Migratory Birds.* North Point Press, 1999.

White, Norval, Elliot Willensky, and Fran Leadon. *AIA Guide to New York City.* Oxford University Press, 2010.

Wilson, Alexander. *American Ornithology*. Otis, Broaders, 1839.

Winger, Benjamin M., F. Keith Barker, and Richard H. Ree. "Temperate Origins of Long-Distance Seasonal Migration in New World Songbirds." *Proceedings of the National Academy of Sciences* 111, no. 33 (2014): 12115–20. https://doi.org/10.1073/pnas.1405000111.

*The WPA Guide to New York City: The Federal Writers Project Guide to 1930s New York*. New Press, 1995. First published in 1939 by Random House.